Foundation Course in English

FEG-01/BEGF-101

For

B.A., B.Com., B.Sc.

Useful For

IGNOU, KSOU (Karnataka), Bihar University (Muzaffarpur), Nalanda University, Jamia Millia Islamia, Vardhman Mahaveer Open University (Kota), Uttarakhand Open University, Kurukshetra University, Seva Sadan's College of Education (Maharashtra), Lalit Narayan Mithila University, Andhra University, Pt. Sunderlal Sharma (Open) University (Bilaspur), Annamalai University, Bangalore University, Bharathiar University, Bharathidasan University, HP University, Centre for distance and open learning, Kakatiya University (Andhra Pradesh), KOU (Rajasthan), MPBOU (MP), MDU (Haryana), Punjab University, Tamilnadu Open University, Sri Padmavati Mahila Visvavidyalayam (Andhra Pradesh), Sri Venkateswara University (Andhra Pradesh), UCSDE (Kerala), University of Jammu, YCMOU, Rajasthan University, UPRTOU, Kalyani University, Banaras Hindu University (BHU) and all other Indian Universities.

GULLYBABA PUBLISHING HOUSE PVT LTD.

ISO 9001 & ISO 14001 CERTIFIED CO.

Published by:

GullyBaba Publishing House Pvt. Ltd.

Regd. Office:
2525/193, 1st Floor, Onkar Nagar-A,
Tri Nagar, Delhi-110035
(From Kanhaiya Nagar Metro Station Towards Old Bus Stand)
Call: 9991112299, 9312235086
WhatsApp: 9350849407

Branch Office:
1A/2A, 20, Hari Sadan,
Ansari Road, Daryaganj,
New Delhi-110002
Ph.011-45794768
Call & WhatsApp:
8130521616,8130511234

E-mail: hello@gullybaba.com, **Website**:GullyBaba.com

New Edition

ISBN: 978-93-86276-10-0

Author: Gullybaba.com Panel

Preface

Language is the source of communication. It's the way through which we share our ideas and thoughts with others. There are uncountable languages in this world.

There are several factors that make us to learn English Language to go through in the current time. If we see Educational field, we will find much of the syllabus is written in English. Children are taught and encouraged to learn English on starting levels. And accordingly, as they promote to the next levels they study almost all the subjects in English.

We see the Internet and find more than 90 per cent of websites written and created in English. There is another factor that make English very important in this world is it is the easiest language of the world to learn. In today's global world, the importance of English cannot be denied and ignored since English is the most common language spoken everywhere. With the help of developing technology, English has been playing a major role in many sectors including medicine, engineering, and education, which is the most important arena where English is needed.

This book has been written to help students in attaining their goals perfectly in English learning. This book is mainly targeted for the exam of *'Foundation Course in English (BEGF-101)'*. This book has the ability to transport its readers into a world of imagination. The book aims to provide an enriching experience, which can help students to enhance various realms of life. The book will also provide excellent material, critical essays on various topics and information that will provide growth to its readers, and enjoyment at the same time.

In this book, we have tried to solve all possible questions from the exams' point of view. It is enriched with useful and to-the-point matter. We hope that this effort will fulfil the readers' expectations and help them to do well in respective exams.

Feedback in this regard is solicited.

– Author

Acknowledgement

Our compliments go to the **GullyBaba Publishing House (P) Ltd.**, and its meticulous team who have been enthusiastically working towards the perfection of the book.

Their teamwork, initiative and research have been very encouraging. Had it not been for their unflagging support, this work wouldn't have been possible. The creative freedom provided by them along with their aim of presenting the best to the reader has been a major source of inspiration in this work. Hope that this book would be successful.

– GPH Panel of Experts

Publisher's Note

The present book BEGF-101 is targeted for examination purpose as well as enrichment. With the advent of technology and the Internet, there has been no dearth of information available to all; however, finding the relevant and qualitative information, which is focussed, is an uphill task.

We at **GullyBaba Publishing House (P) Ltd.,** have taken this step to provide quality material which can accentuate in-depth knowledge about the subject. GPH books are a pioneer in the effort of providing unique and quality material to its readers. With our books, you are sure to attain success by making use of this powerful study material. Provided book is just a reference book based on the syllabus of particular University/Board. For a profound information, see the textbooks recommended by the University/Board.

Our site **gullybaba.com** is a vital resource for your examination. The publisher wishes to acknowledge the significant contribution of the Team Members and our experts in bringing out this publication and highly thankful to Almighty God, without His blessings, this endeavor wouldn't have been successful.

– Publisher

Topics Covered

Contents

Question Papers

Reading and Listening Comprehension

Reading unseen passages test the student's ability to understand the given passage. The passage may be descriptive, literary or global.

Reading is a master technique to judge the understanding of the students. In order to get mastery in reading, one must be efficient in the basic tenets of reading. They are:

(1) **Skimming** refers to reading quickly in order to get an idea of the passage.

(2) **Scanning** means going through a certain text for gathering specific information.

(3) **Intensive reading** means to study a prescribed text thoroughly to comprehend the meaning at the surface level as well as at a deeper level.

(4) While **extensive reading** refers to reading for pleasure.

The passage can come in the form of prose or poem. Therefore, there is a great need to understand the passage properly. Following are given some steps, which should be taken to answer the asked questions in the comprehension (whether prose or poem) properly:

- First of all, read the passage with concentration. "Intelligent reading" is fast as well as perfect. You should take three to five minutes to read a passage of moderate difficulty.
- Next, look at the questions on the given passage, paying great attention to the key words. You may be able to locate some of the answers immediately. Mark these portions with a pencil and write the question number alongside.
- Look at the questions again which you have not been able to find the answer. Read the passage once again looking for key words, locate the answer and mark the answers as before.
- Now, it's the turn of the questions related to vocabulary. If you can locate the word, well and good, otherwise an intelligent guess is better than leaving a question unanswered. Try to use

the word in a sentence to guess the meaning.

- Now, you can answer the questions easily and write them down in your own words.
- The key to answering any question well is good reading for the first time whether it is prose or poem.

Some Important Points:

(1) Usually, the first sentence of the passage or an individual paragraph or stanza states its main idea. Generally, all questions are based on the main idea dealt within the passage.

(2) Often, the questions follow the same logical sequence as the paragraph or stanza in the passage. This should help you a great deal in locating the answer.

(3) These are the high scoring questions, so attempt all these at any cost.

(4) Do not copy the language of the passage when comes in the form of prose. This will help you in gaining good marks.

(5) Further, also remember that you have to create your own answers when the passage comes in the form of poem.

Read the following passages or poems or other extracts and answer the questions that follow:

Mr. Jones, of the Manor Farm, had locked the hen-house for the night, but was too drunk to remember to shut the pop-holes. With the ring of light from his lantern dancing from side to side, he lurched across the yard, and made his way, up to bed, where Mrs. Jones was already snoring.

As soon as the light in the bedroom went out, there was a stirring and a fluttering all through the farm buildings. Word had gone round during the day that old Major, the prize Middle White boar, had a strange dream on the previous night and wished to communicate it to the other animals. It had been agreed that they should all meet in the big barn as soon as Mr. Jones was safely out of the way. Old Major was so highly regarded on the farm that everyone was quite ready to lose an hour's sleep in order to hear what he had to say.

All the animals were now present except Moses, the tame raven, who slept on a perch behind the back door. When Major saw that they had all made themselves comfortable and were waiting attentively, he cleared his throat and began:

'Comrades, you have heard already about the strange dream that I had last night, But I will come to the dream later. I have something else to say first, I do not think, comrades, that I shall be with you for many months longer, and before I die, I feel it my duty to pass on to you such wisdom as I have acquired. I have had a long life, have had much time for thought as I lay alone in my stall, and I think I may say that I understand the nature of life on this earth as well as any animal now living. It is about this that I wish to speak to you.'

'Now, comrades, what is the nature of this life of ours? Let us face it; our lives are miserable, labourious and short. We are born, we are given just so much food as will keep the breath in our bodies, and those of us who are capable of it are forced to work to the last atom of our strength; and the very instant that our usefulness has come to an end we are slaughtered with hideous cruelty.'

'But is this simply part of the order of nature? Is it because this land of ours is so poor that it cannot afford a decent life to those who dwell upon it? No, comrades, a thousand times no! This single farm of ours would support a dozen horses, twenty cows, hundreds of sheep- and all of them living in a comfort and a dignity that are now almost beyond our imagining. Why then do we continue in this miserable condition? Because nearly the whole of the produce of our labour is stolen from us by human beings. There, comrades, is the answer to all our problems. It is summed up in a single word — Man. Man is the only real enemy we have. Remove Man from the scene, and the root cause of hunger and overwork is abolished forever.'

Man is the only creature that consumes without producing. He does not give milk, he does not lay eggs, he is too weak to pull the plough, he cannot run fast enough to catch rabbits. Yet he is lord of all the animals. He sets them to work, he gives back to them the bare minimum that will prevent them from starving, and the rest he keeps for himself. Our labour tills the soil, our dung fertilise it, and yet there is not one of us that owns more than his bare skin. You cows that I see before me, how many thousands of gallons of milk have you given during the last year? And what has happened to that milk which should have been breeding up your sturdy calves? Every drop of it has gone down the throats of our enemies. And you hens, how many eggs have you laid this last year, and how many of those eggs ever hatched into chickens? The rest have all gone to market to bring in money for Jones and his men. And you, Clover, where are those four foals you bore, who should have been the support and pleasure of your old age? Each was sold at a year old – you will never see one of them again. In return for your four confinements and all your labour in the field, what have you ever had except your bare rations and a stall?

Is it not crystal clear, then, comrades, that all the evils of this life of ours spring from the tyranny of human beings? Only get rid of Man, and the produce of our labour would be our own. Almost overnight we could become rich and free. What then must we do? Why, work night and day, body and soul, for the overthrow of the human race! That is my message to you comrades: Rebellion! I do not know when that Rebellion will come, it might be in a week or in a hundred years, but I know, as surely as I see this straw beneath my feet, that sooner or later justice will be done. Fix your eyes on that, comrades, throughout the short remainder of your lives. And above all, pass on this message of mine to those who come after you, so that future generations shall carry on the struggle until it is victorious.

'And remember, comrades, your resolution must never falter. No argument must lead you astray. Never listen when they tell you that Man and the animals have a common interest, that the prosperity of the one is the prosperity of the other. It is all lies. Man serves the interests of no creature except himself. And among us animals let there be perfect unity, perfect comradeship in the struggle. All men are enemies. All animals are comrades.

Answer the following questions on the passage you have read:

Q1. Why was the ring of light from Mr. Jones's lantern dancing from side to side?

Ans. The ring of light from Mr. Jones's lantern was dancing from side to side because he was drunk and his movement was not steady.

Q2. Where had the animals agreed to meet?

Ans. The animals agreed to meet in the big barn.

Q3. Why had they assembled there?

Ans. They assembled there to hear what Major had to say.

Q4. What does old Major want to share with the animals?

Ans. Old Major wants to share his understanding of the nature of life.

Q5. Pick out the three words Major uses to describe the lives of the animals. Why does he use these words?

Ans. The three words Major uses to describe the lives of the animals are miserable, labourious and short. He uses these words because he wants to tell the animals how bad their condition is.

Q6. How is Man different from the animals?

Ans. Man is different from the animals because the animals produce all the wealth and Man takes it away from them. He does not produce anything himself.

Q7. Does Major depict Man as:

(i) selfish?

(ii) greedy?

(iii) a weakling?

(iv) mean?

(v) the lord of all the animals? or

(vi) cruel?

(There can be more than one choice. Give a reason for your choice).

Ans. Major depicts Man as selfish and cruel because he makes the animals work and gives them just enough to keep them alive.

Q8. How, according to Major, could animals be rich and free?

Ans. According to Major, animals could be rich and free by getting rid of Man, so that they could keep all the things they produced.

Q9. Does Major know when this rebellion will take place? Does this show that Major is:

(i) a realist?

(ii) an idealist? or

(iii) A dreamer?

Ans. No, Major does not know when this rebellion will take place. This shows that he is a dreamer.

Q10. How does Major describe all men?

Ans. Major describes all men as enemies.

Q11. How does he describe all animals?

Ans. He describes all animals as comrades.

Q12. Why do you think Major call the animals 'Comrades'?

Ans. Major calls the animals 'Comrades' to remind them that they are all united against Man.

2

The early 1940s saw people setting out for a journey, carrying their possessions in oversised steel or brass trunks and wooden crates. While boarding a train, it was a common sight to see passengers clutching their precious cloth bags and bundles of queer shapes and sizes and porters balancing gunny sacks and hardboard boxes which would burst open any moment, if not for the strong ropes that bound them. It was only the Queen's men and the royal Sahibs who were proud owners of sophisticated luggage cases. Independent India's elite had access to foreign goods and their travel cases wore a significant aristocratic look. With the second five-year plan advocating industrial expansion, good quality and durable goods were available to the Indian consumer. The voluminous steel trunks and unwieldy hardboard boxes gave way to stylish suitcases and compact travel bags. Come 90s, the era of liberalisation threw open the doors to multinationals which saw an influx of foreign goods and technology.

Today, the markets are flooded with elegant, sleek and stylish travel suitcases of a variety of brands. Travel bags and accessories are no more mere carriers of clothes and your belongings. They are much more of a fashion statement. As is for branded apparels, sunglasses and footwear, your brand of travel bags defines your taste.

The beginning stages saw hard shell suitcases which were strong but brittle, and rough use could make them prone to cracks and scratches. The passage of time and technology evolved quality control techniques of manufacturing with an affordable price line catering to all segments of society.

Travellers now carry bags in colours they please, as multi-colours such as platinum, olive green, carbon black, pewter grey, driftwood, cadet blue, cherry red, brown, sky blue, tan, purple and even yellow, though flamboyant, are in vogue. Innovative designs, colours and patterns adorn the various bags which are the cynosure of all eyes.

Duffels, backpacks, small-sized to large-sized travel suitcases, expandable totes, wheeled luggage, convertible satchels, everyday bags, packing cubes, garment bags, handbags, upright roller carry-ons, executive and computer bags, airbags and all other travel accessories comprise a lion's share of the economy.

Answer the following questions on the passage you have read:

Q1. What sort of bags, according to the passage, were available to the average Indians in the past, and what kinds are popular today.

Ans. In past, Indians used to carry their possessions in oversised steel or brass trunks and wooden crates. While travelling, it was a common sight to see passengers clutching their precious cloth bags and bundles of queer shapes and sizes. Today, the markets are flooded with elegant, sleek and stylish travel suitcases of a variety of brands.

Q2. What words would go together? Think of more adjectives.

Elegant, sleek, stylish, ..., ..., ...

Brittle, ..., ..., ...

Strong, ..., ..., ...

Ans. Elegant, sleek, stylish, graceful, well-designed, chic
Brittle, fragile, easily broken, weak, delicate, breakable
Strong, tough, well-built, durable, hard, robust, stiff

Q3. Look at the paragraph 4, where all the colours are described. Order the colours according to the darkest on one side going to the lighter on the other.

Ans. Carbon black, olive green, cherry red, purple, brown, cadet blue, yellow, tan, pewter grey, driftwood, sky blue, platinum.

Q4. List the various luggages or bags in order of their size.

Ans. Wheeled luggage, travel suitcase, upright roller carry-ons, backpack, garment bag, executive bag, computer bag, tote and handbag.

Q5. Pick out the words from the paragraph which mean the same as the following:

(a) starting

(b) graceful and stylish

(c) levels

(d) baggage

Ans. (a) Beginning
(b) Elegant
(c) Stages
(d) Luggage

One cannot be truly human and civilised unless one looks upon not only all fellow men, but all creation with the eyes of a friend. Throughout India, edicts carved on rocks and iron pillars are reminders that 22 centuries ago the Emperor Ashoka defined a king's duty as not merely to protect citizens and punish wrong-doers but also to preserve animal life and forest trees.

Ashoka was the first and perhaps the only monarch until very recently, to forbid the killing of a large number of species of animals for sport or food. He went further, regretting the carnage of his military conquests and enjoining upon his successors to find "their only pleasure in the peace that comes through righteousness."

Along with the rest of mankind, we in India in spite of Ashoka have been guilty of wanton disregard for the sources of our sustenance. We share your concern at the rapid deterioration of flora and fauna. Some of our own wild life has been wiped out, miles of forests with beautiful old trees, mute witnesses of history, have been destroyed. Even though our industrial development is in its infancy, and at its most difficult stage, we are taking various steps to deal with incipient environmental imbalances; the more so because of our concern for the human being-a species which is also imperiled. In poverty he is threatened by malnutrition and disease, in weakness by war, in richness by the pollution brought about by his own prosperity.

On the one hand, the rich look askance at our continuing poverty; on the other, they warn us against their own methods. We do not wish to impoverish the environment any further and yet we cannot for a moment forget the grim poverty of large numbers of people. Are not poverty and need the greatest polluters? For instance, unless we are in a position to provide employment and purchasing power for the daily necessities of the tribal people and those live in or around jungles, we cannot prevent them from combing the forest for food and livelihood, from poaching and from despoiling the vegetation. When they themselves feel deprived, how can we urge the preservation of animals? How can we speak to those who live in villages or slums about keeping the oceans, the rivers and air clean when their own lives are contaminated at the source? The environment cannot be improved in conditions of poverty. Nor can poverty be eradicated without the use of science and technology.

Must there be conflict between technology and a truly better world or between enlightenment of the spirit and a higher standard of living? Foreigners sometimes ask what to us seems a very strange question, whether progress in India would not mean a diminishing of her spirituality or her values. Is spiritual quality so superficial as to be dependent upon the lack of material comfort? As a country we are not more or less spiritual than any other but traditionally our people have respected the spirit of detachment and renunciation.

The Government of India is one of the few which has an officially sponsored programme of family planning and this is making some progress. We believe that planned families will make for a healthier and more conscious population but we know also that no programme of population control can be effective without education and without a visible rise in the standard of living. Our own programmes have succeeded in the urban or semi-urban areas. To the very poor, every child is an earner and a helper. We are experimenting with new approaches and the family planning programme is being combined with those of maternity and child welfare, nutrition and development in general.

It is an over-simplification to blame all the world's problems on increasing population. Countries with about a small fraction of the world population consume the bulk of the world's production of minerals, fossil fuels and so on. Thus, we see that when it comes to the depletion of natural resources and environmental pollution the increase of one inhabitant in an affluent country, at his level of living, is equivalent to an increase of many Asians, Africans or Latin Americans at their current material levels of living.

Answer the following questions on the passage you have read:

Q1. What is the main idea of the speech?

Ans. The main idea of the speech is 'Preservation of environment–problems and solutions.'

Q2. How does Indira Gandhi establish India's long history of peaceful co-existence?

Ans. Indira Gandhi establishes India's long history of peaceful co-existence by referring to King Ashoka and his edicts. According to him, a king's duty is not merely to protect citizens and punish wrong-doers but also to preserve animal life and forest trees.

Q3. The environment around us has been destroyed. What are the three examples given?

Ans. The environment around us has been destroyed. The three examples are as follows:

(i) Some of the wild animals have been destroyed completely,
(ii) Some of the forests have also been destroyed, and
(iii) Industrial development has upset the balance in our environment.

Q4. It is not only the environment but human beings also who are in danger.

(i) What dangers face them when they are poor?

Ans. They face the danger of poor nutrition and disease.

(ii) What dangers face them when they are politically weak?

Ans. They face the danger of war.

(iii) What dangers face them when they are rich?

Ans. They face the danger of an impure environment.

Q5. Mention the ways in which the poor are complicated to spoil the environment.

Ans. When the poor people living around the jungles cannot get employment and cannot afford their basic necessities, they have to search for food in the forests, kill animals and cut down trees and plants.

Q6. How can poverty be removed?

Ans. Poverty can be removed by the use of science and technology.

Q7. What have Indians down the ages respected?

Ans. Traditionally Indians have respected the spirit of detachment and renunciation.

Q8. When can a programme of population control be successful?

Ans. A programme of population control can be successful when we spread education and raise the standard of living of the people.

Q9. Why do some poor people want large families?

Ans. Some poor people want large families because they think every child is an earner and a helper.

Q10. Natural resources are being depleted.

(i) How are the developed countries responsible for this?

Ans. The developed countries are responsible for natural resources depletion because they consume most of the world's production of minerals and fossil fuels.

(ii) How are the developing countries responsible for this?

Ans. In developing countries, people are so poor and their lives are so contaminated that they cannot think of keeping the air, the rivers and the oceans clean.

The frail man who won India her freedom preached non-violence. To Gandhiji though, non-violence, or ahimsa, was a way of life. He wore 'ahimsa' leather sandals and promoted 'ahimsa' silk; the former made from the hide of cows that had died a natural death. He also hoped that the Indian silk industry would use only those cocoons whose worms had already matured into moths and flown out into the world, not boiled to death for the sake of the rich yarn known all over the world as a symbol of India.

Twelve years ago, the APCO (Andhra Pradesh Handloom Weavers' Cooperative Society) in Hyderabad first realised the value of ahimsa silk when its best silk had to be rushed to a high profile visitor. Mrs. Janaki Venkatraman, wife of the then President of India, Mr. R.Venkatraman, wanted to buy the beautiful silk but would do so only on one condition the silk should have been woven without killing the silkworm before it turned into a moth.

Stumped by the request, the APCO manager, a non-technical person, rushed to his technical assistant, Mr. Kusuma Rajaiah, who confirmed that the process of procuring the silk is a violent one. In fact, one silk saree can mean up to 50,000 silkworms. The irony is that the very cocoon, created by nature to safeguard the growing insect, is made up of the fine silk thread that can be spun into lustrous silk yarn. Just seven days before maturity, the cocoons are collected, put into heat chambers, and treated at 70°C-90°C for three to four hours, thus killing the insect and making the cocoon pliable for spinning.

Over the decades, since Gandhiji first promulgated the idea, there have been movements within the Khadi cottage industry and institutions such as Kalashetra in Tamil Nadu to actually popularise this form of silk, where only those cocoons are used that have been discarded by the resident silkworm. At Kalashetra, the traditional art and craft institution begun by the famous danseuse and activist Mrs. Rukmini Devi Arundale, there is a half-a-century old weaving centre, which produces traditional Kalashetra sarees in cotton and ahimsa silk.

As often seen with alternative methods that are eco-friendly and which require new technology or way of thinking, the costs are high. It is easy to produce a single saree but mass production requires bulk procurement of the special cocoons. The process was exhausting and it was only in January 2001 that Mr. Rajaiah managed to purchase 105 kg cocoons from the Sericulture Federation in Hyderabad. Funds were also a problem. So Mr. Rajaiah mobilised the funds from his provident fund and personal savings. After much persuasion, the Indorama mills at Raipur, Chattisgarh agreed to spin this silk. Finally, in Nalgonda district, Andhra Pradesh, 30 samples of ahimsa silk sarees were ready for market trial.

Many experts from the textile industry supported the concept. Mr. N V R Nathan, Director, NIFT (National Institute of Fashion Technology), Hyderabad is one amongst them. He feels that "forbearance, compassion, a vegetarian diet, avoiding injury and avoiding killing are the five concepts of ahimsa, or non-violence, and ahimsa silk sarees fall under these principles." Also, ahimsa silk is as good as any other silk in quality.

Ahimsa silk is costlier than ordinary silk, simply because when the moth leaves home it punctures the cocoon and this breaks the silk thread. During the spinning process, cocoons without the moth lead to a lot of wastage. From an ordinary cocoon, 80 per cent of the thread can be procured as yarn, but from an empty one, this goes down to an abysmal 16 per cent. The finished saree reflects this cost and is one and half times costlier than a regular silk saree. Therefore, to make it accessible to the ordinary customer on the street, there is a need to work on not just bringing the cost down, but also on spreading awareness about the good deed s/he does by buying such a saree.

Answer the following questions on the passage you have read:

Q1. Complete the sentences given below. Select the most appropriate phrase from those given.

(a) Gandhiji preferred to wear ahimsa leather because

(i) it was processed in a natural way.

(ii) it did not require the killing of cows.

(iii) it was made in Gandhi Ashram.

(iv) it was soft and did not hurt the feet.

Ans. (ii) it did not require the killing of cows.

(b) Silk is usually prepared by

(i) unwinding the cocoons after the adult moth has flown out.

(ii) boiling empty cocoons after the adult moth has flown out.

(iii) by using the broken thread of the cocoon after the moth had flown out.

(iv) boiling the cocoons along with the worms a few days before they fly out.

Ans. (iv) boiling the cocoons along with the worms a few days before they fly out.

(c) The idea of non-violent methods of making silk was first spread by

(i) Gandhiji

(ii) Mrs. Janaki Venkatraman

(iii) Mrs. Rukmini Arundale

(iv) Mr. Rajaiah

Ans. (i) Gandhiji

(d) Ahimsa silk is different because of the way

(i) its patterns are designed.

(ii) its yarn is obtained.

(iii) it is marketed.

(iv) it is worn.

Ans. (ii) its yarn is obtained.

(e) Ahimsa silk is costlier because

(i) all the machines used in making it are new.

(ii) there are very few people making it.

(iii) the yarn obtained from the punctured cocoon is very little.

(iv) it is needs special care to store it.

Ans. (iii) the yarn obtained from the punctured cocoon is very little.

(f) Ahimsa silk is valuable because

(i) the thread obtained from the discarded cocoons is broken.

(ii) it upholds the value of life.

(iii) so many great minds attempted to popularise it.

(iv) new technology is used to make it.

Ans. (ii) it upholds the value of life.

Q2. Ahimsa silk is a beautiful concept but it is not easy to make and popularise. State four reasons why?

Ans. Four reasons are:

(i) the moth punctures the cocoon when it leaves it, thus leaving very little of thread for yarn.

(ii) making the yarn is a tedious process.

(iii) during the making process there is a lot of wastage.

(iv) since the silk is produced with such difficulty the saree is expensive.

Q3. Mention two places where ahimsa silk is being made.

Ans. Two places where ahimsa silk is being made are Kalashetra in Tamilnadu and Nalgonda District, Andhra Pradesh.

Q4. What is the irony in the life of a silk worm?

Ans. The irony is that the very cocoon, created by nature to safeguard the growing insect, is made up of the fine silk thread that can be spun into lustrous silk yarn. Something that is used to protect the moth becomes the cause of its death.

Rising an alarm bell on the city's water situation, Delhi Jal Board chief P K Tripathi said that the gap between the demand and supply of water in the city was widening incessantly. As the gap is being met by drawing groundwater, the water table is falling at an alarming rate.

Instead of the earlier demand and supply figures of 800 million gallons a day (mgd) and 650 mgd, respectively, Tripathi said: "Those figures were based on the 2001 Census figures. But as the population has increased in the last two years, the demand is now over 830 mgd. And due to the 20 per cent loss in our supply of 650 mgd, only about 520 mgd reaches people."

As a result, the difference of over 300 mgd is being partially met by drawing up to 200 mgd of the sub-soil aqua reserves. And as Delhi's dependence on groundwater grows, its over-exploitation has left the water table severely depleted.

Experts say that groundwater should be left alone as a contingency reserve and not a source of regular supply. This year the Central Ground Water Board has recorded some of the lowest ever post-monsoon water table in the city.

Central Ground Water Board (CGWB) state unit in-charge S B Singh said: "There's a very thin layer of sweet groundwater left in some parts of the city that will be over if the exploitation goes on at the current pace, without making any efforts to recharge it."

Answer the following questions on the passage you have read:

Q1. What is the demand for water in Delhi?

Ans. The demand for water in Delhi is over 830 mgd.

Q2. What is the actual supply?

Ans. The actual supply in Delhi is 520 mgd.

Q3. Do you think twenty per cent of water is lost every day because of

(a) stealing?

(b) leaking taps?

(c) clogging?

Ans. (c) Leaking taps

Q4. How is the gap between the demand and supply of water met?

Ans. The gap between the demand and supply of water is met by drawing up the sub-soil water.

Q5. "The water table is falling at an alarming rate." Why has the word "alarming" been used?

Ans. The word 'alarming' has been used because soon the sub-soil water will fall so low that even in an emergency, water cannot be drawn.

Q6. Why has the demand for water increased during the last two years.

Ans. The demand for water increase during the last two years because the population has increased.

Q7. What do you think is the only way to survive?

Ans. Rain harvesting is the only way to service.

Ever since the villagers got together and built a johad or check dam in Sawai Madhopur zila, two years ago, problems of women in that region have been halved, says Sugna (40) from Dangarwar village, Rajasthan.

"Earlier, the water level in our wells was so low that our hands used to ache while drawing water. But since we have started harvesting rain water by building the small earthen dam in the vicinity, all it takes is a push of the village hand pump to draw water", she says with relief.

Easy availability of water has helped them grow two cash crops a year. "We grow wheat, bajra, chana and even vegetables," she says. This translated into greater savings and micro-credit banks with assistance from the National Bank for Agricultural and Rural Development. These banks help villagers through loans for 'development and other constructive activities'.

Answer the following questions on the passage you have read:

Q1. What did the women build in Sawai Madhopur?

Ans. The women in Sawai Madhopur built a 'johad' or check dam.

Q2. Does it require a lot of stamina to draw water from this dam? Pick out words from the paragraph in support of your answer.

Ans. No, it does not require a lot of stamina to draw water from this dam. "... all it takes is a push of the village hand pump to draw water."

Q3. Why can they now grow two cash crops in a year?

Ans. They can now grow two cash crops in a year because water is easily available.

Q4. Do the banks give loans to the villagers?

Ans. Yes, the banks give loans to the villagers.

Q5. How do the villagers use the loans?

Ans. The villagers use the loans for development and constructive activities.

Q6. Has rain harvesting made villages

(i) more modern?

(ii) more advanced?

(iii) more prosperous?

(Select the best alternative.)

Ans. (iii) more prosperous

The greater part of all food you eat
Is chemically poisoned! This is so,
You sicken upon very doubtful meat;
Your beer is made; I am prepared to show,
Of SO_3 With H_2O
And that's the reason you have stomach cold.
But these are things that people do not know;
They do not know because they are not told.
So grin and bear it, Stupid, do not bleat;
You hungered after progress years ago;
You wanted science and you've got it–neat;
You certainly desired 'Hygiene' and lo!
You have it now–and mutter in your woe
Of bitter knowledge dearer bought than gold
These are the things that people do not know.
They do not know because they are not told.

(Hillaire Belloc)

Answer the following questions on the poem that you read:

Q1. The poet talking about

(i) progress

(ii) food

(iii) poison

Ans. (ii) food

Q2. Is the food that we eat

(i) state?

(ii) hygienic?

(iii) polluted?

Ans. (iii) polluted

Q3. Are people not aware that their food is polluted because

(i) they do not want to know?

(ii) it is tasty?

(iii) they are not told?

Ans. (iii) they are not told

Q4. Does the poet want to

(i) shock us?

(ii) make us laugh?

(iii) make us contradict him?

Ans. (iii) make us contradict him

Stem cells are one of the most fascinating areas of biology today. Research on stem cells has shown how an organism develops from a single cell and how healthy cells replace damaged cells in adult organisms. Stem cells can be used effectively in the treatment of many diseases. Such cell-based therapies are called regenerative or reparative medicine.

Stem cells have two important characteristics that distinguish them from other types of cells. First, they are unspecialised cells that renew themselves for long periods through cell division. The second is that under certain physiologic or experimental conditions, they can be induced to become cells with special functions such as the beating cells of the heart muscle or the insulin-producing cells of the pancreas.

Scientists primarily work with two kinds of stem cells from animals and humans: embryonic stem cells and adult stem cells, which have different functions and characteristics. Scientists discovered ways to obtain or derive stem cells from early mouse embryos more than 20 years ago. Many years of detailed study of the biology of mouse stem cells led to the discovery, in 1998, of the process of isolating stem cells from human embryos and growing the cells in the laboratory. These are called human embryonic stem cells. The embryos used in these studies were created to treat infertility through in vitro fertilisation procedures and when they were no longer needed for the purpose, they were donated for research with the informed consent of the donor.

Stem cells are important for living organisms for many reasons. In the 3-to 5-day-old embryo, called a blastocyst, stem cells in developing tissues give rise to the multiple specialised cell types that make up the heart, lung, skin, and other tissues. In some adult tissues, such as bone marrow, muscle, and brain, discrete populations of adult stem cells generate replacements for cells that arc lost through normal wear and tear, injury, or disease.

Scientists believe that stem cells may, at some point in the future, become the basis for treating diseases such as Parkinson's disease, diabetes, and heart disease.

They want to study stem cells in the laboratory so they can learn about their essential properties and what makes them different from specialised cell types. As scientists learn more about stem cells, it may become possible to use the cells not just in cell-based therapies, but also for screening new drugs and toxins and understanding birth defects. In order to develop such treatments, scientists are intensively studying the fundamental properties of stem cells, which include:

- determining precisely how stem cells remain unspecialised and self renewing for many years; and
- identifying the signals that cause stem cells to become specialised cells.

Answer the following questions on the passage you have read:

Q1. Select the most appropriate phrase from those given:

(i) Stem cells can be used profitably in treating .... diseases.

(a) contagious

(b) degenerative

(c) infectious

(d) none of the above

Ans. Stem cells can be used profitably in treating **degenerative** diseases.

Q2. Give two important characteristics of stem cells.

Ans. Two important characteristics of stem cells are as follows:

- Stem cells are unspecialised cells that renew themselves for long periods through cell division.
- Stem cells can be induced to become cells with special functions under certain physiologic or experimental conditions.

Q3. What do scientists believe?

Ans. Scientists believe that stem cells may become the basis for treating diseases such as Parkinson's disease, diabetes and heart disease at some point in the future.

Q4. Define blastocyst.

Ans. The 3 to 5 day old embryo is known as blastocyst.

Q5. Special cells can do special functions like make the heart beat and produce insulin. (State True/False)

Ans. True

In India as elsewhere every girl or boy has fond and warm memories of his childhood, from the day he begins to talk to his mother and father in broken syllables. Invariably a child learns and recognises the faces of his mother and father, of sisters and brothers who play with him constantly or the servants who prepare his meals or watch him play in the nursery. He must also remember the rich colours of the butterflies and birds which children everywhere always love to watch with open eyes. I say must, because when I was three and a half, all these memories were expunged, and with the prolonged sickness I started living in a world of four senses — that is, a world in which colours and faces and light and darkness are unknown.

If my age and the length of the sickness deprived me of the treasured memories of sight, they also reduced things which are valued so much in the sighted world to nothing more than mere words, empty of meaning. I started living in a universe where it was not the flood of sunshine streaming through the nursery window or the colours of the rainbow, a sunset or a full moon that mattered, but the feel of the sun against the skin, the slow drizzling sound of rain, the feel of the air just before the coming of the quiet night, the smell of the grass on a warm morning. It was a universe where at first – but only at first – I made my way fumbling and faltering.

It was good that I lost my sight when I did, because having no memories of seeing there was nothing to look back to, nothing to miss. I went blind in November 1937. At that time we were living in Gujarat, in the province of Punjab in northern India. After my sickness we moved to Lahore, a few miles away, but the procession of relatives who came to sympathise made my father ask for another transfer, this time to Karnal, where we had neither friends nor relatives. There we got a cottage on the canal bank, built in very peaceful and quiet surroundings.

As might be expected, in the beginning it was tough for all of us – for my mother and my father, for my three sisters and my brother and for me, too. The illness had left me weak. The servants shirked me as though I was an evil eye personified. My sister treated me with care, as though I were a fragile doll, and my mother wept. My father, who was a doctor in the public health service, was grateful that my spine had been tapped in time, for a delay in the lumber puncture would have affected my mind or endangered my life. But he, like that rest, despaired.

A state of complete inaction therefore followed my blindness. In part, this was due to the immediate shock of the illness, but more important still, the impasse was caused by ignorance of the potentialities of a blind child, since the only blind persons my parents saw were beggars.

My father's wide medical experience had prepared him for an acceptance of this tragedy, and he understood that any course of action must begin with the realisation that I would be blind for the rest of my life. My mother, on the other hand, neither would nor could convince herself that my sight would never return; she did not have the medical experiences of my father, and she blamed something in her past for the tragedy.

Answer the following questions on the passage you have read:

Q1. What are some of the things children everywhere learn and recognise?

Ans. Some of the things children everywhere learn and recognise are faces of members of the family and colours of butterflies and birds.

Q2. The author's childhood was different from that of other children. Why?

Ans. The author's childhood was different from that of other children because he was blind. He lost his sight at the age of three and a half.

Q3. The author's perception of the world was confined only to four senses. Pick out phrases which highlight the use of the senses of

(i) Hearing

Ans. The sound of rain.

(ii) Touch

Ans. The feel of the sun against the skin.
The feel of the air before the coming night.

(iii) Smell

Ans. The smell of grass.

Q4. Why does he say "It was good that I lost sight when I did"?

Ans. He lost his eyesight at a very tender age. He almost began life as a blind child, and his mind had stored nothing much which he could have missed later.

Q5. From Lahore the family moved to Karnal, where they had neither friends nor relatives. But they were happy. Why?

Ans. The new surroundings were quiet and peaceful, and no relatives or friends came to offer sympathies, which used to be embarrassing.

Q6. 'The servants shirked me as though I were an evil eye personified.' This means that the servants thought I was

(i) blind

(ii) a curse on the family

(iii) a spoilt child

(Select the correct alternative.)

Ans. (ii) a curse on the family

"THE AGEING OF the world's population is one of the most important demographic phenomena of our time," says United Nations Secretary-General Javier Perez de Cuellar. He was speaking on 1st October at a UNFPA-organised symposium on population ageing held to mark the first International Day for the Elderly.

The world's elderly population–defined as persons 60 years and older – is growing rapidly, in developing countries as well as in the industrialised countries commonly characterised as "graying". By the year 2025, seven in ten older persons will come from developing countries, the UN predicts. These countries are faced with a quandary: How to take care of their elders and invest in economic development with limited resources.

The needs of the elderly range from continued employment for those sometimes referred to as the "younger older", to health care for the chronic ailments that come during "old-old age".

"If all the world's elderly were considered as a single nation, that nation would be the world's third most populous, coming immediately after China and India," says David Horlacher, chief of the Population and Development Section of the UN Population Division.

"However", says Horlacher, the age structures of sub-Saharan African countries are getting younger. "Population ageing is unlikely to be a significant problem for them before 2020. Age structures in a majority of countries in Latin America and Asia became younger in the 1950s and 1960s, but the trend was reversed around 1970 when substantial fertility decline started."

"The proportions of elderly are not changing markedly, but their sheer numbers are increasing rapidly" in the developing countries, says William Seltzer, chief of the UN Statistical Office. "At the same time, changes in social and cultural patterns, such as the flight of young people to towns and the spread of the nuclear family, mean that the traditional resources to care for the elderly are being undermined."

Elderly persons make up some 12 per cent of the population of industrialised countries, 4.5 per cent in developing countries. By 2025, according to UN projections, the proportions will be 19 per cent and 8 per cent, respectively.

Answer the following questions on the passage you have read:

Q1. When is one considered to be 'aged'?

Ans. Persons who are 60 years and above are considered to be 'aged' people.

Q2. What are the challenges that the younger older face and the 'old-old age' people face?

Ans. "Younger older" people face challenges of employment and "old-old aged" people face health-care for chronic ailments.

Q3. Suggest some reasons why people live longer today than they did some years ago.

Ans. Some of the reasons people live longer today than they did some years ago are better health care, better food and nutrition, general improvement in the quality of life, etc.

Q4. What problem does this pose for developing countries?

Ans. Developing countries have limited resources. Should they invest these resources in taking care of their 'aged' persons or in economic development of their country?

Q5. Why didn't they face this problem in the past?

Ans. The population of the elderly people was not so vast. Moreover, they were taken care of by their children in the joint family system.

Q6. What are the needs of 'aged' people? How were these needs met traditionally in the past?

Ans. Their needs are (i) economic (ii) health care, and (iii) social and psychological.

Q7. When is the "International Day for the Elderly" celebrated?

Ans. The "International Day for the Elderly" is celebrated on 1st of October.

Jay Tee, 30, has been a drug addict since he was a teenager. He has tried to kick the habit many times; going in and out of rehabilitation centers. He managed to stay clean for a month before suffering a relapse. There are many drug addicts like Jay Tee. Why are they into it in the first place? It doesn't matter if you are white or black or Asian or Latin, every race has their share of drug abuse problems.

Some people say that it is due to the perception of drugs being "bad and illegal" and therefore something so irresistible that you just have to try it. Somehow, teenagers are more curious to discover the "forbidden fruit". Some manage to kick the habit early but there are many others who are trapped.

For many teenagers, drug abuse is a mere escape. They use drugs to get out of their misery, pain, confusion and loneliness. Some teenage drug addicts grow up without guidance from their parents, and so they resort to drugs. Some are physically or mentally abused and drugs become the only thing that they are able to count on. Many succumb to drug addiction because of the need to feel like they belong. They try drugs to please their friends or to be part of a group. Many teenage drug abusers are also low achievers in schools and have low self-esteem.

There are also teenagers who claim that they were first exposed to different kinds of drugs at parties and discos. These drugs were distributed freely the first few times and they kept coming back for more. As a result, many of them became addicted even before they knew it. In certain cases, these teenagers might resort to committing crimes to support their expensive habit.

One effective tool in the fight against teen drug abuse is communication. Troubled teens need some form of outlet from the problems or depression they are facing. Parents should take time out from their busy schedules to spend time with their children and listen to their problems. Communication, however, should go beyond words. Parents should show their children that they really care. Adequate parental supervision has also been found to be a deterrent to drug use in youth. Parents should know who their children's friends are and what is going on in their social lives. School counselors should also play an active role in providing information on drug abuse and also provide emotional support.

One common belief is that drug abusers should be able to stop taking drugs if only they are willing to change their behaviour. However, drug addiction is a disease that affects the brain and because of that,

stopping drug abuse is not simply a matter of willpower. Drug abuse can affect a person's self-control and ability to make sound decisions, and at the same time send intense impulses to take drugs. Through scientific advances, we now know that the abuse of drugs leads to changes in the structure and function of the brain and at the same time, we also know that drug addiction can be successfully treated to help people get over their addiction and resume productive lives.

At the end of the day, the best way to prevent drug addiction is by educating teenagers about it. The more they learn about the bad effects, the less their excuses to take it. This may even dissuade them from using it.

Answer the following question on the passage that you have read:

Q1. From paragraph 1, who does 'they' refer to?

Ans. 'They' refers to teenage drug abusers.

Q2. From paragraph 2, what is the reason cited for teenage drug addiction?

Ans. The perception that drugs are 'bad and illegal', and since they are forbidden, it becomes irresistible.

Q3. From paragraph 3,

(a) what are teenage drug abusers escaping from?

(b) give two other reasons for drug abuse among teenagers.

(c) give two characteristics of teenage drug abusers.

Ans. (a) They are using drugs to escape from misery, pain, confusion and loneliness.

(b) No guidance from parents and Peer pressure.

(c) Low achievers in schools and have low self-esteem.

Q4. From paragraph 5, name one way in which parents could help their troubled children.

Ans. Parents should take time to listen to their children's problems.

Q5. In your own words, explain why stopping drug abuse is not simply a matter of willpower.

Ans. It is because drugs can affect a person's self-control and s/he will not be able to think wisely.

12

A little over a hundred years ago, on February 29, 1904, exactly at noon, a baby girl was born to Neelakanta Sastri and Seshammal. They named her Rukmini Devi. She would one day be known the world over as Rukmini Devi Arundale, a respected authority on dance, music and culture.

Though she lived in a house next to a Bharatanatyam dancer, she was not drawn to dance as a child. A nattuvanar (conductor of bharatanatyam) lived behind her house, and she grew up listening to music and the beat of the thattukazhi (a wooden block and stick instrument used for beats), but it did not mean anything to her. Later she wrote, 'I am sometimes surprised that my destiny led me to be a dancer'.

Her father was an engineer with the Public Works Department. It was a transferable job and the family moved frequently. In 1906, her father was introduced to the Theosophical Society. Though Rukmini Devi's sisters were married even before they entered their teens, he and a group of his friends took an oath under Dr. Annie Besant (who headed the Society) that they would not allow child marriage in their families.

Dr. Besant helped Rukmini Devi's elder sister Sivakamu, who was married at the tender age of 12, complete her studies at Banaras. Later, Sivakamu went to London where she earned her medical degree.

Rukmini Devi's father became a firm believer in Dr. Besant's movement. The whole family moved from Chengalpet to Chennai (then known as Madras), bought a piece of land next to the Theosophical Society in Adyar, built a house and named it Buddha Vilas.

It was only after shifting to Madras that Rukmini Devi began attending regular school. She spent most of her free time on the grounds of the Theosophical Society. Slowly, Rukmini was drawn to art, nature and animals.

Rukmini Devi was just 14 when she first met Dr. George Arundale in 1917. Dr. Arundale's aunt Francesca was a leading figure in the Theosophical Society movement. He worked closely with Dr Annie Besant and was in charge of her paper, *New India*. What attracted Rukmini Devi to Dr. Arundale was his 'striking personality and sense of humour'. They met quite often. After a couple of years, Dr. Arundale proposed to her. Rukmini Devi wrote, 'I really cannot tell why I decided to marry Dr. Arundale. Maybe there is a destiny in these matters. I did not even think that it was a revolutionary step that I was taking'.

After they decided to get married, Dr. Arundale took her to meet Dr. Annie Besant. Rukmini Devi's mother also was with her. When Rukmini Devi saw Dr. Besant at close quarters, she felt she was looking at a 'maharishi'.

Though Rukmini Devi's mother was supportive of her decision (her father had passed away by then), there were strong protests from relatives and the community. The public protest was so bad that the couple were forced to marry in Mumbai. Dr Besant stood by them. At her instance, the governor of Madras hosted a reception for the Arundales when they returned. It amused Rukmini Devi to see all those people who opposed her marriage at the reception.

It was Anna Pavlova, the legendary ballet dancer, who first suggested she learn dance. Rukmini Devi was in her late twenties then. Meenakshisundaram Pillai, her guru, was quite old so he would remain seated as he taught her. Once she made up her mind to learn dance, she worked very hard. She began practising from seven in the morning till seven in the evening, with an hour's break for lunch. Still, her guru felt she was not working hard enough. Sometimes, he would call her again for training at night.

Initially, conservative Madras could not accept the fact that a Brahmin girl had taken up dancing. But her astounding performances converted them.

She also revolutionised many things connected with dance. She made the musicians sit on the side of the stage. She designed her own costumes.

Her performance at the Diamond Jubilee convention of the Theosophical Society amazed Dr. Arundale, who had till then thought dance was a delightful hobby his young wife had picked up. After the performance, he realised it was more of a spiritual experience like meditation. He also felt dance could be a part of Theosophical Society's work.

They decided to start a dance academy. Pandit Subramanya Sastri suggested the name Kalakshetra. At Kalakshetra, Rukmini Devi wanted the best of music by the greatest of musicians. She wanted Sanskrit classics set to pure classical music and made into dance dramas. She wanted everything - the music, the dance, the story - to be pure and classical. Kalakshetra grew to become a pioneering institution; path-breaking artists from all over the country taught there.

Even as a child, Rukmini Devi loved animals. She was horrified to see goats being sacrificed in temples. She would say, "The frightened look in the eyes of the animals used to haunt me in my dreams for a long time."

The person who used to jokingly say that she would one day be elected to Parliament by her friends, the animals, became a member of the Rajya Sabha in 1952. She said, "I should like to be the chosen representative of the tiger, the lion, the dog and the deer, the helpless and the voiceless."

She was instrumental in getting the Prevention of Cruelty to Animals Act (1960) passed as a Central Act. As a result of her effort, the Animal Welfare Board of India was established in 1962 as a statutory body under the PCA Act. Her landmark achievement was making sure Act 51 (G) of the Constitution of India was included under Part IV, making it the fundamental duty of every citizen to show kindness and compassion to all living beings. She also started a powerful national vegetarian society in India.

On February 20, 1986, Rukmini Devi was admitted to the Vijaya Hospital in Chennai. It is said she refused to use allopathic medicines or injections as she was against testing the medicines on animals. On February 23, 1986, early in the morning, she breathed her last. She was 82.

Answer the following questions on the passage you have read:

Q1. Complete the sentences given below. Select the most appropriate phrase from those given:

(i) As a young girl Rukmini

(a) was very interested in dance and was encouraged by her family.

(b) was very interested in dance but was not encouraged by family.

(c) was not interested in dance even though she had a dancer as a neighbour.

(d) disliked dance even though she was surrounded by dancers and artistes.

Ans.(c) was not interested in dance even though she had a dancer as a neighbour.

(ii) In Rukmini's house child-marriage was a custom

(a) even after her father was introduced to Dr. Annie Besant and the Theosophical Society.

(b) till her father was introduced to Dr. Annie Besant and the Theosophical Society.

(c) because her father was a follower of the Theosophical Society.

(d) because her father was not a follower of the Theosophical Society.

Ans.(b) till her father was introduced to Dr. Annie Besant and the Theosophical Society.

(iii) Rukmini was attracted to art, nature and animals

(a) when she was a small child.

(b) when she met Dr. Arundale.

(c) when she began learning to dance.

(d) when she was at school in Chennai (Madras).

Ans. (d) when she was at school in Chennai (Madras).

(iv) Rukmini Devi wrote, "I really cannot tell why I decided to marry Dr. Arundale. Maybe there is a destiny in these matters. I did not even think that it was a revolutionary step that I was taking'. It was a revolutionary step because (More than one answer may be correct here.)

(a) she was very young to get married.

(b) she was marrying outside caste and religion.

(c) her family did not like him.

(d) she was marrying for love.

Ans.(b) she was marrying outside caste and religion.
(d) she was marrying for love.

(v) "It amused Rukmini Devi to see all those people who opposed her marriage at the reception in Chennai (Madras)." Why do you think they had come to the reception?

(a) because they realised that they had been wrong.

(b) because it was a reception of a different kind.

(c) because Dr. Besant requested them to attend.

(d) because it was a reception thrown by the governor of Madras.

Ans. (d) because it was a reception thrown by the governor of Madras.

(vi) Dance for Rukmini was:

(a) a noble and spiritual experience.

(b) just a hobby.

(c) a little more than a hobby.

(d) a good way to achieve something in life.

Ans. (a) a noble and spiritual experience.

(vii) Rukmini Devi's institution became a pioneering institution because:

(a) it was the first institution of its kind.

(b) it helped to preserve our culture.

(c) it was devoted to classical dance forms.

(d) it took the help of great masters of dance.

Ans. (a) it was the first institution of its kind.

Q2. Chronological Sequence: Read the statements given below and arrange them in the correct sequence according to the passage.

(a) On February 29, 1904, Rukmini was born to Seshammal, an engineer in the public works department and his wife Neelakanta Sastri.

(b) They moved to Chengalpet in Chennai (then called Madras) where they built a house close to the Theosophical Society.

(c) When she was fourteen, Rukmini met Dr. Arundale who was in charge of Annie Besant's paper 'New India'.

(d) Though she had a Bharatanatyam dancer and a Bharatanatyam conductor as neighbours she was not really attracted to dance.

(e) She began attending school regularly here and spent most of her free time in the grounds of the Theosophical Society.

(f) She married Dr. Arundale to the displeasure of most of her family members except her mother who supported her.

(g) While she was only two, her father was influenced by Dr. Annie Besant and took a vow not to allow child marriage in his family.

(h) She was inspired to learn dance from the legendary ballet dancer, Anna Pavlova.

(i) Rukmini Devi was elected to the Rajya Sabha where she espoused the cause of animal rights.

(j) She mastered dance and brought about many innovations in it.

(k) She and her husband opened a dance academy called Kalashetra where the best artistes from all over the country were invited to teach.

(l) Rukmini Devi died at the ripe old age of 82 and not before she had let everyone know that her heart was always with the poor animals that suffered as a result of our medical experiments.

Ans. Chronological Sequence is a, d, g, b, e, c, f, h, j, k, i, l

Q3. Rukmini Devi Arundale was a revolutionary in many ways. Describe how?

Ans. She learnt to dance although she belonged to a Brahmin family where dance was not considered respectable. Fell in love and married the love of her life while being in a conservative society. She married outside her religion and caste. Pioneered the movement of animal rights in an age when animals were considered as creatures to be utilised for human comfort or research.

Q4. Even as a child, Rukmini Devi loved animals. She was horrified to see goats being sacrificed in temples. She would say, "The frightened look in the eyes of the animals used to haunt me in any dreams for a long time." What did she do to prove her love for the animals?

Ans. She was instrumental in getting the Prevention of Cruelty to Animals Act (1960) passed as a Central Act. The Animal Welfare Board of India was established in 1962 as a statutory body under the PCA Act. She made sure that showing kindness and compassion to all living beings became a fundamental duty of every citisen in our Constitution. Even when she lay dying she refused to take allopathic medicines as they had been developed using experiments on animals.

Q5 How did Dr. Annie Besant help in the uplifting the cause of women in our country in her time?

Ans. Dr. Annie Besant helped in the uplifting the cause of women in our country in her time in following ways:

- She ensured that girls also received education.
- Started a movement to end child marriage.
- Supported Rukmini in marrying the person she liked, thus symbolically announcing that women too have their freedom of choice.

13

If you ever had the opportunity to witness a Yakshagana performance in Karnataka you would know what a rich art form it is, both acoustically and visually, since like an opera it tells its story through song and dance. Yakshagana, a theatre form, which is pronounced as *yaksha-gaana* is an art form popular in the coastal areas of Malnad, Karnataka and nearby areas of Kerala. Yakshagana shares many characteristics with other art forms of the neighbouring states of Andhra Pradesh, Kerala, Tamilnadu and Maharashtra.

The name of this performing art, 'Yakshagana' literally means the song of the Yaksha. According to mythology, Yakshas were a class of benevolent nature spirits who were the custodian of the treasures that are hidden in the earth and in the roots of trees. A Yakshagana performance, called Aataa in Tulu language, goes on all through the night.

It normally begins at the twilight hours with the beating of drums. After the beating of drum has gone on for about a couple of hours, the 'actors' get on the stage. They offer a breathtaking view with their resplendent costumes, head-dresses and painted faces which they themselves would have painstakingly painted. A performance usually depicts a story from the Hindu epics and puranas. It consists of a narrator, who narrates the story in a song-like fashion. Musicians play on traditional instruments to which the actors dance. The actors do not have much of dialogue. They portray the story through their actions as they dance.

It is difficult to classify Yakshagana into any one category of folk, classical or rural. In fact, it has characteristics of all depending upon how we look at it. Being a theatre form, unlike a pure dance form, it is more plural and dynamic, exhibiting many types and varieties in its performances. Certainly, Yakshagana can be rightly called a traditional form.

The origin of Yakshagana can be traced back to the Vaishnava Bhakthi movement which spread with vigour after the 10th Century. The Bhakti Movement took religion to the common man, to the lower strata of society, those classes to whom the highly formalised and Vedic religion was beyond reach. Hence, Bhakthi movement was a social movement as well.

In order to propagate and spread the message of devotion, it adopted and adapted the existing folk as well as classical literary forms and performances. In doing so, it created its own forms. Most of the traditional theatre forms are the result of this phenomenon. Hence, a clear resemblance can be noticed among the members of the 'Traditional

Theatre Family'. These are Ankhia Nata (Assam), Jathra (Bengal), Chau (Bihar, Bengal), Prahlada Nata (Orissa), Veedhinatakam & Chindu (Andhra), Terukoothu Bhagawathamela (Tamil Nadu) and Kathakkali (Kerala). These theatre forms also differ from each other in various ways. Like these theatre forms, the origin of Yakshagana too is connected with a wider historical situation, namely the Bhakti movement.

Yakshagana is said to have originated somewhere between the 11th Century to 16th Century. It is said that Sage Narahari Thirtha started a Dasvathara Ata performance and a performing troupe in Udupi around 1300 circa. It later spread to other places and grew into what we call Yakshagana today. As it spread, it slowly evolved, drawing upon elements from the ritual theatre, temple arts, secular arts like Bahurupi, the royal courts and artists' imagination.

The 1930s saw some changes in compositions, organisations and presentation. Dance and the spoken word was further developed and refined. But in costume, a type of transformation started with the use of 'modern' clothing and stone jewellery, which replaced handloom clothing and wooden ornaments. A Yakshagana artiste wears a *pagaDe*, a kind of head-wear. Among the head-wears, *pagaDe* and *kireeTa* are worn by male characters and only small *pagaDe* by female ones. Exceptionally different head-wears are also used by comedians and some side artists.

By the early decades of this century, the structure of Yakshagana had reached a definite shape and form. The year 1950 saw the birth of 'tent' troupes, who gave performances to audience, using 'tent theatres' and furniture for seating. These troupes ushered in the commercialisation of Yakshagana.

Yakshagana saw major changes in form and organisation. Electrical lights replaced the 'gas lights' or 'petromax' lamps. Seating arrangements improved. Major changes came in the themes, with the inclusion of folk epics, Sanskrit dramas and imaginary stories often formed the thematic base. Popular entertainment became the criterion in place of 'classical' presentation. Performances were now held in Tulu as well, and Kannada was no longer the exclusive language of Yakshagana. This helped Yakshagana to gain great popularity. Today, it exists in various forms and styles which include puppetry as well.

Answer the following questions on the passage you have read:

Q1. Read the first sentence of the first paragraph. Can you predict what the text is going to be about?

Ans. The first paragraph tells us the theme of the text 'Yakshagana', which is a classical folk art form of Southern India. The text would be a description of this art form.

Q2. Read the text quickly once and say which paragraphs are talking about the following. There may be more than one paragraph

The actors and costumes:

Origin of Yakshagana:

Similarity with other art forms:

Relationship with religion or 'Bhakti':

The meaning of the word Yakshagana:

The stage of Yakshagana:

Ans. The actors and costumes: **Paragraphs 3 and 8**
Origin of Yakshagana: **Paragraphs 5 and 7**
Similarity with other art forms: **Paragraphs 6**
Relationship with religion or 'Bhakti': **Paragraphs 5**
The meaning of the word Yakshagana: **Paragraphs 2**
The stage of Yakshagana: **Paragraphs 10**

Q3. Pick words from the text that are associated with 'theatre' or 'drama'.

Ans. Words from the text that are associated with theatre or drama are as follows: opera, costumes, roles, performances, actors, painted faces, narrator, musician, dance, tune, action, portray, dialogue, classical, folk, traditional theatre, troupe, artiste, character, comedians, audience, lights, seating arrangements, furniture, themes, folk epics, stage, dramas and stories.

Q4. Pick sentences from the text which mean the following:

(i) Yakshagana is an art form which grew and flourished in southern India.

Ans. Yakshagana (pronounced as *yaksha-gana*) is a classical folk art form of the state of Karnataka in India, mostly popular in the coastal and Malnad areas of Karnataka and in adjacent areas and Kerala.

(ii) The performance of Yakshagana is not a brief affair.

Ans. The actors of Yakshagana wear costumes and enact various roles in plays that would, traditionally, go on all night.

A Yakshagana performance begins at the twilight hours with the beating of drums for up to a couple of hours before the 'actors' get on the stage.

(iii) The costumes are elaborate and attractive.

Ans. The actors wear resplendent costumes, head-dresses and painted faces which they paint themselves.

A Yakshagana artiste wears a *pagaDe*, a kind of head-wear. Among the head-wears *pagaDe* and *kireeTa* are worn by male characters and only small *pagaDe* by female ones. Exceptionally different head-wears are also used by comedians and some side roles.

(iv) Traditional stories are used in the plays and performances.

Ans. A performance usually depicts a story from the Hindu epics and puranas.

(v) There is more narration and music rather than dialogue unlike a normal play.

Ans. It consists of a narrator who narrates the story in a song-like fashion, backed by musicians playing on traditional musical instruments while the actors dance to the tune. Their actions portray the story as it is being narrated. The actors have limited dialogue during the course of the performance.

(vi) Yakshagana cannot be classified into any one category.

Ans. Yakshagana, like many other forms, defies neat classification into categories like folk, classical, rural. It can be included into each of these, or all of them together, depending upon our line of approach. Being a theatre form, unlike a dance form, it is more plural and dynamic. And hence it exhibits many types and varieties itself.

(vii) Yakshagana helped in the spread of religion.

Ans. It took religion to the common man, to the lower strata of society, those classes to whom the highly formalised and Vedic religion was beyond reach.

(viii) The Yakshagana draws its style from many sources.

Ans. It underwent a slow evolution drawing its elements from ritual theatre, temple arts, secular arts like Bahurupi, royal courts of the time and artists' imagination – all interwoven over a period of time.

Q5. Describe the costume of a Yakshagana actor.

Ans. In Yakshagana, use of 'modern' clothing and stone jewellery replaced handloom clothing and wooden ornaments. A Yakshagana artiste wears a *pagaDe*, a kind of head-wear. Among the head-wears, *pagaDe* and *kireeTa* are worn by male characters and only small *pagaDe* by female ones. Exceptionally different head-wears are also used by comedians and some side artists.

Q6. How was the Yakshagana performance modernised after the 1950's?

Ans. The year 1950 saw the birth of 'tent' troupes, who gave performances to audience, using 'tent theatres' and furniture of seating. Electrical lights replaced the 'gas lights' or 'petromax' lamps. Seating arrangements improved. Major changes came in the themes, with the inclusion of folk epics, Sanskrit dramas and imaginary stories often formed the thematic base.

<u>To be able to communicate across cultures it is important to know and understand the cultural background of the person you need to</u>

communicate with. Intercultural communication principles guide the process of exchanging meaningful information across cultural boundaries, in a way that preserves mutual respect and minimises ill feeling or misunderstanding.

Globalisation has brought the world closer together and helped to reduce cultural diversity. Yet globalisation also makes it necessary for us to study and understand cultures that are different from ours.

In a country like India, which has 18 major languages, over 200 dialects, 4 major religions, 29 states and 7 union territories, weather ranging from - 35°C to + 45° C, there is an unusual diversity of culture which impacts the way we express ourselves and reach out to people who are different from us in many ways.

To begin with, one needs to understanding what constitutes culture. Culture is a complex concept, with many different definitions. Hofstede has called it 'collective mental programming' or 'software of the mind'.

Culture is not just about our food, clothing and behaviour; it has a great deal to do with our beliefs, attitudes and values. It is about those aspects of us which are outwardly visible, such as food, language, clothing and behaviour. But it is also about those aspects of us which are not outwardly visible such as attitudes, values and perceptions. Various models have been used to illustrate this concept. It is often likened to an iceberg where only the tangible aspects of our culture are above the surface of water. In fact what is seen outwardly is a result of what we are and what we believe in.

But, simply put, 'culture' refers to a group or community with whom we share common experiences that shape the way we understand the world and relate to it.

It includes groups that we are born into, such as gender, race, religion or national origin. It also includes groups we join or become part of. For example, we can acquire a new culture by moving to a new region, by a change in our economic status or the society in which we move.

Learning about different cultures and ways that people communicate can enrich our lives infinitely.

Answer the following questions on the passage you have read:

Q1. Read the underlined sentences in the above reading passage carefully and formulate suitable questions to which these sentences could serve as answer.

Ans. Why is it important to know the cultural background of the person you communicate with? (para 1)

What has globalisation done? OR What has happened due to globalisation? (para 2)

What is culture? (para 5)

What does culture include? (para 6)

Q2. Complete these sentences that have been begun for you, based on the information given in the text. Do not copy the text. Use your own words.

(i) We can make meaningful conversation with people from other cultures by

(ii) Globalisation has helped cross cultural communication by

(iii) In India culture impacts the way we communicate because

(iv) Culture is likened to an iceberg because

(v) Culture can also be indicated through a tree because

(vi) We can acquire a new culture by

Ans. (i) We can make meaningful conversation with people from other cultures by *learning and understanding intercultural communication principles.*

(ii) Globalisation has helped cross cultural communication by *reducing the distance between countries, people and cultures.*

(iii) In India culture impacts the way we communicate because of *our cultural diversity.*

(iv) Culture is likened to an iceberg because *only a part of it is outwardly seen.*

(v) Culture can also be indicated through a tree because *just like a tree its roots are not visible from the outside.*

(vi) We can acquire a new culture by *changing our physical or social environment.*

Q3. What do these numbers denote in paragraph (3) of the text?

(i) 18

(ii) 200

(iii) 4

(iv) 28

(v) 45

Ans. (i) 18 – major languages of India

(ii) 200 – major dialects spoken in India

(iii) 4 – major religions followed in India

(iv) 29 – states of India

(v) 45 – degrees Celsius, the highest temperature in many parts of India

Q4. The reading passage here has several word partnerships. Can you make eight word partnerships without looking back at the text?

(i) cultural __________

(ii) intercultural __________

(iii) _________ information

(iv) cultural _________

(v) _________ respect

(vi) cultural _________

(vii) mental _________

(viii) _________ experiences

(ix) national _________

(x) economic _________

Ans. (i) cultural background
(ii) intercultural communication
(iii) meaningful information
(iv) cultural boundaries
(v) mutual respect
(vi) cultural diversity
(vii) mental programming
(viii) common experiences
(ix) national origin
(x) economic status

15

For about six weeks each year, a Bangalore restaurant creates a menu it calls 'veggie chic'. It is an appropriate name because the special menu features vegetables – including a few totally unexotic ones – that have been given chic makeovers. The menu, not only includes dishes like an avocado and mint gazpacho and ratatouille – stuffed grilled Portobello mushrooms, but also a carrot and fennel soufflé, cauliflower and roast garlic risotto and a beet and honey caramel-centred sponge cake.

The restaurant owner says the idea was to take vegetarian food to the next level. 'We also wanted to show people that gourmet vegetarian food is not just about so-called 'exotic' ingredients, and that even the humble eggplant and pumpkin can be given a new value'. 'The 'veggie chic' menu was a hit – the restaurant initially planned to run it for two weeks and had to extend it to six to meet demand.

Other Indian restaurants, especially those serving up Western cuisines, are also moving beyond the usual pasta-pizza routine and creating exciting choices on the green-dotted side of the menu.

While not eschewing meat, many other chefs across the world are letting vegetables be the stars of a meal rather than being relegated to appetisers and side dishes.

However, persuading vegetarians to pay prices that are at par with those on the non-veg side of the menu is a tricky job. "For meat eaters, it's very easy to quote pricing relevant to the meat you are serving, but for vegetarians, one has to be creative with the use of ingredients to justify pricing. This limits your usage of products – some restaurants feel only stuff like exotic cheeses and international products like couscous and polenta can justify fine-dining prices." Some restaurants have tried to move away from this trend by using everyday veggies like jackfruit, bael and raw papaya creativity. The surprise element is of elevating seemingly "common" produce into a gourmet experience.

Fine dining restaurants have the bandwidth to take more risks. Mid-range restaurants tend to play it safe as their menus are larger (encompassing multi-cuisine), which therefore requires the stocking of ingredients that can be used across all cuisines. Fine-diners have smaller menus, are usually cuisine-specific and therefore, have the room to play around with ingredients.

Surprisingly, given Indian cuisine's dependence on vegetarian dishes, it has shown the highest reluctance to innovate with vegetables, preferring to stay with the tried-and-tasted dals, a few greens like spinach and the inevitable paneer dishes. Yet, a few restaurants and hotels chains are beginning to change this.

Answer the following questions on the passage you have read:

Q1. Why do you think the menu is called 'veggie chic'?

Ans. The menu is called 'veggie chic' because it features vegetables not frequently eaten. Those which are frequently eaten are made in interesting ways.

Q2. Mention any three "unexotic vegetables" mentioned in the paragraph.

Ans. Three 'unexotic vegetales' are carrot, eggplant and pumpkin.

Q3. What does the restaurant owner mean when he says, "The idea was to take vegetarian food to the next level."

Ans. The restaurant owner means 'to make vegetarian food as part of gourmet, fine-dining experience'.

Q4. Why does the writer call eggplant and pumpkin "humble"?

Ans. The writer call eggplant and pumpkin 'humble' because they are commonly used in most Indian households.

Q5. Why do you think the vegetarians do not like to pay as much as non-vegetarians for the food they order in restaurants?

Ans. The vegetarians do not like to pay as much as non-vegetarians for the food they order in restaurants because they think vegetables cost less than meat products.

Q6. What is the difference between fine-dining restaurants and mid-range restaurants?

Ans. Fine dining restaurants are generally highly priced restaurants. The waiters are usually highly trained and wear more formal attire.

These restaurants have certain rules of dining which guests are usually expected to follow, and this may include a dress-code as well. The decor of such restaurants is rather stylish. These restaurants serve gourmet meals with specified dedicated meal courses. The food served is visually appealing using higher quality ingredients.

The mid-level restaurants are moderately priced. The atmosphere in these restaurants is friendly and informal. The appearance is neat and clean without being stylish. The food is wholesome consisting of normal ingredients.

Q7. Find words from the text which mean the same as the following:

(i) Stylish

Ans. chic

(ii) Introduced from abroad; unusual

Ans. exotic

(iii) Good, interesting food

Ans. gourmet

(iv) Was successful

Ans. was a hit

(v) Vegetarian side of the menu

Ans. green-dotted side

(vi) Avoiding

Ans. eschewing

(vii) Place at an inferior position

Ans. relegated

(viii) Raising the standard

Ans. elevating

(ix) Introduce new ideas

Ans. innovate

(x) Tried and tasted

Ans. commonly used

It has been found that although the world's population is almost equally divided between women and men, there are only 79 elderly men to every 100 elderly women.

"In all regions bar South Asia, women live longer than men", says Catherine Pierce, chief of UNFPA's Special Unit on Women, Population and Development. "In consequence, a higher proportion of elderly women are alone than are men."

"In developing countries, women's general health is much worse than men's Health and nutritional deficiencies throughout life mean that women enter old age more unhealthy than men." says Pierce.

She adds that "the culture of poverty follows women even in industrialised countries", where, for example, widows are entitled to only a portion of their husband's pensions.

Tarek Shuman, Director of the International Programme of the Centre for Ageing says, "The key policy question in industrialised and developing countries alike", is "Who is going to pay the bill?"

"The younger generation is paying for the elderly, no matter how you look at it", Shuman told Population during a recent visit to New York. Whereas the economic costs of ageing fall on the young, the social burden is borne by the elderly themselves, most commonly in the form of isolation and immobility.

Industrialised countries are discovering that the best place for the elderly is their own home, rather than some institution. This is the traditional model in many developing countries, where the family is central to the culture and traditions. Family care is more cost-effective and more likely to enhance the lives of the elderly than institutionalisation.

"Developing countries should think twice before investing institutions", says Shuman. This is where the UN comes in. It should emphasise an important message: 'Don't lose the family'."

Answer the following questions on the passage you have read:

Q1. According to Pierce, the plight of elderly women is worse than men in all countries. What reason does she give for this statement?

Ans. Peirce said that the plight of elderly women is worse than men in all countries. In developing countries, they suffer from health and nutritional deficiencies throughout life and so enter old age more unhealthy than men. Even in developed countries where they are entitled to old-age benefits, they get only a portion of their husband's pensions and this is not adequate to meet their economic and health care needs.

Q2. In what sense does the economic burden fall on the young?

Ans. The economic burden falls on the young because it is the younger generation who meets the economic needs of the elderly people.

Q3. What examples does the writer give of 'social burden'?

Ans. According to the writer, examples of 'social burden' are loneliness and immobility.

Games and sports should be an essential part of our school curriculum. Unfortunately, the emphasis in our schools and colleges has been, by and large, on academics alone. Most administrators and academicians think that games and sports should be meant for those who have an aptitude for these. For that matter, academic learning should also be limited to those who have the capacity to learn. We know this logic does not hold good. Again, some people feel that games and sports hamper the academic performance. Those who think on these lines, perhaps equate the pursuit of games and sports with achieving proficiency and excellence. This is not the truth, of course. The purpose is to keep you physically fit and mentally alert. Besides, education does not mean the acquisition of bookish knowledge alone. It is the harmonious development of an individual's personality that we are always aiming at. If, therefore, mental growth and development is important to professional growth then physical culture is equally necessary for the maintenance of proper health and physique. We should not, therefore, underestimate the value of sports and games in the large interests of our national growth.

Answer the following questions on the passage you have read:

Q1. What does the present educational system emphasise upon?

Ans. The present education system emphasises only on academic achievement of the students.

Q2. What is the view of most educational administrators regarding sports and games?

Ans. Most educational administrators are of the opinion that games and sports hamper the academic performance of students. Such activities should only be given secondary importance and should be meant for a few students who have an aptitude for it.

Q3. According to the writer, what should be the aim of education?

Ans. According to the writer, the aim of education should be the overall development of an individual's personality and not the acquisition of bookish knowledge alone.

Q4. What possible damage will take place if we neglect sports and games?

Ans. If we neglect sports and games, the maintenance of proper health and physique will become difficult.

Q5. Complete the following statements:

(i) Acquisition of knowledge along with physical well-being leads to____________.

Ans. Acquisition of knowledge along with physical well-being leads to harmonious development of an individual's personality.

(ii) In the interest of our national growth, it is important ____________.

Ans. In the interest of our national growth, it is important to understand the value of sports and games.

Q6. Give a suitable title to the passage.

Ans."Importance of sports and games in student's life"

The great defect of our civilisation is that it does not know what to do with its knowledge. Science has given us powers fit for the gods, yet we use them like small children. For example, we do not know how to manage our machines. Machines were made to be our servants; yet we have grown so dependent upon them that they are in a big way becoming our masters. Already most people spend most of their lives looking after and waiting upon machines. And, the machines are very stern masters. They must be fed with coal and petrol to drink, and oil to wash with, and they must be kept at the right temperature. And if they do not get their meals when they expect them, they grow sulky and refuse to work, or burst with rage, and blow up, and spread ruin and destruction all around them. Therefore, we have to wait upon them very attentively and do all that we can to keep them in good temper. Already we find it difficult either to work or play without the machines, and a time may come when they will rule us; just as we rule the animals.

And this brings me to the point at which I asked what do we do with all the time which the machines have saved for us, and the new energy they have given us? Overall it must be admitted, we do very little. For the most part, we use our time and energy to make more and better machines; but more and better machines will only give us still more time as well as energy, and what are we to do with them? The answer, I think is that we should try to become more civilised. For the machines themselves, and the power which the machines have given us, are not civilisation but aids to civilisation.

Answer the following questions on the passage you have read:

Q1. Give a suitable title to the passage.

Ans."Man and Machine"

Q2. Pick out any two human features which the machines have.

Ans. The machines have the following two human features:

(a) They are very stern masters; and

(b) They grow sulky and refuse to work.

Q3. Is the writer happy with the way human beings have used machines? Discuss.

Ans. The writer is not happy with the way the human beings have used machines because the machines are meant to provide better facilities and ease the tensions of men. However, they have become our masters.

Q4. Why does the writer call machines, "stern master"? Give reasons.

Ans. The writer calls the machines as stern masters because the machines need regular servicing, oil and petrol. If proper care is not taken, the machines stop working and give trouble like a stern master.

Q5. What are the benefits that we get from machines? Have these benefits really helped us become more civilised? Discuss.

Ans. The machines have saved our valuable time. We do very little work and save energy. But this has not helped us to become more civilised as we only make new machines by using the time and energy saved by machines. We do not attempt to improve ourselves. Hence, we have become the slaves of machines.

19

Many people in Europe think that they are much civilised and the people of Asia are quite barbarous. Is this because the people of Europe put on more clothes than the people of Asia and Africa? But clothes depend on the climate. In a cold climate men put on more clothes than in a hot climate. Or is it because the man with a gun is stronger than the man without a weapon and, is therefore, more civilised than him? Whether he is more civilised or not, the man who is weak dare not tell him that he is not or else he might get shot.

You know that only a few years ago there was a great war. Most of the countries of the world were in it, and every one of them was trying to kill as many people on the other side as possible. The Englishman was trying his best to kill Germans, and the Germans were killing Englishmen. Millions of people were killed in this war and many thousands were maimed for life. You must have seen many of these war-wounded people in France and elsewhere. Do you think, it was a very civilised or sensible thing for people to kill each other like this? It is just like two savages fighting in the jungles. Moreover, if the savages are called barbarous, how much more barbarous are the countries that behave in that way?

So, it is not easy to understand what civilisation means. Fine buildings, fine pictures and books and everything that is beautiful are certainly signs of civilisation. But an even better sign is a fine man who is unselfish and works with others for the good of all.

Answer the following questions on the passage you have read:

Q1. What do Europeans think of Asians?

Ans. The Europeans think that they are much civilised people and the Asians are quite barbarous.

Q2. What price may a weak person have to pay for expressing his views frankly?

Ans. The weak person may get killed if he expresses his views frankly. The writer says that even when a person is more civilised, he should remain silent if he is weak, or he might get shot.

Q3. What were the consequences of the war referred to in paragraph 2?

Ans. In paragraph 2, the writer explains the consequences of war and says that when most of the countries of the world fought, millions of people were killed. And many thousands were maimed for life. Such wars can only destroy lives and reflect the barbarous nature of mankind.

Q4. With whom does the writer compare the nations who fought in the war? What does he think of these nations?

Ans. The writer compares the nations who fought with two savages fighting in the jungle. He considers such nations as barbarous and not at all civilised.

Q5. What are some signs of a civilised nation?

Ans. Fine buildings, fine pictures and books and everything that is beautiful are certainly signs of civilisation.

Q6. Who is a civilised person according to the writer?

Ans. According to the writer, a person who keeps away from destruction of any kind and works with others in an unselfish way for the benefit of mankind is a civilised person.

20

How long I remained in the room with the cobra I cannot say. My servant said later that it was only half an hour, and no sound has ever been more welcome to me than the sounds I heard as my servant laid the table for dinner. I called him to the bathroom door, and told him of my predicament and instructed him to fetch a lantern and a ladder. After another long wait, I heard the babel of voices, followed by the scraping of the ladder against the outer wall of the house. When the lantern had been lifted to the window, ten feet above the ground, it did not illuminate the room, so I told the man who was holding it to break a pane of glass and pass the lantern through the opening. The opening was too small for the lantern to be passed in upright. However, after it had been relit three times it was finally inserted into the room and, feeling that the cobra was behind me, I turned my head and saw it lying at the bottom of the bedroom door two feet away. Leaning forward very slowly, I picked up heavy bath-mat, raised it high and let it fall as the cobra was sliding over the floor towards me. Fortunately I judged my aim accurately and the bath-mat crashed down on the cobra's neck six inches from its head.

As it bit at the wood and lashed about with its tail, I took a hasty stride to the verandah door and in a moment was outside among a crowd of men, armed with sticks and carrying lanterns for word had got round to the railway quarters that I was having a life-and-death struggle with a big snake in a locked room.

Answer the following questions on the passage you have read:

Q1. Read the following statements and say which statement is true and which is false.

(i) The writer remained in the company of the cobra for an hour.

Ans. False.

(ii) The writer instructed his servant to fetch a ladder.

Ans. True.

(iii) The lantern illuminated the room.

Ans. False.

(iv) The writer hit the cobra on its tail with the bath-mat.

Ans. False.

(v) The writer managed to escape when he found the cobra biting the mat.

Ans. True.

Q2. Answer the following questions briefly.

(i) What did the writer hear after a long wait?

Ans. The writer heard the babel of voices, followed by the scraping of the ladder against the outer wall of the house.

(ii) What did the writer ask the man holding the lantern to do?

Ans. The writer told the man who was holding the lantern to break a pane of glass and pass the lantern through the opening.

(iii) What did the writer discover when the room got lighted?

Ans. When the room got lighted, the writer discovered that the cobra was behind him.

(iv) In what manner did the writer hit the cobra?

Ans. The writer hit the neck of the cobra with the heavy bath-mat.

(v) What made the crowd gather outside the house of the writer?

Ans. The crowd gathered outside the house of the writer because they heard that the writer was having a life and death struggle with a big snake (cobra) and they ran to save the writer.

With lifted feet, hands still,
I am poised, and down the hill
Part, with heedful mind

The air goes by in a wind.
Swifter and yet more swift
Till the heart with a mighty lift
Makes the lungs laugh, the throat cry...
'O bird, see, see, bird, I fly!'
Is this, is this your joy?
O bird, then I, thought a boy,
For a golden moment share
Your feathery life in air.

Answer the following questions on the poem you have read:

Q1. Do you think the boy is afraid he might fall off the bicycle? Yes/No/Slightly?

Ans. No

Q2. What does 'poised' mean? (Choose from the alternatives below):

(i) Scared

(ii) Lifted

(iii) Slipping

(iv) Balanced

Ans. balanced

Q3. 'Part, with heedful mind' suggests a mind which is:

(i) Careful

(ii) Fearful

(iii) Hopeful

(iv) Restless

Ans. careful

Q4. What is the difference between *air* and *wind*?

Ans. The air is more or less still, the wind is moving air.

Q5. Who/what is moving swiftly: the wind or the cyclist?

Ans. The cyclist

Q6. Which words suggest the speed is increasing?

Ans. 'and yet more swift'

Q7. To interpret the meaning of lines 6 and 7 indicate the multiple (more than one) meanings of the underlined words:

till the heart with a <u>mighty</u> <u>lift</u>

Makes the lungs laugh, the throat <u>cry</u>

Ans. mighty = strong, heavy, glorious

lift = raise a weight (as of fear), a feeling of lightness i.e., the thrill of going up (as in a lift).

cry = scream from excitement, cry out of fear

Q8. What two meanings of 'feather' are indicated?

Ans. The feathers in the wings of the bird; the lightness of the feathers which help the bird to fly.

22

Indian social etiquette is a strange mix of Western and Indian culture. This is largely because of British influence during the colonial period, which continued in post-colonial India. Hence, India is very much influenced by the British style of etiquette, which is rather formal and somewhat conservative.

On the other hand, India is a multicultural society where religion, region, caste, language, tradition and custom play a large role in the kind of social etiquette prevalent in different parts of the country. These have an impact on the nature of greetings and introductions as well as the degree of formality used in social and business situations.

In addition to this is the impact of globalisation, which is largely felt in the metropolitan cities. With changes in lifestyles as well as business environment, a synthesised form of social behaviour and etiquette has emerged which is more in keeping with international practices. Having said this, it must be admitted that the influence of native culture continues to have its impact even in these environs. Hence, though a great deal of commonality can be seen in the social etiquette of Delhi, Mumbai, Calcutta, Bangaluru and Chennai, one may also observe many differences in the way people address and greet each other.

One may easily conclude that there is no one correct way of introducing and greeting. To communicate effectively and strike the right note at the very beginning, it is advisable to study the social etiquette of different regions so that you may be able to make a good impression from the word go.

Answer the following questions on the passage you have read:

Q1. The most appropriate title for the passage is:

(i) The impact of globalisation on social etiquette

(ii) Social etiquette in India

(iii) Effective communication

Ans. (ii) Social etiquette in India

Q2. State whether these statements are true or false:

(i) Indian social etiquette is very different from that of the West.

(ii) Indians are largely formal in their social etiquette.

(iii) All Indians greet each other in the same way.

(iv) The metropolitan cities of India are more influenced by global trends in social etiquette.

(v) It is advisable to follow your own rules in social etiquette.

(vi) Appropriate greetings and introductions can help us make a good first impression.

Ans. (i) False; (ii) True; (iii) False; (iv) True; (v) False; (vi) True

Q3. Find words from the passage, which have similar meanings to these:

(i) traditional

(ii) part of the British Empire

(iii) belonging to several cultures

(iv) large and important

(v) belonging to a specified region or place

Ans. (i) conservative; (ii) colonial; (iii) multicultural; (iv) metropolitan; (v) native

☺☺☺

Grammar Section

Tenses

Tenses are divided into three parts which are as follows:

(1) Present Tense: The running period of time.

(2) Past Tense: The period of time which has already gone.

(3) Future Tense: The period of time which will come ahead.

Each tense is sub-divided into four parts, i.e. Indefinite, Continuous, Perfect and Perfect Continuous.

Present

(1) Present Indefinite (2) Present Continuous

(3) Present Perfect (4) Present Perfect Continuous

Past

(1) Past Indefinite (2) Past Continuous

(3) Past Perfect (4) Past Perfect Continuous

Future

(1) Future Indefinite (2) Future Continuous

(3) Future Perfect (4) Future Perfect Continuous

Each sub-division is divided into three parts, which are as follows:

(1) Affirmative (2) Negative

(3) Interrogative

Sentence

Sentence is a group of words which makes clear sense. It has three parts, Subject/Object/Verb.

Subject: The doer is called the subject.

Object: The work done by the subject is called the object.

Verb: The action words are called verbs.

Order

Order plays a vital role in the construction of sentences. In Hindi language, the three parts of the sentence must be in the order of: Subject/ Object/Verb. While in English language, the three parts of the sentence must be in the order: Subject/Verb/Object.

Note: Like the word 'GOD' can be written as 'DOG' due to change of order. So, perfect order must be maintained.

Number

In English language, there are two types of numbers:

(1) **Singular Number:** It indicates a single person or thing.

(2) **Plural Number:** It indicates more than one person or thing.

Basically there are three kinds of tenses: Present + Past + Future; and the verb is used accordingly. A verb generally has three forms; first form; 2nd form; 3rd form. Every sentence which has a 'no' or 'not', becomes negative.

Verb

A verb has five forms. The students must learn them, e.g.

go – went – gone – goes – going

Now, let us study tenses one by one.

PRESENT TENSE

(1) Present Indefinite.

Recognition: It expresses indefiniteness of action in Present Time.

Affirmative–*Rule:* Subject + verb Ist form + 's' or 'es' (with plural without 's' or 'es') + objective + others.

Examples:

- They eat food.
- Rita sings a song.

Negative–*Rule*: Subject + does or do ('does' with singular and 'do' with plural)+ not + verb Ist form + objective + others.

Examples:

- They do not eat food.
- Rita does not sing a song.

Interrogative–*Rule*: Interrogative word + 'do' or 'does'+ subject+ verb Ist form?

Examples:

- Do they eat food?
- Does Rita sing a song?
- Where does he going?

(2) Present Continuous

Recognition: It expresses continuity of action in Present Time.

Affirmative–*Rule*: Subject+ 'is' or 'are' or 'am' (with singular 'is', plural 'are' and I 'am') + verb Ist form+ ing + objective + others.

Examples:

- She is eating the food.
- They are eating the food.
- I am eating the food.

Negative–*Rule*: Subject+ 'is' or 'are' or 'am' (with singular 'is', plural 'are' and I 'am') + not+ verb Ist form+ ing + objective + others.

Examples:

- She is not eating the food.
- They are not eating the food.
- I am not eating the food.

Interrogative–*Rule*: Interrogative word + 'is' or 'are' or 'am' (with singular 'is', plural 'are' and I 'am') + Subject + verb Ist form+ ing + objective + others?

Examples:

- Are they eating the food?
- What am I eating?

(3) Present Perfect Tense

Recognition: It expresses completion of action in present tense.

Affirmative–*Rule*: Subject + has or have (with singular 'has' and 'have' with plural)+ verb IIIrd form+ object + others.

Examples:

- He has eaten the food.
- They have eaten the food.
- We have already learned the concept of clauses and phrases.

Negative–*Rule*: Subject + has or have (with singular 'has' and 'have' with plural)+ not + verb IIIrd form+ object + others.

Examples:

- He has not eaten the food.
- They have not eaten the food.
- She has not read this novel yet.

Interrogative–*Rule*: Interrogative words + has or have (with singular 'has' and 'have' with plural)+ subject + verb IIIrd form+ object + others?

Examples:

- Has he eaten the food?
- Have they eaten the food?
- Why have they eaten the food?

(4) Present Perfect Continuous

Recognition: It expresses completion of action as well as continuity of action. In this tense, time expression is always given.

Affirmative–*Rule*: Subject + has or have (with singular 'has' and 'have' with plural)+ been + verb Ist form+ ing + object+ 'since' or 'for' + time + others.

Note: Since: For point of time, and **For:** For period of time,

Examples:

- He has been eating the food for two hours.
- They have been eating the food since 2 o'clock.
- They have been manufacturing the scooters here for 8 years.

Negative–*Rule*: Subject + has or have (with singular 'has' and 'have' with plural)+ not + been + verb Ist form+ ing + object+ 'since' or 'for' + time + others.

Examples:

- He has not been eating the lunch for two hours.
- They have not been eating the lunch since 2 o'clock.

Interrogative–*Rule*: Interrogative words + 'has' or 'have' + **s**ubject + been + verb Ist form+ ing + object+ 'since' or 'for' + time + others?

Examples:

- Has he been eating the lunch for two hours?
- Have they been eating the lunch since 2 o'clock?
- What has he been eating for two hours?

PAST TENSE

(1) Past Indefinite

Recognition: It expresses indefiniteness of action in Past Time.

Affirmative–*Rule:* Subject + verb IInd form + objective + others.

Examples:

- He ate the lunch.
- They ate the lunch.

Negative–*Rule:* Subject + did + not + verb Ist form + objective + others.

Examples:

- He did not eat the lunch.
- They did not eat the lunch.
- I did not play hockey.
- They did not write an essay.

Interrogative–*Rule*: Interrogative word + did + subject + verb Ist form + objective + others?

Example:

- Did he eat the lunch?
- Did they play the hockey?
- Why did they write a letter?

(2) Past Continuous

Recognition: It expresses continuity of action in Past Time.

Affirmative-*Rule*: Subject+ was or were (with singular number was and with plural were)+ verb Ist form + ing + object+ others.

Examples:

- He was eating the lunch.
- They were writing a letter.

Negative-*Rule*: Subject+ was or were (with singular number was and with plural were)+not+ verb Ist form + ing+ object+ others.

Examples:

- He was not eating the lunch.
- They were not eating the lunch.

Interrogative-*Rule*: Interrogative words + was or were (with singular number was and with plural were)+ subject + verb Ist form + ing+ object+ others.

Examples:

- Was he eating the lunch?
- Were they playing cricket?
- Where was he going?

(3) Past Perfect

Recognition: It expresses completion of action in Past Time.

Affirmative-*Rule*: Subject+ had (with both singular number and plural number)+ verb IIIrd form + object+ others.

Examples:

- He had eaten the lunch.
- They had written a letter.

Negative-*Rule*: Subject + had (with both singular number and plural number)+ not+ verb IIIrd form + object+ others.

Examples:

- He had not eaten the lunch.
- They had not played football.
- I had not learnt my lesson.
- She had not cooked the food.

Interrogative-*Rule*: Interrogative word + had (with both singular number and plural number)+subject+ verb IIIrd form + object+ others?

Examples:

- Had he eaten the lunch?
- Had they written a letter?
- What had he eaten?

(4) Past Perfect Continuous

Recognition: It expresses completion of action as well as continuity of action in Past Time.

Affirmative-*Rule*: Subject+ had (with both singular number and plural number)+ been + verb Ist form + ing + 'since' or 'for' + time + object+ others.

Examples:

- He had been writing a letter since morning.
- They had been preparing for exams for two months.

Negative-*Rule*: Subject+ had (with both singular number and plural number)+ not + been + verb Ist form + ing + 'since' or 'for' + time + object+ others.

Examples:

- He had not been writing a letter since morning.
- She had not been cooking for ten days.

Interrogative-*Rule*: Interrogative word + had (with both singular number and plural number)+ subject + been + verb Ist form + ing + 'since' or 'for' + time + object + others?

Examples:

- Had he been writing a letter since morning?
- Had they been rehearsing a song for two days?
- Where had he been living for two years?

FUTURE TENSE

(1) Future Indefinite

Recognition: It expresses indefiniteness of action in Future Time.

Affirmative–*Rule:* Subject + will or shall ('I' or 'We' – 'shall' and with all other subjects 'will') + verb Ist form + object + others.

Examples:

- I shall eat the lunch.
- They will write a letter.
- We shall play cricket.
- She will cook the lunch.

Negative– *Rule:* Subject + will or shall ('I' or 'We' – 'shall' and with all other subjects 'will') + not + verb Ist form + object + others.

Examples:

- They will not write a letter.
- She will not cook the food.

Interrogative– *Rule:* Interrogative words + will or shall ('I' or 'We' – 'shall' and with all other subjects 'will') + subject + verb Ist form + object + others?

Examples:

- Will he write a letter?
- Shall we play cricket?
- What will you play there?

(2) Future Continuous

Recognition: It expresses continuity of action in Future Time.

Affirmative –*Rule:* Subject + will or shall ('I' or 'We' – 'shall' and with all other subjects 'will') + be + verb Ist form + ing + object + others.

Examples:

- He will be eating the lunch.
- I shall be writing a letter.

Negative–*Rule:* Subject + will or shall ('I' or 'We' – 'shall' and with all other subjects 'will') + not+ be + verb Ist form + ing + object + others.

Examples:

- He will not be eating the lunch.
- I shall not be writing a letter.

Interrogative– *Rule:* Interrogative words + will or shall (with 'I' and 'We' – 'shall' and with all other subjects 'will') + subject + be+ verb Ist form + object + others?

Examples:

- Will he be eating the lunch?
- Will they be writing a letter?
- What will he be eating?

(3) Future Perfect

Recognition: It expresses completion of action in Future Time.

Affirmative– *Rule:* Subject + will or shall ('I' or 'We' – 'shall' and with all other subjects 'will') + have + verb IIIrd form + object + others.

Examples:

- He will have eaten the lunch.
- They will have written a letter.
- I shall have cooked the lunch.

Negative–*Rule:* Subject + will or shall ('I' or 'We' – 'shall' and with all other subjects 'will') + not + have + verb IIIrd form + object + others.

Examples:

- He will not have written a letter.
- They will not have gone to the market.

Interrogative–*Rule:* Interrogative word + will or shall ('I' or 'We' – 'shall' and with all other subjects 'will') + subject + have + verb IIIrd form + object + others?

Examples:

- Will they have written a letter?
- Shall we have eaten the lunch?
- Why shall we have gone to the market?
- Why will Sita have written a letter?
- Shall I have learnt my lesson?

(4) Future Perfect Continuous

Recognition: It expresses completion of action as well as continuity of action in Future Time.

Affirmative–Rule: Subject + will or shall ('I' or 'We' – 'shall' and with all other subjects 'will') + have + been + verb Ist form + ing + object + 'since' or 'for' + time + others.

Note: Use of 'since' or 'for' for expression of time

Examples:

- He will have been writing a letter since night.
- They will have been playing hockey for five days.

Negative–*Rule:* Subject + will or shall ('I' or 'We' – 'shall' and with all other subjects 'will') + have + not + been + verb Ist form + ing + object + 'since' or 'for' + time + others.

Examples:

- He will not have been writing a letter since morning.
- Mohan will not have been rehearsing a song for nine days.

Interrogative–*Rule:* Interrogative word + will or shall ('I' or 'We' – 'shall' and with all other subjects 'will') + subject + have + not + been + verb Ist form + ing + object + 'since' or 'for' + time + others?

Examples:

- Will he have been writing a letter since morning?
- What shall I have been playing cricket for two hours?

THE SEQUENCE OF TENSES

The Sequence of Tenses is the principle according to which the tense of the verb in a subordinate clause follows the tense of the verb in the Principle Clause. There are two main rules about the Sequence of Tenses:

Rule No. 1. If the verb in the Principle Clause is in the Present or Future Tense, the verb in the Subordinate Clause may be in any tense, according to the sense:

He says or He will say
→ that Mohan goes to school everyday.
→ that Mohan is going to school now
→ that Mohan has gone to school.
→ that Mohan has been going to school since last November.
→ that Mohan went to school yesterday.
→ that Mohan was going to school.
→ that Mohan had gone to school before he (the speaker) arrived.
→ that Mohan had been going to school for two months.
→ that Mohan will go to school.
→ that Mohan will be going to school.
→ that Mohan will have gone to school.
→ that Mohan will have been going to school since two days.
→ that what he is doing.
→ that what he was doing.
→ that what he will be doing
→ that what he had done.
→ that what he will have done.

Rule No. 2. If the verb in the Principle Clause is in the Past Tense, the verb in the Subordinate Clause must also be written in the Past Tense, e.g.

He said
- → that Mohan went to school everyday.
- → that Mohan was going to school then.
- → that Mohan had gone to school.
- → that Mohan had been going to school since November.
- → that Mohan had gone to school the previous day.
- → that Mohan had been going to school for three days.
- → that Mohan would go to school.
- → that Mohan would be going to school.
- → that Mohan would have gone to school.

Special Cases: There are, however, some exceptions to this rule:

(i) If the verb in the Subordinate Clause expresses some universal truths or habitual facts, it is always in the Present Tense, even if the verb in the Principle clause is in the Past Tense; e.g.

- The father told his sons that union is strength.
- I was sorry to hear that he has a bad temper.
- The teacher made it clear that the earth revolves round the sun.
- We learnt at school that honesty is the best policy.
- I told him that I am an early riser.

(ii) Again if the subordinate clause is an adverb clause showing comparison it may have a present tense even after the past tense, in the principal clause:

Examples:

- He liked you better than he likes me.
- He worked harder than I do.
- He liked you better than he has liked me.

Note: If the comparison is expressed by *as well as* instead of *than*, the same rule holds good:

Examples:

- He liked you as well as he likes me.
- He liked you as well as he has liked me.

(iii) In adverbial clauses of purpose, the verb is in the present tense when the verb in the principal clause is in the present or future tense:

Examples:

- He works hard (present) so that he may succeed. (present)
- He will work hard (future) so that he may succeed. (present)

(iv) *Since* as a conjunction of time is followed by a verb in the past tense or the present perfect tense, whereas the verb in the principal clause usually is in the present or the present perfect tense:

Examples:

- Since you left the house no one has lived in it.
- It is long since you left.
- Since you have gone from here things have changed.

(v) *Lest* introducing a subordinate clause is always followed by should:

Examples:

- I speak slowly lest he should be disturbed.
- I spoke slowly lest he should be disturbed.
- I shall speak slowly lest he should be disturbed.

(vi) The conjunctions *as if* and *as though* always take a past tense in the subordinate clause:

Examples:

- He cried as if someone had died.
- He behaved as if he were the boss.

Sentence Connectors

A conjunction is a word which connects words, phrases, clauses or sentences and at the same time brings about relationships between the elements thus joined. In short, the joining words are called conjunctions.

Major conjunctions are:

And, but, unless, lest, therefore, otherwise, when, while, however, since, because, though, yet, neither, nor, either, or, whether, till, as, if.

Examples of their uses:

(i) Words connected by conjunctions:

- Ram and Shyam went out for a walk.

(ii) Phrases connected conjunctions:

- Democracy is a government of the people, by the people and for the people.

(iii) Clauses connected by conjunctions:

- As I was ill, I didn't go to school.

(iv) Sentences connected by conjunctions:

- Kabir had no hope of winning the prize, nevertheless he tried his best.

Kinds of Conjunctions: These are mainly divided into two parts:

(1) Coordinating Conjunctions

(2) Subordinating Conjunctions.

Coordinating Conjunctions: These are the conjunctions which join words, phrases or coordinate clauses of equal rank. These are: Otherwise, nor, or, else, and, for, but, etc.

Examples:

- He worked hard and got the first division.
- His old but he runs fast.
- Two and two make four.

Subordinating Conjunctions: These are the conjunctions which join a sub-ordinate clause and a principal clause of unequal rank. These are: Because, as, than, when, since, though, if, that, etc.

Examples:

- Hardly had he reached the school when the peon rang the bell.
- She knew that she would win the prize.
- I shall not attend his marriage unless he invites me.

Classification of Coordinating Conjunctions: They can connect co-ordinating clauses in four different ways. Hence, we have four types of co-ordinating conjunctions:

(i) Cumulative Conjunctions: These conjunctions add one simple statement or a fact to another. They are: Not only..... but also both.... and as well as, too, now, also, not less than, etc.

Examples:

- Suresh as well as his children has come.
- Not only is he rich but also wise.
- He is both a singer and dancer.
- God made the country and man made the town.

(ii) Alternative Conjunctions: These conjunctions express a choice between two alternatives. They are: Either...... or, Neither... nor, otherwise, else, or, etc.

Examples:

- We have neither a pen nor a pencil.
- Either Radha or her brother has done this mischief.
- Work hard otherwise you will fail.
- Walk quickly else you will miss the bus.

(iii) Adversative Conjunctions: These conjunctions express contrast between two statements. They are: However, whereas, while, only, still, yet, but, nevertheless, etc.

Examples:

- Ramesh worked hard still he failed.
- Kiran was angry, bust she kept quiet.
- Go where you like, only do not stay here.
- Raju is a rich man; while (whereas) his father was very poor.

(iv) Illative Conjunctions: These conjunctions express inference, i.e., those conjunctions which show that one statement or fact is inferred or proved from another. They are: then, for, therefore, so, etc.

Examples:

- His is honest, therefore, he is respected.
- He was innocent, so he was pardoned.
- It must have rained last night, for the ground is wet.
- It is time to go; let us start then.

Classification of Subordinating Conjunctions: These are classified according to the purpose they serve. They are as follows:

(i) Conjunctions showing 'time' – before, after, as, as soon as, while, so long as, as long as, till, until.

Examples:

- The patient had died before the doctor arrived.
- Wait here till I come.
- He did not go away until I came in.
- You must stay indoors as long as it is raining.
- As soon as we left home, it began to rain.

(ii) Conjunctions showing 'cause' or 'reason' – as, since, because.

Examples:

- As Mahesh is an honest boy, I love him.
- I didn't go to school since it was raining.
- Suresh was fined because he broke the window-pane.

(iii) Conjunctions showing 'purpose' – that, so that, in order that, lest.

Examples:

- We eat so that we may live.
- Neelam works hard in order that she may pass.
- Soldiers die that the country may live.
- Walk fast lest you should miss the train.

(iv) Conjunctions showing 'condition' – if, unless, provided, provided that.

Examples:

- If you go to Mumbai, please bring a watch for me.
- We cannot get through the examination unless we work hard.
- You can camp here provided you do not damage the plants.
- We shall play the match provided that it does not rain.

(v) Conjunctions showing 'place' – where, wherever.

Examples:
- I do not know where he lives.
- You may go wherever you like.

(vi) Conjunctions showing 'manner' or 'extent' – as, as..... as, so far as, as if.

(vii) Conjunctions showing 'comparison' – than, so.....as, as.....as.
Examples:
- He did not behave as I expected him to do.
- He is a patriot, as far as I know.
- Do as I tell you.

(viii) Conjunctions showing 'concession' or 'contrast' – although, though, however, yet, notwithstanding.
Examples:
- Though he is weak, he can walk.
- Although he is poor, yet he is honest.
- He cannot catch the train however fast he may run.
- Rubi failed in the examination notwithstanding hard work.

(ix) Conjunctions showing 'result' – that.
Examples:
- He is so weak that he cannot walk.
- The boys made such a noise that nothing could be heard.

Note: Conjunctions which are used in pairs are called 'Correlative Conjunctions'. They are: either....or, neither... nor, both... and, not only... but also, though... yet, whether... or.

Examples:
- Either you or your brother has stolen my pen.
- Neither you nor your brother has come prepared.
- Neither he nor I am taking the examination.

Non-Finites

There are some verbs which do not have subjects. They are also not affected by the number, person and tense of the subjects. Such type of verbs are called Non-Finite Verbs, e.g.

(1) Walking is a good exercise.
(2) Singing is an art.
(3) To drive a car is easy.
(4) I want to play cricket.

In the above sentences 'walking', 'singing', 'to drive and to play' are non-finite verbs because they do not have any subject, neither they express Number, Person and Tenses of the subjects.

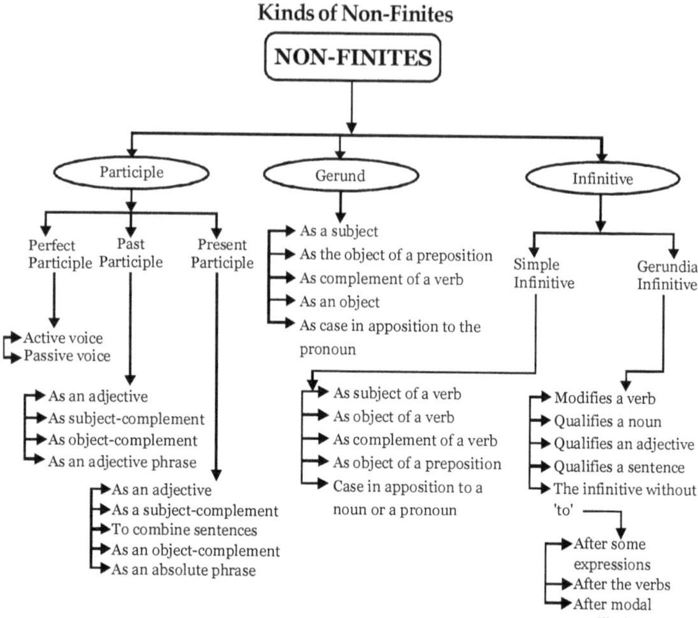

Non-Finite verbs are divided into three parts:

(1) Infinitive
(2) Gerund
(3) Participle

(1) Infinitive

This is the verb without any connection to a subject. Infinitives usually have a 'to' in front of them: to run, to jump, to be, to have, to go.

Example:

- It is not the right time to go to the shops.

Uses of the Infinitive:

(1) The Infinitive may be the subject of a sentence, e.g.
- To respect our teachers is our duty.

(2) The Infinitive may be the complement of a verb, e.g.
- His plan is to keep the affair secret.

(3) The Infinitive may be the object or part of the object of a verb, e.g.
- He wants me to pay.

(4) To convey a plan, e.g.
- She is to be married next year.

(5) Be about + infinitive expresses the immediate future, e.g.
- They are about to start.

(6) The Infinitive can express purpose, e.g.
- We work hard to get a good score.

(7) The Infinitive can be used after certain adjectives, e.g.
- angry, glad, happy, sorry, lucky.

(8) The Infinitive can connect two clauses, e.g.
- He asked me to get first division by working hard.

(9) An important construction for using infinitive.
Verb + Know/what/when/where/which/why + infinitive, e.g.
- I know how to write a letter.

(10) Infinitive can be used after verb + object, e.g.
- He advised me to sing a song.

(11) Verb + Object + Infinitive, e.g.
- She encouraged me to try again.

(12) When the thought concerns a previous action, we use the Perfect Infinitive, e.g.
- They are believed to have landed in Japan.

(13) The Infinitive is used after 'only' to express a disappointing situation, e.g.
- He survived the crash only to die in the desert.

(14) Infinitives + Prepositions, e.g.
- A table to write on.

(15) Adjective + enough + Infinitive, e.g.
- He is old enough to climb on the wall.

(16) Infinitive as the object of a verb, e.g.
- The box is light enough for me to carry.

(17) The object of a preposition, e.g.
- The light was strong enough to read by.

(18) Adverb + enough + Infinitive, e.g.
- He did not jump high enough to win a prize.

(19) Infinitive is used with the following verbs in the Passive Voice: acknowledge, believe, consider, find, know, report, say, suppose, think, understand, e.g.
- He is understood to have left the country.

(20) Infinitive can be used in opposition to a dummy subject, e.g.
- It is a pleasure to see you.

(2) The Gerund

Gerund works as a noun. It is found in the form of 'first form + ing' of the verb, i.e. walk + ing = walking. It is also known as 'Verbal Noun'. It has exactly the same form as the present participle.

It can be used in the following ways:

(1) As subject of a sentence, e.g.
- Walking is a good exercise.

(2) As complement of a verb, e.g.
- Her hobby is painting.

(3) After preposition, e.g.
- He was accused of smuggling.

(4) After certain verbs, e.g.
- He came running.

(5) In noun compounds, e.g.
- A driving boat.

(6) The Gerund is used in short prohibitions, e.g.
- No smoking. No waiting.

Note: Prohibitions involving an object are usually expressed by an imperative, e.g.
- Do not touch electric wires.

(7) Regret, remember, forget are used with a gerund when the action expressed by the gerund is an earlier action, e.g.
- I regret spending so much money.

(8) 'Go on' is normally followed by a gerund, e.g.
- Go on singing.

(9) Verbs followed by the gerund. The most important of such types of verbs are as follows:
admit, appreciate, avoid, consider, delay, deny, dislike, enjoy, escape, excuse, finish, forgive, involve, keep, miss, pardon, postpone, practice, remember, risk, stop, suggest, understand, etc., e.g.
- He admitted taking the money.
- Would you appreciate telling a lie?

(3) The Participle

The Participle works as a verb as well as an adjective. This is why it is also known as Verbal Adjective. The main difference between Gerund and Participle is that the Gerund works as a noun while Participle works as adjective to qualify Nouns or Pronouns.

Kinds of Participle

Participles are divided into three parts:

(1) The Present Participle
(2) The Past Participle
(3) The Perfect Participle

The Present Participle: The Present Participle always expresses continuity of action. It is formed by using 'ing' in the first form of the verb. It does not denote time but an unfinished or incomplete action.

Example:
- I saw him crossing the road.
- I heard someone weeping.

The Present Participle is used as follows:

(1) As an Adjective, e.g.
- Barking dogs seldom bite.

(2) As a subject complement, e.g.
- This poem is interesting.

(3) As an object complement, e.g.
- I saw him leaving the room.

(4) As an absolute phrase, e.g.
- It being a rainy day, we did not go out.

(5) To combine sentences, e.g.
- I heard the news of his death. I went to his house.
- Hearing the news of his death, I went to his house.

(6) After verbs of sensation, e.g.
- I felt the bike skidding.

(7) After catch/find/leave + object, e.g.
- I caught them stealing my mangoes.

(8) When one action is immediately followed by another by the same subject, the first action can be expressed by the Present Participle, e.g.
- He opened the drawer and took out a revolver.
- Opening the drawer he took out a revolver.

(9) In case of three actions, express the last two by the Present Participle, e.g.
- I fell, striking my head against the door and cutting it.

The Past Participle: The Past Participle always expresses completion of action. It is the III form of the verb. It ends in d, ed, t, n or en.

The Past Participle is used as follows:

(1) As an Adjective, e.g.
- The tired traveller lay under a tree.

(2) As a subject compliment, e.g.
- She seems worried.

(3) As an object complement, e.g.
- We found all the people gone.

(4) As an Adjective phrase, e.g.
- The boy selected for the post is my cousin.

The Perfect Participle: The Perfect Participle is found by putting 'having' before the Past Participle, i.e. III form of the verb. It denotes an action, which was finished in the past.

The Perfect Participle is used as follows:

(1) Having + Past Participle, e.g.
- Having taught him, I returned home.
- Having being tired, he took rest.

(2) The Perfect Participle can be used instead of the Present Participle in sentences where one action is immediately followed by another with the same subject, e.g.
- Tying one end of the rope to his bed, he threw the other end out of the window.

Note: The Perfect Participle emphasises that the first action is complete before the second one starts.

Modals

Modals/Auxiliaries are helping verbs that are used with the main verb to express the modes and manners of actions denoted by the main verbs. Modals are the modified forms of helping verbs.

The main modals are as follows:

Shall, will, should, would, can, could, may, might, must, ought to, used to, need, dare, etc.

Features of Modals

- Modals always express the imaginary actions like ability, power, permission, request, possibility, willingness, certainty, etc.
- Modals do not come alone, they always take first form of the verb with them.
- Modals are never affected by the person, number and gender of the subject.

Use of 'Shall' and 'Will'

	First Person my, me, us (I, my, me, us, We, Our, Mine, etc.)	II/III Person (You, Your, he, she, it, they, etc.)
Shall	Simple Future	Threat/Promise/Command Firm determination
Will	Threat/Promise Intention/Firm determination	Simple Future

From the table, it becomes clear that to express simple future tense with the subjects I or We use 'shall' and with all other subjects use 'will', while to express Threat/Promise/Firm determination/Willingness with the subjects I or We, use 'will' and with all other subjects use 'shall', e.g.

- I shall buy a car. (Simple Future)
- I will buy a car. (Firm determination)
- I will surely help her. (Promise)
- I will break your hand. (Threat)
- You shall be punished if you do not change your habits. (Threat)

Uses of 'Should' (Past form of shall)

'Should' is the past tense of 'shall'. It is used in the following ways:

(1) To express the Future in the Past tense, e.g.

- I told him that I should go to Mumbai.

(2) To express duty or obligation, e.g.
- We should respect our elders.

(3) To express advice or suggestion, e.g.
- You should work hard to pass the examination.

(4) To express request, e.g.
- I should like to say that he is not to blame.

(5) To express surprise, e.g.
- It is really sad that he should lose in the first round.

(6) To express supposition or improbable action, e.g.
- Should they work hard, they will pass.

(7) With lest in order to express purpose, e.g.
- I worked hard lest I should fail.

(8) To make conditional sentences, e.g.
- Should it rain, we shall not go out.

(9) To express supposition, e.g.
- Should you go to the market, bring a pen for me.

Uses of 'Would' (Past form of Will)

'Would' is the past tense of 'will' and it is used in the following ways:

(1) As the future tense in the indirect speech, e.g.
- He said that he would not take milk.

(2) To express past habit, e.g.
- Gandhiji would spin every day.

(3) To express determination, e.g.
- I would help him in any trouble.

(4) To express suggestion, e.g.
- Would you take care of your health?

(5) To express polite request, e.g.
- Would you take a cup of tea?

(6) To express wish or desire, e.g.
- Would that I were a king?

(7) To express preference, e.g.
- I would prefer death to dishonour.

(8) To express unreal condition, e.g.
- If I won a lottery prize, I would build a theatre.

Uses of 'Can'

'Can' shows ability. It is used to express strength – physical, mental, of the official authority, of wealth, etc. It is used as follows:

(1) To express ability, e.g.
- I can speak English fluently.

(2) To express strong possibility which is almost a certainty, e.g.
- The Principal can fine him.

(3) To express permission, e.g.
- You can go home now.

(4) To express disposition, e.g.

- Mohan can tell a lie at any time.

[Generally, 'can' is used for seeking permission from someone younger to you.]

Uses of 'Could' (Past Tense of Can)

'Could' is the past tense of 'can' and is used in the indirect form as follows:

(1) To express Power in past tense, e.g.
- I asked him if he could play cricket.

(2) To express Ability in past tense, e.g.
- I could solve the whole paper in one hour.

(3) Past Tense of Polite Request, e.g.
- Could you lend me your pen?

(4) Past Tense of Possibility, e.g.
- You could have caught the train if you had run fast.

(5) Feeling of Impatience, e.g.
- How could it happen?

(6) Past Tense phrase, e.g.
- The Principal couldn't help giving him admission.

Uses of 'May'

May means 'to be able to'. It is used to express:

(1) To express Permission, e.g.
- May I come in sir?

(2) To express Possibility, e.g.
- It may rain today.

(3) To express Purpose, e.g.
- We eat so that we may live.

(4) To express Wish or Prayer, e.g.
- May you live long!

Uses of 'Might' (Past Tense of May)

(1) The Past tense of May, e.g.
- I asked him if I might take his book.

(2) Purpose, e.g.
- He ran fast so that he might catch the train.

(3) Doubtful Possibility, e.g.
- He is working hard, he might win a scholarship.

(4) Possibility of Past Tense, e.g.
- The tortoise said that he might win the race.

(5) Permission in Past Tense, e.g.
- The captain said that we might play match.

(6) Future condition, e.g.
- If I get money, I might go to England.

(7) To express good wishes in the Past, e.g.
- The teacher wished that I might live long.

Uses of 'Must'

Must is used to express:

(1) Necessity, e.g.
- You must work hard to get good marks.

(2) Obligation, e.g.
- Parents must look after their children.

(3) Determination, e.g.
- I must finish this work today.

(4) Compulsion, e.g.
- We must follow the rules of the road.

(5) Certainty or belief, e.g.
- Geeta must have broken my slate.

(6) Emphatic advice, e.g.
- You must give up bad habits.

(7) Possibility, e.g.
- The teacher must have finished this course by this time.

(8) Expectation, e.g.
- There must be something wrong in his mind.

(9) Prohibition, e.g.
- You must not leave the class without my permission.

(10) Necessity or obligation in Future Tense, e.g.
- We must do our work by tomorrow.

Uses of 'Ought to'

The modal is 'Ought' but 'to' is always used with it. That is why it is called 'ought to'.

Ought to is used to express the following:

(1) Moral duty or obligation in Present Tense, e.g.
- We ought to respect our elders.

(2) Moral duty or obligation in Past Tense, e.g.
- You ought to have worked hard.

(3) Advice, e.g.
- We ought to walk fast as we are getting late.

(4) Strong probability, e.g.
- He is very hard working; he ought to win a scholarship.

Uses of 'Need'

Need is used as the Principal verb and also as a Defective verb.

(1) When it is used as Principal verb, it means 'to stand in need of', e.g.
- I need his help.

(2) Need as a defective verb is used in the negative and interrogative sentences.
- In negative and interrogative sentences, need is used to express weakness, necessity, obligation, etc.
- In this form it can be used only in the present tense.
- An 's' is added to need if the subject is in the third person and the sentence is in the present tense, e.g. He needs to study.

Uses of 'Dare'

Dare is used both as the Principal Verb and as Defective Verb.

Dare as a Principal Verb

(i) As a Principal Verb, dare means challenge.

(ii) As a Principal Verb, it will have the following three forms: dare, dares, dared.

(iii) It is used with all the tenses and is followed by 'to' in the affirmative sentences, e.g.

- He dares to face his enemy.

Dare as a Defective Verb

(i) As a defective verb, dare means 'to venture'.

(ii) As a defective verb, it will have the following three forms: dare, durst, durst.

(iii) As a defective verb, it is used only in the negative and interrogative sentences.

(iv) In this form it does not take 'to', e.g.

- He dare not face his enemy. (Present Tense)
- He durst not face his enemy. (Past Tense)

Uses of 'Used to'

Used to is used to express some past habit. It is used in the following types of sentences.

(1) Affirmative Sentences, e.g.

- Gandhiji used to spin for an hour every morning.

(2) Negative Sentences, e.g.

- He used not to tell lies.

(3) Interrogative Sentences, e.g.

- Did he use to drink when he was young?

(4) Passive Voice Sentences, e.g.

- I am used to lead simple life.

Narration

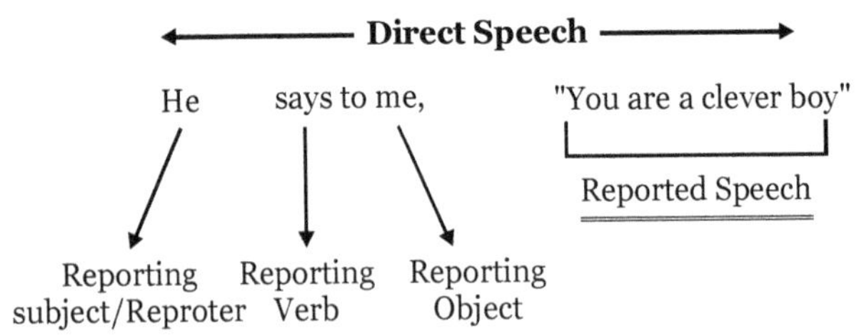

The art of reporting the words of a speaker is called narration.

Direct Speech: The real words of the speaker are called Direct Speech.

Indirect Speech: When we convert the speaker's words in our own words then it becomes Indirect Speech.

As shown above, Direct Speech is divided into two parts, i.e. Reporting Speech and Reported Speech. That part of Direct Speech which is outside the inverted commas is called Reporting Speech and the part of Direct Speech which is inside the inverted commas is called Reported Speech.

Reporting Speech is divided into three parts, i.e. Reporting Subject/Reporter, Reporting Verb and Reporting Object.

- The subject of the Reporting Speech is called Reporting Subject or Reporter.
- The verb of the Reporting Speech is called Reporting Verb.
- The object of the reporting speech is called Reporting Object.

There are basically five types of sentences which can be converted from Direct Sentences to Indirect Sentences.

(1) Assertive Sentences (Statements)
(2) Interrogative Sentences (Questions)
(3) Imperative Sentences (Commands and Requests)
(4) Exclamatory Sentences (Strong feelings)
(5) Optative Sentences (Wishes)

To convert direct sentences into indirect sentences, we have to do four common changes.

Change No. 1: Remove commas and inverted commas, use any conjunction.

Change No. 2: In Reported Speech, there are some words which must be changed when converting into indirect speech. They are as follows:

Words		**Changed into**
here	into	there
now	into	then
this	into	that
these	into	those
today	into	that day
tonight	into	that night
yesterday	into	the previous day
last night	into	the previous night
last week	into	the previous week
tomorrow	into	the following day
next week	into	the following week
ago	into	before
thus	into	so
hence	into	thence
neither	into	thither
either	into	thither
come	into	go

Note: Come is changed into go only in that case when any word showing nearness is given with it.

Change No. 3: Change of Person. There are three types of Person in English language which are as follows:

First Person [I my me / We our us]

Second Person [You Your You]

Second Person [He His Him / She Her Her / They Their Them / It Its It]

In order to make the change simple, here is a word 'SON' which makes the situation clear.

S O N
1 2 3

Where, S – stands for Subject, Subject of the Reporting Speech. O – stands for Object, Object of the Reporting Speech and N – stands for no change. It means, Ist person is always changed according to the Subject, IInd person is always changed according to the object and IIIrd person is never changed.

Change No. 4: If the reporting verb is in Present or in Future Tense, there is no change in the tense of the Reported Speech but if the reporting verb is in Past Tense, there is always a change in the tense of the Reported Speech, which is as follows:

(1) Present Indefinite is changed into Past Indefinite
(2) Present Continuous is changed into Past Continuous
(3) Present Perfect is changed into Past Perfect.
(4) Present Perfect Continuous is changed into Past Perfect Continuous
(5) Past Indefinite is changed into Past Perfect
(6) Past Continuous is changed into Past Perfect Continuous
(7) Past Perfect and Past Perfect Continuous remain unchanged.
(8) In case of Future Tense, there are only four words which are changed, *i.e.*

will	into	would
shall	into	should
may	into	might
can	into	could

Note: In all types of sentences, use all the four common changes as mentioned above with their individual changes.

(1) Assertive Sentences (Statements)

Change No. 1: Remove commas and inverted commas, use conjunction 'that'.

Change No. 2: Change the reporting verb say into tell, says into tells, said into told, if the reporting object is given in the sentence. However, do not change the reporting verb if reporting object is not given in the sentence.

Change No. 3: 'Said to' can be changed into replied, informed, stated, added, remarked, asserted, assured, pleaded, reminded, complained and reported according to the meaning.

- **He said to me, "I cannot help you in this matter."**
  He told me that he could not help me in that matter.
- **He said, "My sister's marriage comes off next month.**
  He said that his sister's marriage would come off the following month.

(2) Interrogative Sentences

Change No. 1: Change the reporting verb said or said to into asked or 'inquired of'. In case of a single question, change it into 'asked' but in case of more than one question, change it into 'inquired of'.

Change No. 2: Use conjunction 'if' or 'whether' if the reported speech starts with a helping verb. But do not use any conjunction if the reported speech starts with an interrogative word.

Change No. 3. Change the Interrogative sentence or word into Assertive sentence or word.

Change No. 4. Remove question mark '?' and use full stop '.', *e.g.*

- **She said to her servant, "Is tea ready for me?"**
  She asked her servant that if tea was ready for her.
- **She asked me, "Who teaches you English?"**
  She asked me who taught me English.

(3) Imperative Sentences

Change No. 1: Change the reporting verb 'said' or 'said to' into ordered, commanded, requested, advised, warned, forbade, suggested, etc. according to the tense.

Change No. 2: Remove commas and inverted commas, use conjunction 'to'.

Change No. 3: Change the Imperative sentence into Infinitive sentence.

Change No. 4: Remove 'do' and use 'not to' in case of Negative Imperative, *e.g.*

- **The teacher said to me, "Stand up on the bench."**
  The teacher ordered me to stand up on the bench.
- **The General said to the soldiers, "March forward and attack the foe."**
  The General ordered the soldiers to march forward and attack the foe.

- **The gardener said to the boys, "Do not pluck the flowers."**
  The gardener forbade the boys to pluck the flowers.

(4) Exclamatory Sentences

Change No. 1: Change the reporting verb 'said' or 'said to' into 'exclaimed with joy' or 'exclaimed with sorrow', *etc.* according to the sense, *i.e.*

Exclaimed with joy: in case of Aha! Ha! Hurrah!
Exclaimed with sorrow: in case of Ah! Alas!
Exclaimed with surprise: in case of Oh! What! How!
Exclaimed with regret: in case of Sorry!
Exclaimed with contempt: in case of Pooh! Pshaw!
Applauded with saying: in case of Bravo! Hear!

Change No. 2: Use very or great by removing what or how.
Change No. 3: Use conjunction 'that'.
Change No. 4: Remove exclamatory word and exclamation sign '!', *e.g.*

- **They said, "Hurray! We have won the match."**
  They exclaimed with joy that they had won the match.
- **She said, "Alas! I have lost my bridal ring."**
  She exclaimed with sorrow that she had lost her bridal ring.
- **She said, "How charming the scenery is!"**
  She exclaimed with surprise that it was a very charming scenery.

Optative Sentences

Change No. 1: Change the reporting verb 'said' or 'said to' into 'wished' in case of Good morning. Good noon, Good afternoon, Good evening and into 'bade' in case of Good night, Good bye, Farewell, *etc.*
Change No. 2: Use 'that' to introduce the reported speech.
Change No. 3: Change the Optative Sentence into the Assertive Sentence and replace the sign of exclamation (!) by a full stop (.), *e.g.*

- **She said, "If I were a queen!"**
  She wished that she would be a queen.
- **She said to me, "May God bless you with a son!"**
  She prayed that God might bless me with a son.
- **He said, "Good God! The fellow has come to life again."**
  He exclaimed with surprise that the fellow had come to life again.
- **The General said to his men, "Bravo! You fought bravely."**
  The General applauded his men saying that they had fought bravely.

Change of Voice

Voice refers to the form of the verb that indicates whether the doer of an action is the subject or object. In a sentence, there may be two voices:

- Active
- Passive

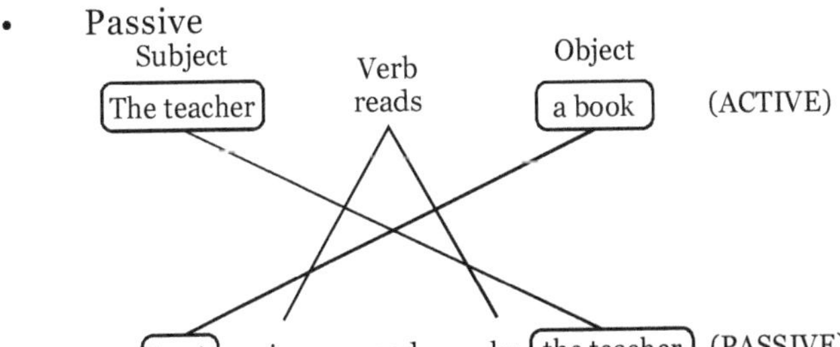

The verbs that take an object can be used in the Passive Voice. In Active Voice, the primary focus is on the subject while object is in focus in Passive Voice.

Rules for changing Voice: (Passive)

- The 'object' of the verb in the Active Voice becomes the 'subject' of the verb in the Passive Voice and the 'subject' in the Active Voice becomes the 'object' in the 'Passive Voice'.
- The main verb is changed into the Past Participle (the IIIrd form) and an appropriate form of the helping verb according to the 'Tense' of the sentences is used.

The 'subject' in the 'Active Voice' becomes the 'object' in the Passive Voice and generally takes 'by' before it.

Tense	Voice	Indefinite	Continuous	Perfect	Perfect Continuous
Present	**Active**	He reads a book	He is reading a book	He has read a book	He has been reading a book
	Passive	A book is read by him	A book is being read by him.	A book has been read by him	No Passive
Past	**Active**	He read a book	He was read -ing a book	He had read a book	He had been reading a book
	Passive	A book was read by him	A book was being read by him	A book had been read by him	No Passive
Future	**Active**	He will read a book	He will be reading a book	He will have read a book	He will have been reading a book
	Passive	A book will be read by him	No Passive	A book will have been read by him	No Passive

The Nominative case of the pronoun is changed into the objective case.

For example:

He	-	him
She	-	her
I	-	me
We	-	us
They	-	them
You	-	you
It	-	it

If a transitive, verb has two objects either of them may be made the subjects in the Passive Voice and the other remains unchanged.

PRESENT INDEFINITE TENSE

Affirmative Sentences

Active Voice	Passive Voice
• I read a story.	A story is read by me.
• The boys play hockey.	Hockey is played by the boys.
• You hide a bat.	A bat is hidden by you.

Negative Sentences

Active Voice	Passive Voice
• Sima does not solve the questions.	The questions are not solved by Sima.
• Hari does not open the window.	The window is not opened by Hari.

Interrogative Sentences

'Yes' or 'No' type.

Active Voice	Passive Voice
• Does he break the window?	Is the window broken by him?
• Do they beat you?	Are you beaten by them?
• Does Ravi sing a song?	Is a song sung by Ravi?

'Wh' Questions:

Active Voice	Passive Voice
• Where does he hide your money?	Where is your money hidden by him?
• Who writes a story?	By whom is a story written?
• Who teaches you English?	By whom are you taught English?

PRESENT CONTINUOUS TENSE

Affirmative Sentences

Active Voice	Passive Voice
• Mina is singing a song.	A song is being sung byMina.

Active Voice	Passive Voice
• Rahul is writing a book.	A book is being written by Rahul.
• They are buying a new bus.	A new bus is being bought by them.

Negative Sentences

Active Voice	**Passive Voice**
• He is not playing Hockey.	Hockey is not being played by him.
• Arpita is not doing her home work.	Home work is not being done by Arpita.
• Parit is not cleaning the room.	The room is not being cleaned by Parit.

'Yes' or 'No' type questions

Active Voice	**Passive Voice**
• Is Gita telling a story?	Is a story being told by Gita?
• Is Mahesh accusing Ram?	Is Ram being accused by Mahesh?
• Are children plucking flowers?	Are flowers being plucked by the children?

'Wh' Questions

Active Voice	**Passive Voice**
• Why is Sita singing a song?	Why is a song being sung by Sita?
• Why are the children making a noise?	Why is a noise being made by the children?
• Who is breaking this wall?	By whom is this wall being broken?
• How is she preparing coffee?	How is coffee being prepared by her?

PRESENT PERFECT TENSE

Affirmative Sentences

Active Voice	**Passive Voice**
• Harish has made a toy.	A toy has been made by Harish.
• Ramesh has broken the glass.	The glass has been broken by Ramesh.
• Sarad has written a song.	A song has been written by Sarad.
• Mr. Verma has vacated this house.	This house has been vacated by Mr. Verma.

Negative Sentences

Active Voice	**Passive Voice**
• Arjun has not beaten the dog.	The dog has not been beaten by Arjun.

- Shyam has not typed this copy. This copy has not been typed by Shyam.
- Vinu has not decorated this house. This house has not been decorated by Vinu.

'Yes' or 'No' type Questions

Active Voice	Passive Voice
• Has Rajni helped the poor?	Have the poor helped by Rajni?
• Has Shami painted the pot?	Has the pot been painted by Shami?
• Have the children closed the door?	Has the door been closed by the children?

'Wh' Questions

Active Voice	Passive Voice
• Why have you planted trees here?	Why have the trees been planted here?
• Who has damaged the crop?	By whom has the crop been damaged?
• Where have you seen this movie?	Where has this movie been seen by you?

PAST INDEFINITE TENSE

Affirmative Sentences

Active Voice	Passive Voice
• Mahesh broke the glass.	The glass was broken by Mahesh.
• Mamta rang the bell.	The bell was rang by Mamta.
• Ragini gave me a gift.	A gift was given to me by Ragini.

Negative Sentences

Active Voice	Passive Voice
• They did not cook the food.	The food was not cooked by them.
• Heena did not learn German.	German was not learnt by Heena.
• The Minister did not attend the party.	The party was not attended by the Minister.

'Yes' or 'No' type Questions

Active Voice	Passive Voice
• Did Meeta invite you to the function?	Were you invited to the function by Meeta?
• Did your mother punish the mischievous boys?	Were the mischievous boys punished by your mother?
• Did Asha sing a song in the party?	Was a song sung in the party by Asha?

'Wh' type Questions

	Active Voice	Passive Voice
•	Who painted these pots?	By whom were these pots painted?
•	Why did your father scold you yesterday?	Why were you scolded by your father yesterday?
•	How did you plan your journey?	How was the journey planned by you?

PAST CONTINUOUS TENSE

Affirmative Sentences

	Active Voice	Passive Voice
•	Mohit was reading a book.	A book was being read by Mohit.
•	Heena was writing a letter.	A letter was being written by Heena.
•	Deepak was playing piano.	Piano was being played by Deepak.
•	The women were washing clothes.	Clothes were being washed by women.

Negative Sentences

	Active Voice	Passive Voice
•	The ladies were not attending the workshop.	The workshop was not being attended by the ladies.
•	Kali was not cleaning the room.	The room was not bein cleaned by Kali
•	Ajay was not painting the pots.	The pots were not being painted by Ajay.

'Yes' or 'No' type Questions

	Active Voice	Passive Voice
•	Was Anjana opening the cupboard?	Was the cupboard being opened by Anjana?
•	Were the children playing hockey?	Was hockey being played by the children?
•	Was Rahul knitting a sweater?	Was a sweater being knitted by Rahul?

'Wh' type Questions

	Active Voice	Passive Voice
•	When were you singing a song?	When was a song being sung by you?
•	How were you preparing the food?	How was the food being prepared by you?
•	When were they watching T.V. ?	When was the T.V. being watched by them?

PAST PERFECT TENSE

Affirmative Sentences

Active Voice	Passive Voice
• Sujal had painted the room.	The room had been painted by Sujal.
• Dinesh had invited me to the party.	I had been invited to the party by Dinesh.
• The labourers had built the house.	The house had been built by the labourers.

Negative Sentences

Active Voice	Passive Voice
• Ajit had not deposited his fees.	His fees had not been deposited by Ajit.
• Anita had not torn the book.	The book had not been torn by Anita.

'Yes' or 'No' type Questions

Active Voice	Passive Voice
• Had Manjit played the match?	Had the match been played by Manjit?
• Had the children written a story?	Had a story been written by the children?
• Had the servant closed the door?	Had the door been closed by the servant?

IMPERATIVE SENTENCES

(a) When the verbs expressing command, advice or request are changed into the Passive Voice, we use the verb 'let' followed by the Passive Infinitive without 'to'. The form of the verb in the passive is : Let + be + III Form.

The subject is put between 'let' and 'be' + III From.

Active Voice	Passive Voice
• Do it.	Let it be done.
• Type this letter.	Let this letter be typed.
• Put out the lamp.	Let the lamp be put out.
• Let him run a race.	Let a race be run by him.
• Let him sell the book.	Let the book be sold by him.
• Do not inform the police.	Let the police not be informed.

(b) However, when the imperative sentence begins with *please* or *kindly*, the sentence in the passive voice takes the words 'you are requested', followed by the active infinitive; as,

Active Voice	Passive Voice
• Please help him.	You are requested to help him.
• Kindly show me your new watch.	You are requested to show me your new watch.

• Please read out the letter.	You are requested to read out the letter.
• Kindly go through this book.	You are requested to go through this book.

(c) When the advice/order is limited upto the subject and the action is not carried forward to the object, the sentence in the passive voice takes the words 'you are advised/ordered' followed by the active infinitive, as,

Active Voice	**Passive Voice**
• Work hard.	You are advised to work hard.
• Stand up on the bench.	You are ordered to stand up on the bench.
• Keep to the left.	You are advised to keep to the left.
• Shut the widows.	You are ordered to shut the windows.

Clauses

What is a CLAUSE?

Clause is a part of a sentence which has a subject and a finite verb, e.g.

- This is the place where I was born.

In this sentence, there are two clauses. In the first clause 'this' and 'is' are the subject and verb respectively.

In the second clause 'I' and 'was born' are the subject and verb respectively.

In this way, the more finite verbs, the more the clauses in a sentence. If there is single 'finite verb' in a sentence, then it is not a clause but only a simple sentence, e.g.

- He goes to school. (Simple Sentence-No Clause)

Note: If there, are more than one finite verb in a sentence, that is either a Complex or Compound sentence.

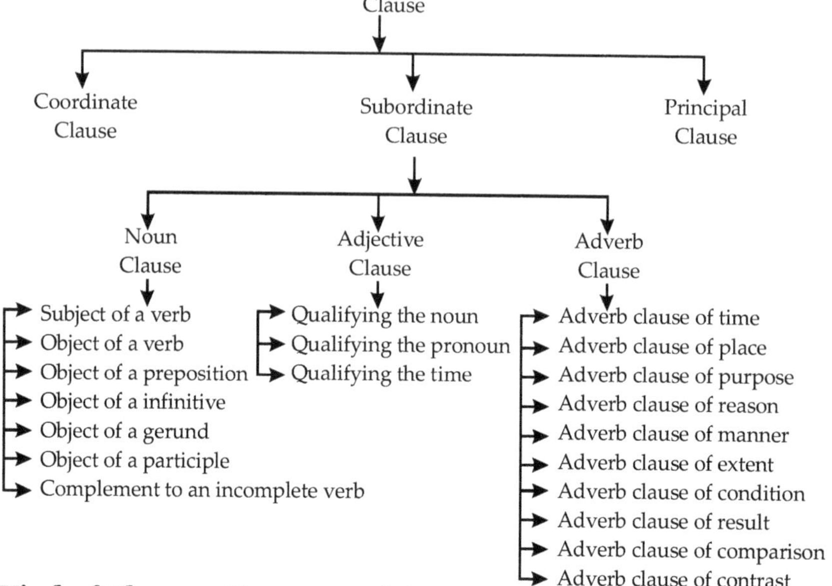

Kind of Clauses: Clauses are of three types:

(1) The Principal Clause: The Principal Clause is a clause which is complete in itself and expresses its meaning clearly. It does not take any support from any other clause for clearing its meaning. So, it is also known as 'the main clause' 'the independent clause' or 'complete clause', e.g.

- I do not know where he lives.

In this sentence, 'I do not know' is the Principal clause because it provides clear meaning.

Note: The Principal Clause never begins with any Conjunction.

(2) The Subordinate Clause: The subordinate clause is a clause which is not complete in itself for expressing its clear meaning. It cannot provide its meaning clearly without the help of the Principal Clause. So, it is also known as 'the dependent clause' or 'the incomplete clause', e.g.

- I asked her why she came late.

In this sentence, the clause 'why she came late' does not provide its clear meaning that is why it is the subordinate clause.

(3) The Coordinate Clause: This clause is totally independent. It does not take any support from any other clause for making its meaning clear. They are like simple sentences joined by coordinate conjunctions, e.g.

- I shall go and she will come.

In this sentence 'I shall go' and 'She will come', both are independent clauses. But the first one is Principal Clause and the second one is Co-ordinate clause.

Note: As the coordinate clause has no more importance due to its identity, we have to understand only 'the Principal Clause' and 'the Subordinate Clause'.

Kinds of Subordinate Clause: The Subordinate clause is divided into three parts:

- **The Noun Clause:** The Noun clause is a clause which does the work of a noun in the sentence.
- **The Adjective Clause:** The Adjective clause is a clause which does the work of an adjective in the sentence.
- **The Adverb Clause:** The Adverb clause is a clause which does the work of an adverb in the sentence.

The Noun Clause

Recognition: Ask the question 'what' to the main verb, the answer is always the noun clause, *e.g.*

- He told me that he was feeling unwell.
  Question: He told me________what?
  Answer: That he was feeling unwell. (Noun Clause)

The Noun Clause generally begins with the connectives like, who, whose, whom, when, where, which, what, why, how, that, if and whether.

Functions of the Noun Clause: The Noun Clause functions in the following ways:

(1) Subject of a Verb: If any clause takes place as a subject of a verb and does the work of a noun, it is called subject of a verb, *e.g.*

- (It) is uncertain________Principal Clause.
- When he will return________Sub. Noun Clause.

In the above example, 'When he will return' is used as a subject of the Principal Clause 'is uncertain'.

It is doing the work of a noun in the sentence, that is why it is called 'Subject of a verb'.

(2) Object of a Verb: If any clause takes place as an Object of a Verb and does the work of a noun, it is called object of a verb, *e.g*

- I cannot say what he wants.
  (*a*) I cannot say________Principal Clause.
  (*b*) What he wants________Sub. Noun Clause.

In the above example, 'What he wants' is used as an object to the Principal Clause 'I cannot say'. It is doing the work of a noun in the sentence that is why it is called object of a verb.

(3) Object of an Infinitive: If any clause begins after infinitive and does the work of an object, such type of clause is called object of an infinitive, *e.g.*

- I want to know how far he is right.
  (a) I want to know________Principal Clause.
  (b) How far he is right________Sub. Noun Clause.

In the above example, 'How far he is right?' has taken place after infinitive and is doing the work of an object to the Principal Clause, 'I want to know'. That is why, it is called object of an infinitive.

(4) Object of a Preposition: If any clause takes place after a preposition as an object, such types of clause is called noun clause, Object of a Preposition, *e.g.*

- Please attend to what I say.
  (a) Please attend to________Principal Clause.
  (b) What I say________Sub. Noun Clause.

In the above example, 'What I say' has taken place after the preposition 'to' as an object of the Principal Clause, 'Please attend to'. That is why it is called Object of a Preposition.

(5) Object of a Participle: If any clause takes place after a participle as an object, the clause is called Noun Clause, Object of a Participle, *e.g.*

- Hoping that he would be in the park, I went there.
  (a) I went there hoping________Principal Clause.
  (b) That he would be in the park________Sub. Noun Clause.

In the above example, 'That he would be in the park' has taken place after the participle 'hoping' and is doing the work of an object. That is why it is called 'Object of a Participle.

(6) Complement of an Incomplete Verb: If there is any helping verb after the Principal Clause, the clause after the helping verb is called Complement of an Incomplete Verb, *e.g.*

- Life is what we make it.
  (a) Life is________Principal Clause
  (b) What we make it________Sub. Noun Clause.

In the above example, 'What we make it' has taken place after the helping verb 'is', that is why it is called Complement of an Incomplete Verb.

(7) Object of a Gerund: If any clause takes place after a Gerund and does the work of an object, it is called Noun Clause Object of a Gerund. Example:

- It depends on your giving what I want.

In the above example, 'What I want' has taken place after the

Gerund 'giving' and is doing the work of an object. That is why it is called object of a gerund.

(8) In Apposition to a Noun or a Pronoun: If any clause takes place to clarify the sense of a noun or a pronoun, it is called 'In Apposition to a Noun or a Pronoun'. Example:

- It is strange that you should say so.
  - *(a)* It is strange________Principal Clause
  - *(b)* That you should say so________Sub. Noun Clause.

The Adjective Clause

Recognition

(1) The Adjective Clause generally begins with relative pronouns – who, whose, whom, that, which, as, as well as relative adverbs – when, where, why and how.

(2) The Adjective Clause always qualifies the Principal Clause, e.g.

- He is the boy who had made a noise.
  - (a) He is the boy________***Principal Clause.***
  - (b) Who had made a noise_____***Sub. Adjective Clause.***

  Qualifying the noun 'boy', e.g.
- You know the time when he is coming.
- This is the place where I was born.
- This is the boy whose father has been appointed Collector.
- God helps those who help themselves.

The Adverb Clause

Recognition: The Adverb Clause is used to modify verb, adjective or adverb given in any other clause. It expresses the following things:

(1) Time: Adverb Clause of time indicates time and generally starts with the Subordinating conjunctions – when, whenever, till, until, before, after, since, while, as, as soon as, as long as, so long as, etc., *e.g.*

- As soon as he saw me, he began to weep.
  - (a) He began to weep________***Principal Clause.***
  - (b) As soon as he saw me________***Sub. Adverb Clause***, showing 'time', e.g.
  - When the cat is away, the mice will play.
  - I get up before the sun rises.

(2) Place: Adverb Clause of place indicates place and generally starts with the subordinating conjunctions – where, wherever, whither, whence, etc. Example:

- I shall go where he goes.
  (a) I shall go________***Principal Clause.***
  (b) Where he goes________***Sub. Adverb Clause*** showing 'place'.
- He will follow you whither you go.
- Where there is a will, there is a way.
- He makes friends wherever he goes.
- I go where I like.

(3) Purpose: Adverb clause of Purpose indicates purpose. It generally starts with the subordinating conjunctions – that, so that, in order that, lest, etc., e.g.

- We eat so that we may live.
  (a) We eat________***Principal Clause.***
  (b) So that we may live________***Sub. Adverb Clause*** showing 'purpose'.
- Walk carefully lest you should fall.
- Work hard so that you may pass.
- Run fast lest you should miss the train.
- Be active lest you should miss the chance.

(4) Reason: Adverb clause of Reason shows reason. It generally starts with the subordinating conjunctions – since, because, for, as, that, etc. Example:

- He cannot understand it because he is dull.
  (a) He cannot understand it________***Principal Clause.***
  (b) Because he is dull________***Sub. Adverb Clause*** showing 'reason'.
- I am glad that you have passed.
- Since you are my friend, I must help you.
- I am sad that you have failed.
- She is happy that Gita has topped the class.

(5) Manner: Adverb clause of Manner shows manner. It generally starts with the subordinating conjunctions – as, as...so, as if, as though, according as, etc. Example:

- As you sow, so shall you reap.
  (a) So shall you reap________***Principal Clause.***
  (b) As you sow________***Sub. Adverb Clause*** showing 'manner'.
- He spoke as if he had gone mad.
- I did as I was told.
- Try to finish it as I have shown you.
- Plants breathe as animals do.

(6) Extent: Adverb clause of Extent shows extent of a thing. It generally starts with the subordinating conjunctions – as far as, so far as, etc., e.g.

- As far as I think, he will not betray you.
  - (a) He will not betray you________***Principal Clause.***
  - (b) As far as I thin________ ***Sub. Adverb Clause*** showing 'extent'.
- This is false so far as he could.
- He sang as far as I know.

(7) Condition: Adverb clause of Condition shows condition. It generally starts with the subordinating conjunctions – if, unless, provided, in case, whether....or, etc. e.g.

- If you work hard, you will pass.
  - (a) You will pass________***Principal Clause.***
  - (b) If you work hard________***Sub. Adverb Clause*** showing 'condition'.
- I shall let you go provided you speak the truth.

(8) Result: Adverb clause of Result shows result of a thing. It generally starts with 'that' but so or such is used before in the Principal Clause, e.g.

- He is so poor that he cannot pay his fee.
  - (a) He is so poor________***Principal Clause.***
  - (b) That he cannot pay his fee________***Sub. Adverb Clause*** showing 'result'.
- I am so tired that I cannot walk further.
- It was so cold that many died.

(9) Comparison: Adverb clause of Comparison shows comparison between two objects or things. It generally starts with the subordinating conjunctions – than, as, etc., e.g.

- She is not so intelligent as you think.
  - (a) She is not so intelligent________***Principal Clause.***
  - (b) As you think________***Sub. Adverb Clause*** showing 'comparison'.
- He is not as foolish as you.
- No one is a better monitor than Mohan.

(10) Contrast: Adverb clause of Contrast shows difference between two objects. It generally starts with the subordinating conjunctions – though, although, even if, however, all the same, etc., e.g.

- Although it was raining, I went to school.
  - (a) I went to school________***Principal Clause.***
  - (b) Although it was raining________***Sub. Adverb Clause*** showing 'contrast'.
- However hard he may work, he cannot pass.
- Whatever you may say, I shall not believe you.

Articles

There are two types of articles indefinite 'a' and '*an*' or definite 'the'.

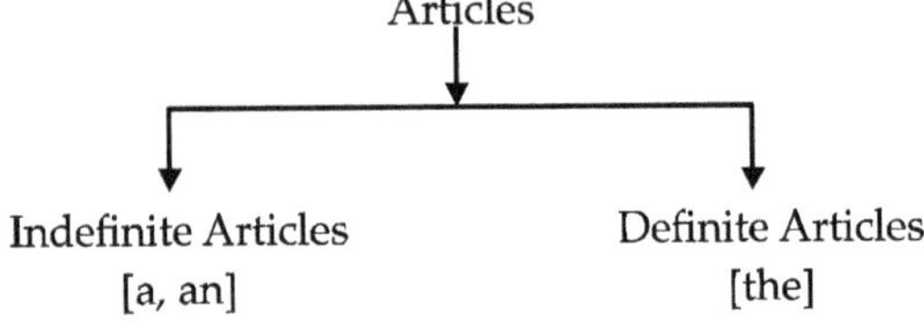

Use of the Indefinite Articles:

A and **an** are the indefinite articles. They refer to something not specifically known to the person you are communicating with.

(1) **A** is used before consonants; **an** before words beginning with the vowel sound:
a dog, **a** girl, **an** umbrella, **a** university

(2) Some words begin with a vowel sound but are pronounced with the same sound as the **y** in **yet**. **A** is used for such words. Some such words are:
a university, **a** European, **a** uniform, **a** one-eyed man, **a** unit, **a** useful item, **a** eucalyptus tree.

(3) The words beginning with unpronounced **h** are preceded by **an**. Some such words with unsounded **h** are:
an honest man, **an** honourable man, **an** hour, **an** heir, **an** heiress

(4) Some consonants are pronounced like vowels. Hence, **an** is used before them:
an M.P., **an** M.A., **an** LL.B. student, **an** S.P., **an** M.L.A., **an** N.D.A. Officer.
In such examples, **M** is pronounced as **em**, N as **an**, **S** as **as** and **L** as **al**.

(5) Before singular countable nouns **a/an** is used:
Wheat is **a** cereal.
There were half **a** dozen pencils.

(6) In its original numerical sense of one, **a/an** is used:
An apple **a** day keeps the doctor away.
Will you like to have **an** orange?

Did **a** European call at my office yesterday?
Mr. Mehra is **an** M.P. from Gujarat.

(7) **A/an** is used with the meaning of each:
My salary has been increased by ₹100 **a** year.
I buy **a** magazine every week.

(8) In the sense of any to single out an individual as the representative of a class, use **a/an**:
A dog is a faithful animal.
Delhi is **a** big city.

(9) **A/an** is used before a proper noun when it is used as a common noun:
He is **a** Kalidas. (As great a poet as Kalidas was)

(10) The names of professions and occupations take the indefinite articles:
He is **a** teacher.
He is **a** principal.

(11) In exclamations before singular countable nouns:
What **a** lovely flower!

The indefinite article is not used at certain points

(1) Before a noun used in its widest sense:
Man is mortal.

(2) Before names of materials
Gold is a precious metal.

(3) When noun is the name of a meal:
We take dinner at 8 O'clock.

(4) Before Proper nouns:
Sonu is a smart boy.
Delhi is the capital of India.

(5) When the noun is uncountable:
Sand is used in making glass.

(6) Before abstract nouns:
Virtue is its own reward.
Honesty is the best policy.

(7) Before languages:
Hindi is her mother-tongue.

Use of the Definite Article

There are two ways to pronounce "the". One is "thuh" and the other is "thee".

(1) Before the names of rivers, valleys, forests, canals, mountains, hills, seas, deserts, etc.:
The Ganges is a sacred river.
The Himalaya is the crown of India.
The Sahara is the largest desert of the world.

(2) When we refer to a particular person or thing:

The boy in blue trousers is my brother.

Beware of **the** dog, he is an Alsatian.

(3) When a singular noun is meant to represent a whole class:

The aeroplane is the fastest means of transport.

An exception to the above rule is the non **man** when it is used to denote the human race as a whole:

Man is mortal.

(4) Before the names of hotels, cinemas, theatres, ships or trains:

London is on **the** Thames.

He crossed **the** Atlantic in **the** Akbar II.

(5) Before common nouns which are names of things unique of their kind:

The Sun rises in the East.

The earth is moving at its axis.

(6) With superlative adjectives which make a noun definite:

She is **the** most beautiful girl.

The most intelligent boy stood first.

(7) Before the names of certain books:

The Ramayana is a holy book of the Hindus.

The Vedas were written by the saints.

(8) Before terms denoting some political party, nationality or community:

The Congress, **The** National Conference, **The** Indians, **The** English, **The** Hindus, **The** Germans.

(9) Before an adjective when it works as a noun:

We should help **the** poor.

(10) With the ordinal numbers:

Read **the** first chapter of this book.

He is **the** second child of his parents.

(11) Before the names of municipal or government departments:

The Principal's office, **The** Public library

(12) Before a proper noun when it is used as a common noun or an adjective:

Shakespeare is **the** Kalidas of England.

The definite article *the* ***is omitted at certain points such as:***

(1) Before proper nouns:

India (not the India)

Philip (not the Philip)

(2) Before the names of substances:
Gold is a precious metal.

(3) Before the names of meals:
I have dinner at 9 O'clock.

(4) Before the plural nouns when used in a general sense:
Apples are good for health.

(5) Before the names of games:
I love hockey.

(6) Before the words of King and Queen:
Queen Victoria, King Henry IV.

(7) Before abstract nouns:
Mercy comes from above.

(8) In certain phrases consisting of a preposition followed by its object:
At home, at sunset, at hand, on time, in bed, on foot.

Repetition of the Article

(1) When two or more adjectives qualify the same noun, the article is used before the first adjectives only; but when they qualify different nouns, the article is used before each adjective:
I have **a** black and white horse.
(a horse which is black and white)
I have **a** black and **a** white horse.
(I have two horses' one black and the other white)

(2) When two or more connected nouns refer to the same person or thing, the article is normally used before the first only; but when two or more connected nouns refer to different persons or things, the article is used before each:
The poet and statesman is dead.
[The poet and statesman are used for the same person]
The poet and **the** statesman are dead.
[Here two persons are dead – the poet and the statesman]

Prepositions

A Preposition is a word placed before a Noun or a Pronoun to show its relation to some other words in the sentence. The Noun or Pronoun which is used with a Preposition is called its object. It is said to be governed by the preposition.

Kinds of prepositions

Prepositions are of **five** kinds :

(1) Simple Prepositions; e.g.,
At, by, of, for, in, on, off, out, till, to, up, with, through, etc.

(2) **Compound Prepositions;** e.g.,
About, across, against, before, beside, into, until, within, etc.

(3) **Double Prepositions**; e.g.,
From among, from beneath, from under, out of, etc.

(4) **Participle Prepositions**; e.g.,
Accepting, considering, during, regarding, notwithstanding, etc.

(5) **Phrase Prepositions;** e.g.,
Along with, according to, away from, because of, by dint of, by virtue of, for the sake of, in addition to, in the course of, in lieu of, in place of, in spite of, on account of, owing to, with a view to, with regard to, etc.

Position of the Preposition

A Preposition is generally placed before a Noun or a Pronoun it governs; e.g.,

- He died of cholera.
- Delhi is famous for the Red Fort.
- Sudhir went up the hill.
- I am tired of writing letters to him.

But there are some exceptions to this general rule.

A preposition is placed at the end of sentences:

(a) Preposition governs a relative Pronoun; e.g.,
- Here is the book which you were looking for.
- This is the man who (whom) I spoke to.

(b) When the Relative Pronoun is **that;** e.g.,
- Here is the pen that you were looking **for.**
- The dog spoiled the paper that I was writing **on.**

The relative pronoun **'that'** cannot take a preposition **before** it.

(c) When a Relative Pronoun is understood; e.g.,
- That is the boy I was speaking about. ('Whom' understood)
- That is the house Mohan lives in. ('Which' understood)

(d) If a Preposition governs an Interrogative Pronoun or adverb; e.g.,
- What are you looking at? (Interrogative Pronoun)
- Where are you going to? (Interrogative Adverb)

Following is the position of a preposition in regard to 'who' and 'whom'; e.g.,
- To whom were you speaking?
- Who were you speaking to?

(e) When the preposition is used with the Infinitive placed at the end, e.g.

- The knife is to cut with.
- Do you have a chair to sit in?
- I have no money to support you with.

SOME IMPORTANT PREPOSITIONS DISTINGUISHED

Particular care should be taken in the use of the following.

Preposition which are given below in pairs for the sake of contrast:

(1) After and **In:**

When we speak of space of time, this distinction is made; e.g.

- Anil came back after a month. (Past)
- Ashok will come back in a week. (Future)

'After' refers to a space of time in the Past.
'In' refer to a space of time in the Future.
Both mean at the close of.

(2) In and **Within:**

'In' means at the end of a given period of time; within means before the end of the given period; e.g.,

- I shall return in a month. (at the end of one month)
- I shall return within a month. (before the end of one month)

(3) In and **into:**

'In' denotes rest or motion inside anything; 'into' shows motion/ movement towards the inside of anything; e.g.

- The boy was in the garden. (Rest inside)
- The boy was walking in the garden. (Act of moving inside)
- He walked into the garden. (Movement towards inside)

Note: Be careful to write the two words 'in' and 'to' separately when the sense is separate:

- He took her into the room (Motion towards inside) but,
- He took her in to dinner. (He took her inside the house for dinner.)

(4) At and **In:**

(a) At and In are used in speaking of things at rest; e.g.,

- The students are sitting at their desks.
- She is lying in her bed.

(b) In speaking of places, 'at' is used for a smaller place and in for a bigger place; e.g.

- I live at Rohtak in Haryana.
- My brother lives at Hissar.
- My uncle lives in Calcutta.

But when we speak of what are known to be big places, we generally use in; e.g.
In Paris; In London; In New York; In Delhi.

(c) In speaking of time, we use 'at' for a point of time and 'in' for a period of time; e.g.
at five, at dawn, at sunset, at midnight.
but in the morning, in May, in 1986
We say, the train will arrive at seven O'clock in the morning.

(5) On and **Upon:**

'On' shows rest; 'upon' shows movement; e.g.,

- He sat in a bench.
- The wolf sprang upon the goat.

(6) By and **With:**

When something has been done by a person with the help of an instrument, a tool or weapon, we use '**by**' for the agent – the doer of the action and '**with**' for the instrument; e.g.

- The loin was killed by the hunter with a sword.
- The king was stabbed by his enemy with a knife.
- The letter will be written by me with a pen.
- You cannot kill two birds with one stone.

(7) Between and **Among:**

'Between refers to two persons or things; while 'among' refers to more than two; e.g.,

- He divided his property between his two sons.
- Bhiwani is between Rohtak and Hissar.
- Sweets were distributed among the children of our class.
- The five robbers divided money among themselves.

(8) Till and **To:**

'Till is used for time and 'to' is used for place; e.g.,

- Farmers work in their fields till evening.
- He walked to the end of the road.

(9) From and **Since:**

'From' and 'Since' denote a point of time. 'From may be used with any tense while 'since' is used with the Perfect or Perfect Continuous Tenses only; e.g.

- I have been living in this house since 1960.
- I have not seen him since he left school.
- Farmer work hard from morning till evening.
- Prem Chand began to write novels from the age of ten.
- From tomorrow, the school will open at 7 A.M.

(10) Beside and **Besides:**

'Beside' means by the side of; 'Besides' means in addition to; e.g.,

- The child walked beside his mother.
- Besides being fined, he was beaten by the teacher.

(11) On, Over and **Above:**

'On' denotes contact with the surface on which something is lying; e.g.,

- The book is lying on the table.

'Above' denotes a higher position but does not imply contact or covering; e.g.,

- This building rises above all the houses in the city.

'Over' means a higher position as well as contact or directly above; e.g.,

- Water flows over plants and bushes.
- At noon, the sun is over us.

Adjectives

An adjective is a word that tells us something about a noun. A noun may have many attributes. For example, 'boy' is a noun, and that boy may be tall or short, intelligent or fool, educated or uneducated, rich or poor. What is the quality of that boy? In order to express the quality of that boy, we use an adjective. E.g., That boy is a rich boy.

In this sentence, the word 'rich' indicates that the boy is a rich boy. That means that the boy has a lot of money.

Words which tell us about the quality of the nouns (which might have been used either as the subject or the object) are known as adjectives.

E.g., India is a country.

India is a democratic country. (Here, 'democratic' is an adjective.)

An adjective can be used in the following two ways:

- **Attributively** (placed immediately before the noun it qualifies)
- **Predicatively** (used after the verb)

E.g., She is a good teacher.

Bimala is intelligent.

Kinds of Adjectives

(1) Adjective of Quality: It answers the question 'what type' and tells the quality of a noun. For example, good, honest, old and big.

(2) Adjective of Quantity: It answers the question 'how much' and tells the quantity of a noun. For example, little, some, much and enough.

(3) Definitive Numeral Adjective: It answers the question 'how many' and tells the number of the noun. For example, one, two, three, four, five, six, seven, etc.

(4) Indefinite Numeral Adjective: It answers the question 'how much/many' and tells the approximate number of the noun. **For example**, all, no one, many, a few and several.

(5) Distributive Numeral Adjective: It answers the question 'who/which'. Some examples are each, every either and neither. **For example:** Each one of you should support this cause.

(6) Demonstrative Adjective: It answers the question 'where' and tells the position of the noun. Some examples are this, that, these, those and such.

(7) Interrogative adjective: It asks a question related to the noun. Some examples are what, which, whose and when.

(8) Adjectival Phrase: Sometimes, a phrase may be used as an adjective. Very often, an adjectival; phrase appears after the noun that it qualifies. For example: The chief lived in the house built of stone.

(9) Adjectival Clause: Often, a full clause may add meaning to a noun. **For exmaple,** John is the boy who broke the window.

EXERCISES

(1) Replace the personal pronouns by possessive adjectives :

Q1. Where is (I) ______ book?
Ans. my

Q2. Here is (we) ______ teacher.
Ans. our

Q3. She goes to school with (she) ______ brother.
Ans. her

Q4. (They) ______ father works in a car factory.
Ans. Their

Q5. (You) ______ laptop is very expensive.
Ans. Your

Q6. (He) ______ favorite hobby is tennis.
Ans. His

Q7. (I) ______ husband and I want to go to Paris.
Ans. My

Q8. We want to see (it) ______ historical monuments.
Ans. its

Q9. Leila likes (she) ______ dog!
Ans. her

Q10. (It) ______ name is Bobby.
Ans. Its

(2) Choose the right possessive adjective:

Q1. Two students didn't do ______ mathematics homework.
Ans. their

Q2. I have a car. ______ colour is black.
Ans. Its

Q3. We have a dog. ______ name is Pancho.
Ans. Its

Q4. Nancy is from England. ______ husband is from Australia.
Ans. Her

Q5. Ann and Nadia go to a high school. ______ little brother goes to primary school.
Ans. Their

Q6. Alan has a van. ______ van is very old.
Ans. His

Q7. We go to a high school. ______ high school is fantastic.
Ans. Our

Q8. I like singing ______ mother sings with me.
Ans. My

Q9. Francois and Alain are French. ______ family are from France.
Ans. Their

Q10. Mary likes ______ grandmother. She often visits her.
Ans. her

(3) Make the comparative form. If it's possible, use 'er'. If not, use 'more'.

Q1. Dogs are ______ (intelligent) than rabbits.
Ans. more intelligent

Q2. Lucy is ______ (old) than Ellie.
Ans. older

Q3. Russia is far ______ (large) than the UK.
Ans. larger

Q4. My Latin class is ______ (boring) than my English class.
Ans. more boring

Q5. In the UK, the streets are generally ______ (narrow) than in the USA.
Ans. narrower

Q6. London is ______ (busy) than Glasgow.
Ans. busier

Q7. Julie is ______ (quiet) than her sister.
Ans. quieter

Q8. Amanda is ______ (ambitious) than her classmates.
Ans. more ambitious

Q9. My garden is a lot ______ (colourful) than this park.
Ans. more colourful

Q10. His house is a bit ______ (comfortable) than a hotel.
Ans. more comfortable

(4) Choose the correct answer from the given options:

Q1. Rajesh is feeling very ______ .

(a) angry **(b) angrier**

(c) angriest

Ans. (a) angry

Q2. Nokia is a ______ company.

(a) good **(b) better**

(c) best

Ans. (a) good

Q3. Rajat is ______ than Ramesh.

(a) fast **(b) faster**

(c) fastest

Ans. (b) faster

Q4. Amongst the three brothers, Aditya is the ______

(a) tall **(b) taller**

(c) tallest

Ans. (c) tallest

Q5. She will live ______ than him.

(a) Long **(b) Longest**

(c) Longer **(d) Larger**

Ans. (c) longer

Q6. What about this? Isn't it ______ ?

(a) Beautiful **(b) Beauteous**

(c) Beauty

Ans. (a) beautiful

Q7. The test was ______ than I thought it would be.

(a) Difficult **(b) More difficult**

(c) Most difficult

Ans. (b) more difficult

Q8. He is the ______ boy in his class.

(a) Old **(b) Older**

(c) Oldest

Ans. (c) oldest

Q9. This locality is ______ than ours.

(a) Expensive **(b) More expensive**

(c) Most expensive

Ans. (b) more expensive

Q10. You are so ______, I am sure you can pick this up.

(a) Strong **(b) Weak**

(c) Fat **(d) Thin**

Ans. (a) strong

Phrasal Verbs

Phrasal verbs are mainly used in spoken English and informal texts. (The more formal a conversation or text, the less phrasal verbs are found.) Phrasal verbs consist of a verb and a particle (preposition, adverb). The particle can change the meaning of the verb completely. For example:

- Look up – consult a reference book (Look a word up in a dictionary.)
- Look for – seek (Look for her ring.)
- Look forward – anticipate with pleasure (Look forward to meeting someone.)

In some cases, the particle is placed either after the verb or after the object.

Examples

- Write ***down*** the word.
- Write the word ***down.***

If the object is a pronoun, however, the particle has to be placed after the pronoun (object).

Examples

- Write it ***down***.
- Your photo album. Put it ***down.***
- Your jacket. Take it ***off.***

Some phrasal verbs are as follows:

- **Back out** — to withdraw from a promise, contract: I felt grieved when he backed out of his promise to help me.
- **Back up** — to support; to sustain: He backed up his report with relevant statistics.
- **Bear upon** — to be relevant to: This argument does not bear upon the subject under discussion.
- **Blow up** — to explode: The mine blew up and all the labourers working inside were killed.
  — To reprimand or scold: If you continue to be negligent, the teacher will blow you up.
- **Break down** — of a car; a piece of machinery; to go wrong so that it will not function: The car broke down on our way to Mumbai.
  — To collapse; to succumb to uncontrollable weeping: She broke down completely on hearing the news of her husband's death.
  — To succumb to a nervous collapse through overwork or worry: He worked so hard that his health broke down near the examination.
- **Break off** — to end; to discontinue; to desist: We had to break off our conversation when he arrived.

She broke off in the middle of the story. She did not like his nature and broke off the engagement.

- **Break up** — to disperse; to dissolve: The college will break up for the Puja holidays on 25th October.
  The meeting will break up after the President has addressed the audience.
- **Bring up** — to rear: Those brought up in adversity are able to cope with life better.
- **Call forth** — to provoke: The minister's views on the disinvestment policy of the government called forth a good deal of bitter criticism.
- **Call out** — to shout: I called out to him but he disappeared in the dark.
  — To announce by calling or shouting: The manager called out to the peon that he was being immediately fired.
- **Call upon** — to order; to require: I was unfortunately called upon to give evidence against him.
- **Carry on** — to continue: If you carry on working hard, your business will soon flourish.
  — To manage: He carried on his business so well that he soon amassed a huge fortune.
- **Cast away** — to throw aside: You must cast away all your apprehensions and accept the offer.
- **Catch up with** — to overtake; to draw level: Last week I had to stay late at the office to catch up with some pending files.
- **Come off** — to take place: The prize distribution came off on Tuesday last.
  — To turn out successful: His speeches at the conference always came off beautifully.
- **Cry down** — to deprecate; to make little of: You must not unnecessarily cry down the conduct of others.
- **Cry out against** — to complain loudly against: The opposition parties cried out against the fast pace of the globalisation of the Indian economy.
- **Cut out** — designed for: You were cut out to be a lecturer in a college.
- **Drop in** — to visit casually: On my way to the college, I dropped in at Mira's place.
- **Drop out** — to leave: As the race progressed, many children dropped out.
- **Fall back** — to recede; to retreat: On seeing the armed guards, the civilians fell back.
- **Fall down** — from a higher position to a lower one: The branch gave way and he fell down into the canal.

- **Fall off** — to withdraw; to drop off: Some of our subscribers have fallen off. Friends fall off in adversity.
- **Fall under** — to come under: This colony does not fall under my jurisdiction.
- **Get along** — to prosper; to progress; to proceed: Well, doctor, how is your patient getting along? It is simply impossible to get along with him.
- **Get on with** — to live pleasantly together; to progress: How are you getting on with your studies?
- **Get into** — to be involved in: It is easy to get into scandals but hard to come out unscathed.
- **Give in** — to surrender; to yield: I gave in for her repeated requests and accepted the offer.
- **Give over** — not doing any longer: It is time you gave over pretending that you have access to the Prime Minister.
- **Go after** — to follow; to pursue: The policeman went after the thief but the latter managed to escape in the dark of the night.
- **Go down** — to be accepted: The terrorist attack on WTC will go down in history as one of the worst acts of terrorism.
- **Go without** — to remain without: He is so poor that sometimes he has to go without food.
- **Go by** — to follow: I am sorry to disappoint you but we have to go by the rules.
  — To elapse (used of time): Months have gone by but I have not called upon him.
- **Hang about** — to loiter near a place: Last evening I say your friend hanging about your house.
- **Hang upon** — to depend upon: The success of any venture hangs upon the seriousness with which it is undertaken.
- **Hold out** — to endure; to refuse to yield: How long can you hold out against starvation?
  — To continue: Sugar stocks are not likely to hold out very long.
  — To offer: She held out her hand to the Prince.
- **Hold to** — abide by: Whatever resistance there might be, I will hold to my decision.
- **Keep off** — to ward off: His stern looks keep off the flatterers.
  — To maintain: They have been trying to keep up their standard of living though there has been a considerable decline in their income.
- **Keep up with** — to keep pace with: You read too fast; I cannot keep up with you.
- **Knock out** — to win by hitting the opponent insensible in a boxing bout: The challenger was knocked out in two minutes.

- **Lay By** — to put away for future use: She has laid by five thousand rupees to celebrate her marriage anniversary.
- **Lay in** — to store for future use: Anticipating scarcity of food grains, they laid in a good store of provisions.
- **Let down** — to fail a friend: Won't I feel grieved if my own friends let me down?
- **Let into** — to suffer to enter; to admit: Despite his pleadings, they did not let him into the meeting. I shall let no one into my secrets.
- **Let out** — to lease on hire: In my neighbourhood, there is a decent house to let out.
  — To loosen: Let us let out the dog for a while.
- **Look about** — to study one's surroundings: The thief looked about himself before entering the house.
- **Look for** — to search for: The old woman was looking for her spectacles.
- **Look up** — to search for and find: Please look up this word in the dictionary.
  — To have an upward tendency (said of prices): The price of sugar is looking up these days.
- **Make off with** — to run away with: The servant made off with the master's watch.
- **Make over** — to transfer: He has made over the building to his son's name.
- **Make up** — to supply what is deficient: You must work hard during the Dussehra holidays and try to make up your deficiency in English.
  — To invent or fabricate: She made up a story to get rid of the visitor.
  — To reconcile: They have made up their quarrel and are now getting on quite well.
- **Pass away** — to die: His sister passed away in the early hours of the morning.
- **Pass by** — to disregard; to omit: He did not invite me to his birthday. It appears that he passed me by.
  — To go alongside of: You passed by my house the day before yesterday.
- **Pick out** — to select or choose: The teacher picked out the best student from the class.
- **Pick up** — to recover or regain health after an illness: He has become so weak that he will take two months to pick up.
- **Play upon** — (a musical instrument): She played upon the harmonium and sang a melodious song.
  — To take advantage of: The blackmailer played upon her love for her husband.

- **Pull down** — to demolish; to destroy: The old house was pulled down to create space for multi-storey flats.
- **Pull up** — to take to task: The teacher was always pulling him up for his bad handwriting.
- **Put off** — to postpone: We had to put off the wedding till the war was over.
  — To lay aside: He put off his shoes before entering the temple.
  — To turn one aside from a purpose or demand: I approached him for some help but he put me off with mere words.
- **Put into** — to drag into: Don't put me into the argument.
- **Put out** — to extinguish: It is time to put out the fire and save the shop.
  — To perturb, to annoy: I was put out on hearing that I had incurred heavy losses in the recent business transactions.
- **Run away** — to flee: The young boy took a necklace and ran away.
- **Run away with** — to steal and depart with: The cashier ran away with twenty thousand rupees.
- **Run off** — to break off from control: The dog broke the chain and ran off.
- **Run over** — to drive over: The car ran over the pedestrian as he was crossing the road.
  — To flow over: The tent is running over.
- **Run through** — to squander or waste: It took him only a few months to run through all the money his father had left for him.
  — To read quickly: I will just run through this lesson and tell you what it is all about.
  — To pierce: The needle ran through her finger when she was stitching her shirt.
- **See into** — to attend to: You can set right the situation if you see into it at an early date.
- **Set in** — to begin: As soon as rains set in, it becomes pleasant.
- **Set up** — to establish; to open a new business: He is soon going to set up as a financier.
- **Speak for** — to recommend somebody or to urge somebody's claims: If you speak for to the Manager, I am sure he will look at my case favourably.
- **Speak on** — to deliver a lecture on: This evening I am going to speak on the changing concepts of morality in various ages.
- **Stand off** — to keep at a distance: Would you please stand off? I brook no interference in my way of work.
- **Strike for** — to stop work for some reason: The labourers have struck for higher wages.

- **Take after** — to resemble: The younger sister takes after the elder one.
- **Take for** — to form an impression about somebody's identity: I was taken for a South Indian.
- **Take in** — to deceive: She thinks her oily tongue can take everybody in.
- **Take to** — to become addicted to: He took to gambling and drinking at a very early age.
  — To form a liking for: Of late she has taken to painting.
- **Tell against** — to prove adverse to; to go against: I am sure these facts are going to tell against your case.
- **Throw about** — to fling here and there; to leave in disorder: The child threw his books about and ran off to play.
- **Throw away** — to lose through carelessness: You have thrown away a golden opportunity.
- **Turn against** — to become hostile to: I shall not give up my principles even if the whole world turns against me.

EXERCISES

(1) Choose the most appropriate option.

Q1. The deal is more than we have bargained _______.

(a) for **(b) at**

(c) off **(d) out**

Ans. (a) for

Q2. My father came_______ an old friend of his last evening.

(a) about **(b) up**

(c) across **(d) along**

Ans. (c) across

Q3. The team of scientists pulled _______ of the expedition because of high costs.

(a) up **(b) down**

(c) out **(d) over**

Ans. (c) out

Q4. The fire that broke _______ in the middle of the night destroyed tens of houses there.

(a) up **(b) out**

(c) along **(d) across**

Ans. (b) out

Q5. The fire was finally put _______ after three hours.

(a) up **(b) on**

(c) across **(d) out**

Ans. (d) out

Q6. The meeting was put ______ because there were not enough members present.

(a) on **(b) off**

(c) in **(d) up**

Ans. (b) off

Q7. The teacher picked ______ the best student from the class.

(a) out **(b) up with**

(c) up for **(d) in with**

Ans. (a) out

Q8. Maya and Manju broke ______ after an intense quarrel.

(a) up **(b) down**

(c) off **(d) along**

Ans. (a) up

Q9. My teacher says that I need to brush ______ on my English.

(a) off **(b) over**

(c) up **(d) away**

Ans. (c) up

Q10. We won't rule ______ the possibility of getting help from Sheela.

(a) off **(b) on**

(c) out **(d) in**

Ans. (c) out

(2) Choose the most appropriate option.

Q1. He is always getting ______ me though I have done nothing wrong.

(a) at **(b) with**

(c) to **(d) on**

Ans. (a) at

Q2. They spent the whole night cooking ______ a plan that they thought could work.

(a) off **(b) away**

(c) out **(d) up**

Ans. (d) up

Q3. I passed ______ Firoz's house but I did not go in because I was in a hurry.

(a) up **(b) along**

(c) by **(d) off**

Ans. (c) by

Q4. Tina's new car broke ______ unexpectedly on the expressway.

(a) up **(b) down**

(c) off **(d) by**

Ans. (b) down

Q5. After the seventh attempt, they finally decided to give ______.

(a) up **(b) away**

(c) off **(d) back**

Ans. (a) up

Q6. His father dropped me______when we reached Manchester Station.

(a) up **(b) out**

(c) off **(d) away**

Ans. (c) off

Q7. The plane took ______ at half past eight.

(a) up **(b) off**

(c) away **(d) on**

Ans. (b) off

Q8. Look ______! There's a bicycle speeding towards us.

(a) up **(b) in**

(c) down **(d) out**

Ans. (d) out

Q9. I cannot make ______ what he wrote. His handwriting is illegible.

(a) off **(b)up**

(c) out **(d) in**

Ans. (c) out

Q10. Do you know what UNICEF stands ______?

(a) for **(b) by**

(c) out **(d) up**

Ans. (a) for

(3) Choose the right option.

Q1. While the women got busy in the kitchen, the men ______ doing nothing.

(a) stood on **(b) stood apart**

(c) stood around **(d) stood between**

Ans. (c) stood around

Q2. "What are you _______, Dipu? You've been rummaging in your closet for hours," said his mother.

(a) looking in **(b) looking for**

(c) looking past **(d) looking to**

Ans. (b) looking for

Q3. "I can't believe I _______ it. I should have known Jitu would never have asked me out if it wasn't for a dare," said a distraught Rosie.

(a) waited for **(b) make for**

(c) look for **(d) fell for**

Ans. (d) fell for

Q4. Once the verdict of guilty was handed down, Rohan _______ to prove that his brother had been framed for a crime that he did not commit.

(a) waited about **(b) planned about**

(c) set about **(d) wished about**

Ans. (c) set about

Q5. The King _______ the witch's spell and she proceeded to tell him to kill the Queen.

(a) fell under **(b) fell into**

(c) fell after **(d) fell over**

Ans. (a) fell under

Q6. When the spy saw that the police officers were catching up with him, he _______ a sprint.

(a) broke apart **(b) broke in**

(c) broke off **(d) broke into**

Ans. (d) broke into

Q7. His refusal to let her look at his passport _______ alarm bells in Mohit's head.

(a) set off **(b) set about**

(c) set between **(d) set on**

Ans. (a) set off

Q8. Mohan's lawyer has arrived to _______ the terms of his prenuptial with his fifth wife.

(a) go with **(b) go over**

(c) go into **(d) go under**

Ans. (b) go over

Q9. "You go ahead, I will _______ with you in a minute", said Kiran to her son.

(a) turn up **(b) catch up**

(c) wake up **(d) walk up**

Ans. (b) catch up

Q10. Navin _______ his old piano teacher at the symposium and caught up with him over lunch.

(a) ran down **(b) ran into**

(c) ran up **(d) ran between**

Ans. (b) ran into

Word Groups

What group do the words belong to? Identify their group and give answer:

(1) Mouse, motherboard, keyboard, monitor: Parts of a Computer
(2) Newcastle, Melbourne, Adelaide, Sydney: Australian Cities
(3) Car, train, tram, bus: Forms of Transport
(4) Polish, Scottish, Australian, Russian: Nationalities
(5) Turnip, carrot, cabbage, onion: Vegetables
(6) Thomas, Eric, Peter, Edward: Names
(7) Ring, necklace, earrings, bracelet: Jewellery
(8) Jaguar, BMW, Honda, Fiat: Car Brands
(9) Heart, liver, brain, kidneys: Organs of Human Body
(10) Tulip, orchid, rose, daisy: Flowers
(11) Tea, coffee, coca cola, coconut water: Beverages
(12) Nepal, Pakistan, Bhutan, Sri Lanka: Neighbouring Countries of India
(13) Michael Johnson, Marcin Urbaœ, Carl Lewis, Ed Moses: Atheletes
(14) Diamond, opal, ruby, emerald: Precious Stones
(15) Rainy, sunny, foggy, cloudy: Weathers
(16) West Ham FC, Arsenal FC, Chelsea FC, Manchester United: English Football Team
(17) Happy, sad, angry, scared: Emotions
(18) Africa, Europe, Asia, America: Continents
(19) Sparrow, peacock, eagle, ostrich: Birds
(20) French, geography, biology, history: Subjects
(21) dalmatian, husky, labrador, boxer: Dog Species
(22) Warsaw, Tokyo, Canberra, Riga: Capital Cities
(23) Chick, puppy, kitten, lamb: Baby Animals
(24) Dolce and Gabbana, Versace, Chanel, Gucci: Fashion Brands
(25) Ben Nevis, Rysy, Fuji, Everest: Mountains
(26) Botswana, Sierra Leone, Chad, Kenya: African Countries
(27) Slippers, sandals, shoes, flip-flops: Footwear
(28) Lipstick, mascara, foundation, eye shadow: Cosmetics
(29) Euro, dollar, pound, yen: Currencies
(30) Scooby Doo, The Simpsons, Mickey Mouse, Tom and Jerry: Cartoon Characters
(31) Strawberry, chocolate, vanilla, coffee: Edible flavours
(32) Apple, mango, banana, grapes: Fruits

Odd Word Out

In each line, choose the word that is different from the others in meaning:

(1) detach, remove, steady, unfasten, eparate: steady
(2) obstacle, dismiss, difficulty, hardship, dilemma: dismiss
(3) sort, kind, type, class, weep: weep
(4) still, hushed, quiet, channel, silent: channel
(5) nature, slender, slim, thin, narrow: nature
(6) determinate, end, finish, conclude, steep: steep
(7) horrible, docile, awful, terrible, dreadful: docile
(8) fertile, common, usual, ordinary, customary: fertile
(9) respect, esteem, regard, confine, honor: confine
(10) opponent, rival, adversary, enemy, slope: slope
(11) wages, draft, salary, earnings, income: draft
(12) awkward, trash, rubbish, junk, garbage: awkward
(13) sensible, weary, wise, prudent, sound: weary
(14) fraction, portion, section, scent, part: scent
(15) consume, urge, persuade, exhort, coax: consume
(16) site, location, spot, damp, place: damp
(17) blunder, mistake, vessel, oversight, error: vessel
(18) succint, bright, radiant, brilliant, gleaming: succint
(19) conceal, hide, smash, camouflage, disguise: smash
(20) omit, prefer, overlook, disregard, neglect: prefer
(21) procedure, method, approach, process, benefit: benefit
(22) hinder, precious, prevent,obstruct, halt: precious
(23) display, show, exhibit, command, demonstrate: command
(24) delete, erase, eliminate, remove, refuse: refuse
(25) tidy, neat, ponder, clean, orderly: ponder
(26) manage, direct, organise, control, various: various
(27) scheme, suitable, plan, design, undertaking: suitable
(28) primary, presume, suppose, assume, believe: primary
(29) foolish, silly, absurd, smooth, ridiculous: smooth
(30) uncertain, marvelous, wonderful, amazing, great: uncertain
(31) pleasant, fragile, delicate, frail, breakable: pleasant
(32) wreck, ruin, destroy, spoil, decent: decent
(33) disaster, catastrophe, tragedy, doubt, calamity: doubt
(34) prompt, immediate, punish, quick, rapid: punish
(35) stretch, private, confidential, personal, secret: stretch
(36) proclaim, announce, declare, publish, chastise: chastise
(37) border, ignore, boundary, edge, margin: ignore
(38) bare, contrary, naked, nude, undressed: contrary
(39) rigid, puzzle, stiff, firm, unbending: puzzle

(40) fragment, splinter, piece, fearful, chip: fearful
(41) vast, huge, enormous, value, immense: value
(42) obtain, gain, lean, acquire, procure: lean
(43) idle, vague, ambiguous, unclear, obscure: idle
(44) narrate, tell, abuse, relate, describe: abuse
(45) soggy, origin, soaked, drenched, wet: origin
(46) supply, gentle, tender, soft, mild: supply
(47) produce, create, make, charge, manufacture: charge
(48) modify, donate, alter, transform, change: donate

Synonyms

Synonyms are the words that are similar or nearly similar in meaning. While choosing a synonym, a student should remember certain things:

- A synonym should be in the same part of speech in which the given word is.
- Sometimes, an antonym is included in the alternative choices. Hence the students must be cautious in choosing a synonym.
- A synonym may have a literal meaning and another implied meaning. So the student should be careful in choosing the right word on the basis of the information given in the passage.

Example of Synonyms

S.No.	Word	Synonyms
(1)	Abandon	abdicate, desert, resign, Jettison
(2)	Abase	bring low, depress, dishonour, lower
(3)	Abash	Bewilder, daunt, humble
(4)	Abate	decline, mitigate, reduce, lower
(5)	Abbreviation	Abridgment, contraction, Condense, Abridge, precise
(6)	Abhor	Detest, hate
(7)	Absurd	Illogical
(8)	Adage	Maxim, saying
(9)	Agile	Active, smart
(10)	Apex	Summit, Zennith
(11)	Appalling	Dreadful, Morbid
(12)	Ardent	Avoid, fervent
(13)	Aspire	Seek, desire
(14)	Assent	Consent
(15)	Austere	Rigorous
(16)	Assimilate	Incorporate
(17)	Avid	Zealous, Ardent
(18)	Awesome	Alarming

(19)	Baleful	Deadly, Malign, Ruinous
(20)	Bashful	Coy
(21)	Beguile	Dupe, cheat
(22)	Belligerent	Warlike
(23)	Betray	Deceive
(24)	Bigot	Fanatic, dogmatist
(25)	Brittle	Fragile
(26)	Brevity	Concise
(27)	Bucolic	Rustic, rural
(28)	Buttress	Strengthen
(29)	Cajole	Coax
(30)	Candid	Frank, out spoken
(31)	Cardinal	Central
(32)	Catholic	Universal
(33)	Censure	Criticise, Disparage
(34)	Chaos	Bedlam
(35)	Circumspect	Discreet
(36)	Colossal	Mammoth, huge, Gigantic
(37)	Commotion	Uproar, Furor
(38)	Condemn	Disapprove
(39)	Conscious	Aware
(40)	Counterfeit	Fake
(41)	Credible	Believable
(42)	Cynical	Distrustful
(43)	Dawdle	Delay
(44)	Defunct	Extinct, expired
(45)	Deity	God
(46)	Delete	Efface
(47)	Deplore	Grieve for
(48)	Deterrent	Hindrance
(49)	Devastation	Destruction
(50)	Dire	Urgent
(51)	Distinguished	Celebrated, Eminent
(52)	Docile	Submissive
(53)	Dormant	Inactive, Languid
(54)	Drudgery	Hard work
(55)	Dubious	Doubtful
(56)	Eccentric	Whimsical
(57)	Effeminate	Unmanly
(58)	Egoist	Self seeker

(59)	Embargo	Ban
(60)	Empirical	Experimental
(61)	Erotic	Sensual, lustful, Passionate
(62)	Erudite	Learned
(63)	Ethnic	Racial
(64)	Exhort	Persuade
(65)	Exotic	Alien
(66)	Explicit	Stated
(67)	Extempore	Impromptu
(68)	Extravagant	Lavish
(69)	Fallible	Erring
(70)	Fallow	Unused
(71)	Famine	Dearth
(72)	Festive	Gay
(73)	Fidelity	Allegiance
(74)	Finesse	Adroitness
(75)	Flamboyant	Ostentatious
(76)	Formidable	Appalling
(77)	Frailty	Feebleness
(78)	Fraudulent	Treacherous
(79)	Fugitive	Deserter
(80)	Futile	Fruitless
(81)	Gangster	Bandit
(82)	Garrulous	Loquacious
(83)	Genial	Amiable
(84)	Gourmet	Connoisseur
(85)	Grandiose	Ambitious
(86)	Grief	Agony, Remorse
(87)	Grimace	Frown
(88)	Grotesque	Bizarre, Outlandish
(89)	Halcyon	Palmy
(90)	Harbour	Nurture, Refuge
(91)	Impede	Hinder
(92)	Impetus	Stimulus
(93)	Inception	Commencement
(94)	Inept	Clumsy
(95)	Linking	Conception
(96)	Innovation	Novelty
(97)	Intermittent	Discontinuous
(98)	Jargon	Slang

(99)	Jeer	Deride
(100)	Jeopardise	Imperil
(101)	Juvenile	Adolescent
(102)	Juxtaposition	Nearness
(103)	Laconic	Brief
(104)	Legible	Readable
(105)	Lethal	Baneful
(106)	Loathsome	Abominable
(107)	Lunatic	Insane
(108)	Luxuriant	Excessive
(109)	Magnanimous	Charitable
(110)	Makeshift	Temporary
(111)	Malice	Animosity
(112)	Menace	Peril
(113)	Meticulous	Detailed
(114)	Mockery	Derision
(115)	Mortification	Humiliation
(116)	Mundane	Earthly
(117)	Nadir	Lowest point
(118)	Niggardly	Mean
(119)	Nomadic	Vagrant
(120)	Novel	Fresh
(121)	Nuptial	Conjugal
(122)	Obnoxious	Disgusting
(123)	Obscure	Hazy
(124)	Obstinate	Stubborn
(125)	Occult	Mystic
(126)	Offspring	Descendant
(127)	Onerous	Burdensome, Onus
(128)	Ordeal	Trial
(129)	Outspoken	Candid
(130)	Overwhelm	Submerge
(131)	Pacifist	Peace lover
(132)	Palatable	Delicious
(133)	Panicky	Frightened
(134)	Paramount	Foremost
(135)	Pastime	Recreation
(136)	Paucity	Deficiency
(137)	Penchant	Leaning
(138)	Perennial	Incessant

(139)	Perilous	Dangerous
(140)	Pernicious	Detrimental
(141)	Perpetuate	Continue
(142)	Perseverance	Diligence
(143)	Pestilence	Epidemic
(144)	Philanthropic	Benevolent
(145)	Picturesque	Charming
(146)	Postulate	Hypothesise
(147)	Precise	Accurate
(148)	Prerogative	Privilege
(149)	Primitive	Primeval
(150)	Profound	Deep
(151)	Promulgate	Circulate
(152)	Proscribe	Ban
(153)	Prudent	Discreet
(154)	Quack	Fake
(155)	Quagmire	Swamp
(156)	Quash	Annul
(157)	Quest	Pursuit
(158)	Quintessence	Essence
(159)	Radical	Fundamental
(160)	Ramshackle	Tottering
(161)	Ransack	Plunder
(162)	Ravage	Demolish
(163)	Rebuke	Admonish
(164)	Recluse	Ascetic
(165)	Rectify	Correct
(166)	Recurrent	Frequent
(167)	Reinforce	Augment
(168)	Relish	Appreciate
(169)	Renounce	Forsake
(170)	Reprieve	Pardon
(171)	Repudiate	Discard
(172)	Resentment	Animosity
(173)	Resolute	Determined
(174)	Reticent	Taciturn
(175)	Revere	Adore
(176)	Ridicule	Laughter
(177)	Riotous	Anarchic
(178)	Robust	Hardy

(179)	Rotund	Bulbous
(180)	Rustic	Rural
(181)	Sabotage	Disrupt
(182)	Sadistic	Brutal
(183)	Salvation	Escape
(184)	Sanguine	Confident
(185)	Savage	Uncivilised
(186)	Scant	Inadequate
(187)	Schism	Split
(188)	Scramble	Struggle
(189)	Scurry	Hurry, sprint
(190)	Segregate	Separate
(191)	Sensual	Carnal
(192)	Serenity	Calmness, Temperate
(193)	Sham	Counterfeit
(194)	Simpleton	Dullard
(195)	Slumber	Sleep
(196)	Soar	Rise
(197)	Solace	Relief
(198)	Somber	Dismal
(199)	Sorcery	Necromancy
(200)	Sparse	Meagre
(201)	Splendid	Magnificent
(202)	Spouse	Companion
(203)	Spruce	Elegant
(204)	Stoop	Incline
(205)	Strident	Harsh
(206)	Studious	Assiduous
(207)	Suave	Agreeable
(208)	Submission	Surrender
(209)	Subsist	Exist
(210)	Sundry	Several
(211)	Surmount	Overcome
(212)	Surveillance	Care
(213)	Swear	Promise
(214)	Taciturn	Tight-lip
(215)	Tangible	Substantial
(216)	Tariff	Tax
(217)	Tedium	Boredom
(218)	Tempt	Entice

(219)	Tenacity	Power
(220)	Tentative	Speculative
(221)	Tepid	Lukewarm
(222)	Terse	Brief
(223)	Therapy	Remedy
(224)	Threshold	Doorstep
(225)	Thrifty	Economical
(226)	Thrive	Flourish
(227)	Ticklish	Awkward, Uncouth
(228)	Topical	Current
(229)	Tornado	Hurricane
(230)	Traitor	Deceiver
(231)	Transitory	Momentary
(232)	Treatise	Dissertation
(233)	Tremor	Shaking
(234)	Trickle	Percolate
(235)	Tumult	Bedlam
(236)	Typhoon	Cyclone
(237)	Unanimity	Agreement
(238)	Unceasing	Continual
(239)	Undue	Disproportionate
(240)	Unification	Union
(241)	Unscrupulous	Corrupt
(242)	Upheaval	Turmoil
(243)	Usher	Initiate
(244)	Utopian	Idealistic
(245)	Vagary	Whim
(246)	Vague	Doubtful
(247)	Valor	Courage
(248)	Vanish	Disappear
(249)	Vehemence	Keenness
(250)	Vendetta	Feud
(251)	Vent	Opening
(252)	Vestige	Multifaceted
(253)	Viable	Practicable
(254)	Vindictive	Rancorous
(255)	Vivid	Distinct
(256)	Volition	Choice
(257)	Voyage	Journey
(258)	Whimsical	Eccentric

(259)	Weird	Grotesque
(260)	Wizard	Magician
(261)	Withstand	Endure
(262)	Woo	Solicit
(263)	Wrath	Agent
(264)	Yearn	Crave
(265)	Yoke	Bandage
(266)	Zest	Pungency

Antonyms

Antonyms are the words that are contrary in meaning to another word. While choosing an antonym, a student should bear in mind certain things:

- An antonym must be in the same part of speech in which the keyword is.
- An antonym must be in the same tense form in which the keyword is.
- A candidate should pay due attention to the fact that generally the examiners include a synonym in the alternative choices given for the answer of the keyword.
- Often the alternative answers are in active as well as in passive voice. The correct answer is that which is similar in voice to the keyword. To be a top scorer — Read only GPH Books.

Examples of Antonyms

S.No.	**Words**	**Antonyms**
(1)	Abandon	Retain, keep
(2)	Abase	Cherish, dignify, exalt, extol, honour, respect, debase, cast down, tumble
(3)	Abash	Immodesty, self-esteem, self-love, self-praise, upgrade
(4)	Abate	Extreme, grow, advance, enhance
(5)	Abbreviation	Amplification, enlargement, extension, increase, spread, stretch
(6)	Abduct	Restore, deliver, adjoin
(7)	Accommodate	Dislodge
(8)	Accord	Discord
(9)	Accurate	Inaccurate
(10)	Adversity	Prosperity
(11)	Aggravate	Diminish
(12)	Aghast	Unsurprised
(13)	Agitation	Stillness, lull, quiet, turmoil

(14)	Amazing	Usual
(15)	Ample	Contracted
(16)	Arbitrary	Reasonable
(17)	Ascend	Descend
(18)	Assail	Defend
(19)	Authentic	Unauthentic
(20)	Babble	Discourse
(21)	Barren	Fertile
(22)	Bleak	Warm
(23)	Blend	Dissolve
(24)	Bore	Interested
(25)	Correct	Inaccurate
(26)	Criminal	Innocent
(27)	Cripple	Help
(28)	Criticism	Approval
(29)	Damage	Reparation
(30)	Defile	Cleanse
(31)	Degree	Unsure
(32)	Descend	Ascend
(33)	Despot	Constitutional
(34)	Destruction	Construction, salvation
(35)	Dictate	Obey
(36)	Difficult	Easy
(37)	Digest	Confuse
(38)	Dire	Harmless
(39)	Disapprove	Approve
(40)	Discern	Misunderstand
(41)	Dissipate	Gather
(42)	Downright	Crooked
(43)	Dwindle	Increase
(44)	Earn	Forfeit
(45)	Earthly	Celestial
(46)	Economy	Wastefulness
(47)	Edge	Inner part
(48)	Effective	Ineffective
(49)	Envy	Goodwill
(50)	Excellence	Inferiority
(51)	Extraordinary	Common
(52)	Extreme	Nearest
(53)	Fade	Flourish

(54)	Fiber	Weakness
(55)	Fictitious	True, fact
(56)	Flexible	Inflexible
(57)	Flinch	Stand firm
(58)	Gaiety	Sadness
(59)	Gale	Calm
(60)	Generous	Ignoble
(61)	Genteel	Rude, imperious
(62)	Genuine	Unnatural
(63)	Glory	Dimness
(64)	Grace	Disfavour
(65)	Graphic	Impricise, uncertain
(66)	Gratify	Refuse
(67)	Greet	Bid farewell
(68)	Haggle	Yield
(69)	Hallucination	Reality
(70)	Hapless	Lucky
(71)	Harmonious	Discordant
(72)	Homogeneous	Heterogeneous
(73)	Hooked	Straight
(74)	Humorous	Dull
(75)	Hypocrisy	Honesty
(76)	Icy	Warm
(77)	Identity	Difference
(78)	Ignorant	Humane, intelligent
(79)	Implicit	Expressed
(80)	Impostor	Honest
(81)	Imputation	Vindication
(82)	Ingenuous	Cunning
(83)	Initiate	End
(84)	Intimate	Unfamiliar
(85)	Irksome	Pleasant, interesting
(86)	Jade	Refresh
(87)	Jaunty	Unaffected
(88)	Jeer	Praise
(89)	Join	Loose
(90)	Journey	Stay-at-home
(91)	Judgment	Stupidity
(92)	Junction	Separation
(93)	Justice	Wrong

(94)	Justify	Condemn
(95)	Kindle	Extinguish
(96)	Knack	Disability
(97)	Knave	Angel, god
(98)	Knotty	Smooth
(99)	Knowledge	Ignorance
(100)	Lack	Plenty
(101)	Laconic	Long-winded
(102)	Lag	Hasten
(103)	Languor	Vigour
(104)	Laudable	Blameworthy
(105)	Linger	Hurry
(106)	Lively	Slow
(107)	Lunacy	Sanity
(108)	Lurid	Cheerful
(109)	Luscious	Unappetizing
(110)	Magnanimous	Ungenerous
(111)	Magnify	Diminish
(112)	Majestic	Undignified
(113)	Malady	Remedy
(114)	Malice	Charity
(115)	Marine	Terrestrial
(116)	Marked	Dubious
(117)	Martial	Civil
(118)	Melancholy	Gaiety
(119)	Memorable	Insignificant
(120)	Monotonous	Melodious
(121)	Moody	Cheerful
(122)	Motley	Homogeneous
(123)	Mount	Descend
(124)	Mournful	Cheerful
(125)	Mystify	Illuminate
(126)	Mythical	Historic
(127)	Native	Exotic
(128)	Nebulous	Clear
(129)	Neighbourhood	Distance
(130)	Niggard	Spendthrift
(131)	Noble	Low
(132)	Notion	Fact
(133)	Notorious	Unknown

(134)	Objection	Agreement
(135)	Obliging	Un-obliging
(136)	Obscene	Pure
(137)	Odium	Love
(138)	Ornate	Plain
(139)	Overrule	Leave alone
(140)	Overt	Covert
(141)	Overture	Withdrawal
(142)	Pacific	Violent
(143)	Pause	Movement
(144)	Plain	Uneven
(145)	Plastic	Stiff
(146)	Plentiful	Scanty
(147)	Pliable	Stiff
(148)	Polish	Stain
(149)	Pressure	Spontaneous
(150)	Produce	Conceal
(151)	Propagate	Be-barren
(152)	Pungent	Mild
(153)	Quack	Professional
(154)	Qualification	Unfitness
(155)	Quell	Arouse
(156)	Quench	Light
(157)	Rack	Torture
(158)	Radial	Superficial
(159)	Real	Apparent
(160)	Redundant	Scanty
(161)	Reform	Retain
(162)	Refresh	Exhaust
(163)	Rescue	Destroy
(164)	Retard	Accelerate
(165)	Revolve	Stand firm
(166)	Righteous	Unjust
(167)	Saddle	Unload
(168)	Salutation	Farewell
(169)	Scandal	Credit
(170)	Sensation	Dullness
(171)	Shocking	Soothing
(172)	Sleek	Rough
(173)	Sloth	Activity

(174)	Soak	Dry
(175)	Solitary	Companionable
(176)	Sordid	Clean
(177)	Steady	Unsteady
(178)	Stingy	Generous
(179)	Sundry	Homogenous
(180)	Surplus	Defect
(181)	Tacit	Explicit
(182)	Tall	Short
(183)	Task	Leisure
(184)	Tease	Please
(185)	Tipsy	Sober
(186)	Tortuous	Straight
(187)	Treachery	Loyalty
(188)	Trenchant	Mild
(189)	Twinkle	Be dull
(190)	Typical	Actual
(191)	Ugly	Beautiful
(192)	Unanimous	Discordant
(193)	Understand	Miss
(194)	Unique	Common
(195)	Utility	Uselessness
(196)	Vacant	Full
(197)	Valid	Ineffective
(198)	Vigilant	Sleepy
(199)	Vile	Worthy
(200)	Vivid	Dull
(201)	Vow	Repudiate
(202)	Wag	Tragedian
(203)	Wail	Rejoice
(204)	Wanton	Serious
(205)	Warp	Straighten
(206)	Wisdom	Folly
(207)	Withhold	Give
(208)	Wonder	Calmness
(209)	Yearn	Be content
(210)	Yoke	Freedom
(211)	Zealous	Cold
(212)	Zenith	Nadir
(213)	Zest	Distaste

☺☺☺

3 Writing Section

Composition

The composition and essay writing is an art to test the ability of one to express his thought properly or logically. The students can combine information with their own opinion and suggestion. Now, the question is how the paragraph develops from a topic or sentence. Paragraph develops from sentence arranged properly and each idea must be logically linked with the next.

While writing a composition/essay the following points must be kept in mind:

- Read the hints/points given in verbal input, carefully.
- To develop an article, arrange them in the order.
- Organise the points properly. Add some new ideas of your own.
- Arrange the points in a logical order.
- Put them under different main headings.
- Add sub-points to the main point.
- Develop each point in a logical way.
- Substantiate your arguments, if you are writing on a debatable issue.
- Try to introduce the main theme or issue in the first few lines.
- Close your composition with a conclusion on the given topic.

Choosing a topic

In an examination there is always a choice given to students in the question. The student should, therefore:

- Carefully choose the topic on which he can write well.
- Do not choose topic where you lack enough matter. General readings and observations will help awareness of various topics.
- Choose the topic about which you feel strongly. What you write, will then seem convincing to the readers.

- Do not choose a topic which does not interest you. You will only come up with an uninteresting essay.
- Limit the scope of your topic, if the topic is too general. For example, a topic like 'Hobbies' may cover far too many things. You may find it easier to discuss various hobbies in your introductory paragraph and then discuss your particular hobby in detail, in the rest of the essay. General topics only make your essays disordered, unless you decide which aspect of it you want to write on.

How to write a Good Essay?

- Choose the proper or most suitable topic.
- Think carefully on the topic.
- Define the subject and its scope –i.e. what you should cover in the essay.
- Understand the topic and what is required thoroughly.
- Jot down all ideas and points, facts, opinions and feelings that come to your mind about the subject.
- Jotting down will help you rearrange the points, remove repetitions and dull information. It will help you organise the point into logical paragraphs. It will also prevent you from missing out on or forgetting some vital point.
- Never start writing down the first thing that comes into your head without knowing what will be the next. This will only result in a badly planned, disorderly essay where there will be much repetition. You may also find that you don't have enough material to write the essay of the required length. Jotting down points will help you decide, whether you have enough material to develop it into a good essay. Otherwise, you could choose another topic.

Organising Your Essay

- Place facts and ideas which you have jotted down into different groups according to their similarities or dissimilarities.
- This will then lead to paragraphs.
- Each paragraph usually conveys and develops one idea, though it may not always be essential to write a paragraph on each item.
- The transition from one paragraph to another should be logical and smooth.
- Your paragraphs can be arranged either according to chronological sequence (time), logical sequence (cause and effect) or spatial sequence (according to place). You can also arrange paragraphs according to the order of importance.

The Format of Composition

All composition and essays must follow the format of:

(1) Introduction

A good introduction is an important part of the essay. It should state your topic and arouse the interest and curiosity of the reader. Often your introduction can convey the pattern your essay will follow or the ideas you will discuss.

An introduction can be in one line – simple and direct or an entire paragraph depending on the topic. An expository essay usually states the topic immediately and comes straight to the point.

(2) The Body

This portion will contain discussion of the ideas you have outlined. In other words, you develop your essay in this section. The style and use of language are most important to convey your ideas with maximum clarity and minimum confusion. There are some points, which we may keep in mind:

- Suit your style to the topic.
- Do not use slang or colloquial terms.
- Sentences should be simple, direct and have a flow.
- Using quotations or proverbs will lend good style to our writing, but do not over indulge in very flowery writing.
- Avoid writing long sentences and use of words, the meanings of which you are not sure of.
- Do not divert from your theme.
- The essay should have your individual opinions and feelings. Do not put content with merely repeating the opinions of others.
- Make your essay interesting with examples and anecdotes. But do not get bogged down in too many details.
- Be brief and clear. Remember you have to write your composition to set a limit of words, though a few extra or less words would not matter too much.

(3) Conclusion

Once you have developed the topic, you should not just end abruptly. A good conclusion is as important as a good introduction. The beginning and end should therefore be well planned out. While the beginning introduces the topic, the end should summarise the main ideas you have discussed. The theme should be repeated to convince the readers you have proved the point, especially in argumentative essays.

Finally revise and read through your essay correcting errors of grammar, punctuation and spelling.

Types of Composition

Composition can be classified into four different types depending upon the topic/subject, approach and the treatment of the topic. No composition however, needs to be of one kind. You may use techniques from other types of composition too. The four main types are:

(1) Expository: The Exposition type of composition usually analyses a character or a situation, give directions, define a term as well as to make something clearer to one presumably does not understand something. Here, the writer tries to expose some information to the readers to make them understand and informed about certain information.

Example:

Ekaterina Gordeeva

There are not many people on this earth that I can say inspire me to achieve my dreams. That is why Ekaterina Gordeeva is so special to me. She inspires me in many ways.

Ekaterina Gordeeva inspires me because she is very brave. When she was just a toddler, she began figure skating. She traveled around the world without her parents throughout her entire childhood. Most kids can't stand one hour without their parents. Many times Ekaterina fell during skating, but she always got back up and continued skating. Ekaterina also survived the loss of her husband, Sergei Grinkov, and if that's not bravery I don't know what is.

Another way Ekaterina inspires me is she is extremely talented. She started skating at a very early age, and held an Olympic title by the time she turned thirteen. She has won many competitions and is a role model for many young figure skaters trying to follow in her footsteps. She also is a wonderful mother. That alone takes much talent.

I also admire Ekaterina Gordeeva because she is such a strong person. The fact that she is still skating after her husband/partner's death is amasing. She had never skated alone in a competition until Sergei's death. She went through tons of mental abuse from Sergei's parents because they blamed her for their son's death. Clearly, it is impossible because the doctors assured it was a heart attack. Most importantly, Ekaterina is staying strong for her daughter, Daria. She has to answer Daria's questions about her father, and that must be extremely hard for a widow.

To me, Ekaterina Gordeeva is a very inspiring person. I believe you don't have to know a person to be inspired by them. People can be inspirational by doing the little things that make them who they are. Ekaterina Gordeeva is a perfect example of what an inspirational person should be.

(2) Argumentative: The Argumentation type of composition appeals to the reader's reasoning capability as well as to the reader's emotion. This type of composition makes the readers change their mind, their attitude as well as their points of views and feelings. In here, the writer tries to persuade the readers by giving an argument that will challenge their reasons with regards to their opinion and thoughts about a certain thing or idea.

Example:

City life is better than country life

'It is often said that God made the country and man made the town', which means that countryside is the handiwork of nature, while town is that of man. This seems to indicate that the country life is better than city life. However, it need not necessarily be true.

There is no doubt that the countryside has many advantages. It is more healthful and natural than the polluted city. The quiet and peace of villages with plenty of greenery, flowing brooks and canals is soothing to the mind unlike the hustle and bustle of city life. The people too are simple and warm hearted, welcoming and helping everyone like a member of the family, whereas in the cities people are impersonal, isolated and keep to themselves. Country life refreshes, while the wear and tear of city life is exhausting.

However, the idyllic picture presented with such regularity, is often a myth. It is hard work and drudgery, often in the villages. Women track miles for water, while they spend hours cooking on charcoal stoves. Medical facilities are minimum and people are generally superstitions and caste ridden. Ignorant, resisting change, they cling to outmoded values, refusing to acknowledge the scientific change in the rest of the world. They often have a 'frog-in-well' attitude. Content with their situation, blaming fate for their misfortunes most of them do not have the will or ability to advance in their life.

Against this, the city has many admirable advantages. Trapped water, electricity, modern means of cooking, refrigerators and such other benefits have greatly reduced the drudgery of the housewife in cities. Best possible medical facilities are available, apart from other modern benefits like quick means of transportation. City life offers greater education privileges and the means of finding suitable work are more numerous and more remunerative. Less prejudiced and less superstitious, the city dweller is ready to change with the times. More alert, energetic and aware of changes all over the world, he is better informed and has more opportunity for intellectual development than a villager in the countryside. Avenues of entertainment are numerous cinema theatres, drama clubs, shopping arcades, restaurants providing food from every corner of India and abroad. Growing environment awareness has led to vast green areas being created in big cities, thus providing city dwellers with benefits of nature too.

From the above argument, it is clear that the city has many more advantages than country life, I feel to city life is definitely better than country life.

Note: In the above essay, we develop the argument by stating the benefits of the village life. But the second para, starting with however, shows that village has its disadvantages – life is not so idyllic after all. The advantages of city life, we reserve for the long, last paragraph, so that its impact is more. Notice how the disadvantages of town life have been given in the first para, but only as a contrast to the main point of the first paragraph, which is advantages of village life. Thus, the impact of the disadvantages is reduced. Finally in the last line of the paragraph on advantages of city-life, we have anticipated a possible counter-argument and have answered it by saying that 'nature' too is now available in the city. The conclusion asserts the topic that city life is better than country life.

(3) Narrative: The Narration type of composition gives the readers with the impression of a particular event as well as gives the readers the sense of actually witnessing it. What happened and how it happened are also discussed. Here, the writer tries to emphasise the story of a particular event by narrating or telling it to the readers.

Example:

Memory of my childhood

Memories of early childhood are hazy. Perhaps, it is because of this that we tend to see it as a rosy, untroubled time of life. My earliest memory is of my mother escorting me to school and the sense of loneliness and terror which used to strike me, when she would leave me behind among the milling, jostling noisy innumerable kids. I was awed by the huge school premises, the teacher in the starched *saree* with a ruler in the hand. But it was a temporary phase.

Later memories of school, where we spend the greater part of childhood, are for the most pleasant. The excitement of taking part in a dance for the first time, the love and pride in my parent's eyes as I danced on the stage are memories which will stay with me forever. So also the quarrels with friends, the quick making up again, playing with dolls are all parts of childhood memories. Studying regularly, the drudgery of daily homework which would never be done without mummy's schooling and Dad's reproving glances remain fresh in the memory.

I remember too, the sadness I felt when my father was transferred and we moved from Mumbai to Delhi. It was tough leaving behind good friends and playmates. But I adapted with the usual childhood resilience, very easily to the new city, new house and new friends.

I cannot forget either, the way I used to rush into father's arms as soon as I heard him return from office or his hearty laughter when I got teased by my elder brother. He never failed to give me a toffee if I happened to be upset or crying. She would prepare mouth-watering dishes and I remember being caught trying to steal a sweet, which she had said should be eaten only after the 'Puja' in the evening.

My childhood like, I believe of most others was a sheltered loving one. I had my share of scoldings, getting caught in mischiefs and of course a terrible predilection to falling and injuring myself, but on the whole there seem to be very sweet recollections of childhood.

Note: The above composition does not follow a strict chronological pattern. Rather we highlight those special memories which stand out because they had some impact on you. An essay like this offers tremendous scope for offering personal comments and observation. Instead of merely listing your memories, the inclusion of observations and comments on the teacher, father and mother (the three main influence of childhood) the essay becomes more interesting.

(4) Descriptive: The Description type of composition usually attempts to make the reader realise how the writer felt under certain circumstances. It further makes the reader see or hear something as the writer saw or heard. It also makes the readers to fell the quality of direct experience. In here, the writer tries to describe what he sees and feel to the readers, making the readers see what he saw and feel what he felt.

Example:

Summer

Everyone has a comfortable place to escape to for relaxation. They go there when they need to be alone and not with people to disturb them. My place is nature in the summer. The summer time relaxes me like no exact place could. Nature, in the summer, relaxes me with its naturedness.

I love sitting in the grass and listening to the nature sounds around me while it's summer. One of the sounds I tune to first is the sound of the birds singing and chirping away as if they are creating a song. After sitting for a few minutes, I'll hear the light breeze coming down through the trees, rustling their leaves. Besides those two things I hear, it is a peaceful quietness that you can't get in a city or town. That's why I love nature, but only in the summer. They are always associated with each other.

When I look around me, in the summer time when I'm outside somewhere, I see beautiful bright clear things. For example, the tall green grass and the leaves on the trees sway in the breeze. Then I see bright or pastel flowers around, never too far away from any one person. Most days, unless rainy, are bright, sunny, and warm. The sky is a beautiful landscape blue with little clouds, if any, in it. If I'm in the forest, I see big tall trees all around me.

The feeling of summer all around me is friendly to me. The sun is so warm against my hot skin. And the breeze cools my skin off again as it lightly touches it from blowing down from the trees. Then, when I am sitting in the grass, I feel either its dryness or its moistness against my body.

Summer is my favourite season, and nature when it's summer is relaxing and comfortable.

Note: Moving from the outer appearance, you can give details of one's habits, his character, his likes and dislikes and general attitude to life.

Some Examples of Composition and Essays

(1) Your favourite novelist/poet in English

Ans. Good books are our best friends. They remain with us in weal and woe. They inspire us to make our life great and sublime. They never fail us like some fair weather friends of this world. I love to read books and my favourite subject is the reading of novels. My favourite novelist is 'Sh. R.K. Narayanan'. I am impressed a lot by his style of presentation. When I started reading his books I was greatly impressed by his ideas. The work of Narayanan has eternal beauty and freshness about them. His appeal is permanent and universal. He is not only liked in India but the whole Asia praises his writing. He is declared as one of the best novelist of English literature in our country. Though he writes many short stories but he is named as a novelist rather than a story teller. No doubt he made no attempt to be original in the plot of his novel, he borrowed it from here and there in one's life but whatever passes through the crucible of his imagination. The novel of Narayanan are illustrations of real life situations in which there is not a smooth ride of live events, rather there is the rock and roll of the fate that plays its due role in the life of the character.

In the novel 'Bachelor of Art' all the characters created by him are so appealing. I feel that the characters are standing in front of me. The simple story of a small town boy, Chander with dreams in his eyes and tension of study and family, the drama with father all are very touching. His romance of young age with a girl, and the method of winning her heart, the way to woo her all attract a person lot. In the character, he showed a deep profound understanding of human nature. The beautiful presentation of lifestyle of southern part of our country helps to understand the cultural of our country. He displays a comprehensive vision and omniscient power.

Whether he presents a few characters or too many characters, he is able to concentrate on all of them. He presents almost all kind of human beings that we find in the real world. I also like the plots of his stories. I am really impressed by the autobiographical element presented in his novels. His stories are always presented in a simple background but there is a serious story with many problems. We feel sorry for almost all the major characters in his novels. I think that Narayanan is the master of pathos. He is also like a social reformer but he is never preaching directly in any of his novels. After reading novels of many other writers, I am greatly impressed by Narayanan. It is rightly said about him that 'he is not for an age but for all times'.

(2) Globalisation and its consequences

Ans. Our world today is characterised by rapid changes, which are reflected in all areas of human relationships and the exchange of ideas and goods of any kind, in scientific discoveries, innovations, in the various life styles, in values and in cultural expressions of any kind, as well as in art and religion. Every day we hear about and experience the consequences of a multi-dimensional phenomenon, the so-called globalisation.

Globalisation undoubtedly brings new challenges to the social, political, and religious institutions of every country, because it has brought about new and complex social, economic, and political processes which, in turn, have accelerated conflicts inherited from earlier times and also created inequalities in the exchanges taking place, which impair the life and development process of people and the marginalised groups considerably.

If we emphasise the negative consequences of globalisation, we cannot deny some of the positive results of internationalising science, technology, and communication. We are well aware of the fact that progress in the area of medicine has made roads on the decline of certain diseases and increased the average lifespan, and that rapid access to information has brought about the exchange of knowledge and skills in the areas of education, production, and employment.

Without being the direct cause of it, globalisation has brought about an acceleration and intensification of several problems from which this continent has suffered for several decades. Let us name a few examples: the decreasing stability of family life; the increase of violence in all its forms; the discrimination of women; the destruction of the environment and the exploitation of natural resources; It would be naive to think that we could contribute to the solution of some of these problems by means of short-term or locally limited endeavours or projects. It is, therefore urgently required that the meeting, in which we are now participating, brings us to the point where we think globally in order to then go forth and act locally. The solidarity which makes it possible to face these challenges requires an open and continuously multi-lateral communication, in order to present analyses and alternatives which include us all, taking up topics such as emigration, protection of natural resources, export of our products under conditions of competition, and technological resources for a sustainable development, etc.

(3) Your favourite scientists/philosopher

Ans. India has produced so many great scientists in the modern age and Dr. APJ Abdul Kalam follows their great tradition. Born on 15 October 1931 at Rameswaram in Tamil Nadu, Dr. Avul Pakir Jainulabdeen Abdul Kalam has specialised in Aeronautical Engineering from Madras Institute of Technology. Initially he wanted to become a pilot, but was rejected and then opted for aeronautical engineering later.

He is often referred to as the 'Missile Man of India' for his work and is considered a leading progressive leader. Dr. Kalam made significant contribution as Project Director to develop India's first indigenous Satellite Launch Vehicle (SLV-III) which successfully injected the Rohini satellite in the near earth orbit in July 1980 and made India an exclusive member of the Space Club.

He was responsible for the evolution of ISRO's launch vehicle programmed, particularly the PSLV configuration. He was responsible for the development and operationalisation of AGNI and PRITHVI Missiles and for building indigenous capability in critical technologies through networking of multiple institutions. He was the Scientific Adviser to Defence Minister and Secretary, Department of Defence Research and Development from July 1992 to December 1999. During this period, he led to the weaponisation of strategic missile systems and the Pokhran-II nuclear tests in collaboration with Department of Atomic Energy, which made India a nuclear weapon State.

Dr. Kalam has served as the Principal Scientific Advisor to the Government of India, in the rank of Cabinet Minister, from November 1999 to November 2001 and was responsible for evolving policies, strategies and missions for many development applications.

In his literary pursuit four of Dr. Kalam's books - "Wings of Fire", "India 2020 - A Vision for the New Millennium", "My journey" and "Ignited Minds - Unleashing the power within India" have become household names in India and among the Indian nationals abroad. These books have been translated in many Indian languages. Dr. Kalam is one of the most distinguished scientists of India with the unique honour of receiving honourary doctorates from 30 universities and institutions. He has been awarded the coveted civilian awards - Padma Bhushan (1981) and Padma Vibhushan (1990) and the highest civilian award Bharat Ratna (1997). Dr. Kalam became the 11th President of India on 25 July 2002. His focus is on transforming India into a developed nation by 2020. He is a very learned and able man. India is proud of such a person being born on its soil.

(4) Problems of a Girl Child

Ans. In India, life of a girl child has never been an easy one. It may happen that she may not even understand her existence. People often hate girls and they do not like a baby girl born in the family. India has exceptionally high rates of girl child malnutrition, because tradition in India requires that women eat last and least throughout their lives, even when pregnant and lactating. Families are far less likely to educate girls than boys, and far more likely to pull them out of school, either to help out at home or from fear of violence. Girls often have to work for longer hours in and outside the home and their work is more arduous than boys. Women have no power to choose whom they will marry and are often married off at a younger age. Legal loopholes are used to deny girl inheritance rights. India is one of the few countries where males significantly outnumber females, and this imbalance has increased over time. India's maternal mortality rates in rural areas are among the world's highest. According to expert estimates "deaths of young girls in India exceed those of young boys by over 300,000 each year, and every sixth infant death is specifically due to gender discrimination". Of the 15 million baby girls born in India each year, nearly 25 per cent will not live to see their 15th birthday. The Indian constitution grants women equal rights with men, but strong patriarchal traditions persist, with women's lives shaped by customs that are centuries old. In most Indian families, a daughter is viewed as a liability, and she is conditioned to believe that she is inferior and subordinate to men. Sons are idolised and celebrated. May you be the mother of a hundred sons is a common Hindu wedding blessing. Women get less healthcare than men. Gender disparities in nutrition are evident from infancy to adulthood. In fact, gender has been the most statistically significant determinant of malnutrition among young children and malnutrition is a frequent direct or underlying cause of death among girls below age 5. Girls are breast-fed less frequently and for shorter durations in infancy; in childhood and adulthood, males are fed first and better. Adult women consume approximately 1,000 fewer calories per day than men according to one estimate from Punjab. It is really a pity that a girl child in a country like India is not given dignity and respect that she truly deserves. An atrocious fact is that even in urban areas it is being done to a large extent.

(5) Advantages and disadvantages of living in a joint Family

Or

Pleasures of family get together

Ans. Man is a social being. Family is the pivot of all civic virtues. The essential themes of Indian cultural life are learned within the bosom of a family. The joint family is highly valued, ideally consisting of several generations residing, working, eating, and worshiping together. Such families include men related through the male line, along with their wives, children, and unmarried daughters. A wife usually lives with her husband's relatives, although she retains important bonds with her natal family. Even in rapidly modernizing India, the traditional joint household remains for most Indians the primary social force, in both ideal and practical.

Large families tend to be flexible and well suited to modern Indian life, especially for the more than two-thirds of Indians who are involved in agriculture. As in most primarily agricultural societies, cooperating kin help provide mutual economic security. You can share your feelings, experience, etc. You can get the advice on any mater you want. The joint family is also common in cities, where kinship ties are often crucial to obtaining employment or financial assistance. Many prominent families, such as the Tatas, Birlas, and Bacchans have retained the joint family arrangements as they cooperate in controlling major financial empires. But there is some disadvantage of joint family that you have to work accordingly to the head of the family. The person loses his personal freedom in a joint family. Your privacy is ruined. You are not allowed to go against the wishes of the family.

The ancient ideal of the joint family retains its power, but today actual living arrangements vary widely. Many Indians live in nuclear families—a couple with their unmarried children—but belong to strong networks of beneficial kinship ties. Often, clusters of relatives live as neighbours, responding readily to their kinship obligation. The lack of joint liability usually leads to disputes and split. The child problem is so common in nuclear family. The children of nuclear family are terrified most of time as nobody cares for them in their loneliness.

As they expand, joint families typically divide into smaller units, which gradually grow into new joint families, continuing a perpetual cycle. Today, some family members may move about to take advantage of job opportunities, typically sending money home to the larger family. However, it still retains the basic culture of our 'Indian society', and somewhere it is important also.

(6) Indian culture at the cross-roads

Ans. India is my motherland. She has brought me up. I love her more than even my life. I wish and pray that she should become a first grade nation of the world. She would regain her ancient glory and become a leader of the world, not by the force of arms but by the force of human values. Our country has a rich historical background and also a rich heritage of our traditions. We respect our elders, we value our relations more than money, we try to be compassionate and polite, we have the feelings of brotherhood and we are well known as the best host. Our historical monuments are still visited by foreigners and they often come to India for their research on Indian culture. Anything that is India, is worth appreciating for many others. We have learnt from history about the ancient Indian culture and civilisations. There was society tied with the stronger ties in which individual person felt secured. What the whole world feels today, the concept to save the environment was followed by our ancient ruler, certain animal species were not allowed to be killed, most of them were prayed as God. So many trees, rivers, mountains were treated as our protector God and worshipped by local communities. The 'Atithi Devo Bhava' was the slogan of every family. Can we say the same thing today? If we look at the present generation, we feel that the time is changing very fast. Everybody seems to be in a hurry. We forget the teachings of our elders, and order of protecting the environment. In short, we are standing at a place where we have the chances of getting lost. Our culture may get lost if we do not have the mental balance and the maturity to respect our culture. Much is expected from the younger generation to save our culture but they are not free from the influence of others. It is a matter of great concern that our culture is facing a time where we do not feel like saying anything with surety.

(7) How safe is Rail Travel?

Ans. The issue of rail safety is on the agenda of every meeting between of railway officials. The possibility that travel by train is becoming more perilous will no doubt be closely examined, as will the role of the operators in making it as safe as possible. In the 1990s, 97 people have been killed and 250 have been injured as a result of train incidents. Train Protection System uses a target speed indication and audible warnings to warn the train driver if they are likely to exceed a speed profile that will cause the train to pass a red signal or exceed a speed restriction. However, the perception that rail travel is becoming less safe in general is not supported by statistics.

Serious accidents on the rail network remain rare, and in general terms, before today's incident, the annual rate of deaths on the railways has dropped back to the level of the early-1980s. Serious train incidents are defined as those collisions and derailments which affect passenger lines, and are therefore considered to be life threatening. They do not include incidents involving freight lines. The nature of rail travel, as opposed to travel by road, means that a single accident may result in higher casualties and fatalities than individual road accidents. The road fatalities however, are much greater annually. They are therefore more shocking, and attract more media attention than the much greater number of accumulated casualties and fatalities which happen on the roads every year.

A lot of people criticise train travel, and say it's not what it used to be. But it can still be a fast, often inexpensive form of transport, not only between cities, but between countries. Like anything else, though, we need to think a little to keep ourself safe in the station and on the train.

However, by putting a few simple rules into practice, we can ensure a pleasant, trouble-free journey.

(8) The Menace of Corruption

Ans. Corruption in India has assumed such large proportions and variegated forms that large numbers of the public have come to believe that it is impossible to get rid of this malaise. Lack of public participation in decision-making, non-transparent administration, promotion of officials on the basis of caste and absence of visionary leaders have contributed to poor governance and ineffective delivery of public goods, are some causes of corruption. Although it may hurt the pride to admit it, India is one of the most corrupt countries in the world. The latest Corruption Perception Index ranks India a lowly 95 out of a list of 178 nations.

Other countries have been notoriously corrupt in the past (for example, Britain in the 18th century) but have succeeded in tackling the problem through a mixture of administrative and electoral reforms. The situation in America during the late-19th century *vis-a-vis* corruption bears a strong causal resemblance to that which exists in India and many other developing countries today. In dispelling the gloomy but widespread notion that corruption in India cannot be curtailed.

Although it may hurt the pride to admit that India is one of the most corrupt countries on the world map. It is small comfort that nations such as Bangladesh or Uganda rank lower in this list of infamy. In 1964, the Santhanam Committee, which was set up to examine the increasing menace of corruption in the administration, observed that the "tendency to subvert integrity in the public services instead of being isolated... is growing into an organised well-planned racket". If anything, it has grown much larger and become even better organised since.

(9) Importance of Books In Our Life

Or

Pleasures of Reading Books

Ans. Since ages, books have been the real partners of human beings. They have always been proven to be a source of knowledge and learning. Books have always been good companions in both good and bad phases of life of people. They have always been impartial as far as their friendship is concerned. They are the same for both rich as well as poor. Books also help humans in reducing their stress, depression, and some other sorts of tension.

Books are the greatest source of entertainment and recreation. Books are of many types and it is the interest of an individual which he finds the most interesting to spend time with. Some love reading novels, some are passionate about current magazines, and some are fond of articles and quotation related books. Library considered as the temple of books. Lover of books finds calm and a quiet environment to interact with the books effectively there. Whenever we are little depressed, there are several books that boost us and encourage us at that bad juncture of life. We get to learn from the writings of many famous personalities how to recover from difficult situations. If we look into our career point of view, books keeps up abreast with current affairs and provides us with each and every subject to prepare for the competitive. Their friendship is so selfless and pure that they do not demand their reader nothing in return. Books are the most sincere, faithful and never falling friends.

Therefore, we can say that "Books open our mind, broaden our mind, and strengthen us as nothing else can do".

(10) Dangers of Global Warming

Ans. Global environmental change is detrimental to the health of human being, and would result in hotter summers, colder winters, rise in sea levels, change in monsoon pattern, drought, extinction of bio diversity level, and devastating floods. In the wake of intensification of the problem of global environmental change, the mankind faces environmental dilemma. Global environmental change is common concern of mankind and possesses inherent capability of transcending national boundaries. Therefore, the international regulation and control of the phenomenon of global environmental change is legitimate.

Scientists agree the Earth's climate is being directly affected by human activity, and for many people around the world, these changes are having negative effects. Carbon dioxide levels today are nearly 30 per cent higher than they were prior to the start of the Industrial Revolution, polar ice cap is now melting at the rate of 9 per cent per decade. Global warming has been of great concerns of the environment and other scientists concerned about the disadvantages of fund following of any sort of development that brought up economic growth. Global warming is a state when the general temperature of the environment is growing from its normal levels. Global warming is said to be the result of unrestricted use of fossil fuels which left too much of carbon dioxide that forms the main component of green house gas. There are many things we can do to help slow anthropogenic climate change, which is caused by emissions of greenhouse gases such as carbon dioxide. A few small changes can make a big difference Continued scientific and technological research is critical to help us understand, mitigate, and adapt to changes. However, it is widely felt that it's not a lack of science but rather a lack of public understanding and political will preventing us from taking actions that could be taken today to stem human forced climate change. Sustainable development is one of the concepts which assumed immense importance against the backdrop of the growth of industrialisation and exploitation of environment to gratify his ever growing hunger for prosperity.

(11) Life in a Metropolitan City

Or

Hazards of living in a big city

Ans. Life in a metropolitan city is very pleasant and attractive. It has many advantages. So great is the charm of a metropolitan city life that people from the rural areas are everyday migrated to the cities in large number. A city life provided comforts and luxuries that we can never dream of in villages. The first of, the means of transportation, like cars, scooters, buses, metros and other means of conveyance that take us from one place to other. Metropolitan cities have big and large number of sources of recreation. We can enjoy cinema show and various plays and art galleries. Articles of our daily needs can be easily available in one departmental store. We have now home delivery system. Again we have in cities medical facilities that we cannot even dream of in a village. The school and colleges in a metropolitan city offer facilities of education. The city life provides us with various avenues for the increase of our knowledge. We have easy access to a variety of newspaper, libraries and study circles. We meet people of different races and cultures and learn a lot of things from them.

This however does not mean that a metropolitan city life does not have any disadvantages. Life in cities is mechanical. With lifestyles becoming progressively frenzied, people are devoting lesser time to their families. There is more trouble for children facing physical and behavioural challenges. People in metropolitan cities are always running. Their routine is always busy. People do not have time for gossips and they do not mix well with others. The competition in each and every field is great and they have to try to cope up with new challenges. The work load is too much and the expectations at work place increases. The rush of traffic on the roads tells on our nerves. The noise in the streets, the hooting of the sirens of the factories and shrieks and cries of people everywhere irritate us. We cannot even dream of fresh air and fresh vegetables. The houses in city are huddled together and one finds it, sometimes, difficult even to breathe freely. Life in metropolitan is artificial and purely material. Everybody is after show and money. The values of life are ignored in these cities. Thus, in spite of having all attractions and facilities in metropolitan cities, a metropolitan city life fails to provide real peace of mind and heart.

(12) A book that has influenced you greatly

Ans. Good books are our best friend; they inspire us to make our life great and sublime. They never fail us like some fair weather friends of this world. Happy is the man who keeps books as his constant companion.

I have great love for books. I have some general books. I go through these books in my spare time. Books on travel increase my knowledge. I have a great liking for the Ramayana. It is my favourite book. I read it in order to learn some noble lessons. The Ramayana is full of wisdom. It contains a lot of useful advices. Mahatma Gandhi also liked this book. He regarded Rama to be an ideal man, ideal king, ideal brother, ideal husband, and ideal son. That is why he was eager to set up 'Ram Rajya' in this country.

The Ramayana is the story of the life of the Rama and his family. Rama was an ideal son. He obeyed his father and mother. He went to forest for 14 years. His noble wife, Sita also went with him. Lakshmana was an ideal brother. He remained by his side through thick and thin. His sacrifice inspires the readers. Bharat was also a loyal brother. He was not at all selfish. He wept when Rama left for the forest. He ruled over the kingdom for 14 years on behalf of Rama. Though he was a king for 14 years, yet he lived like a servant of Rama.

The Ramayana tells us the story of victory of good over evil. The path of truth and goodness leads to glory. The path of evil leads to death and destruction. Ravana, the demon king of Lanka, was full of noble persons. He took away Sita to Lanka. He was proud and cruel. He troubled the good and fight against them. Ravana and his companion were killed at last. The Hindus celebrate Dussehara every year and burn the effigies of these bad persons. In this way, we can learn that ultimately good and noble person win in this world. We should also remain good and noble forever. The Ramayana is a very useful book. If we follow its advice, we can lead a happy and noble life. I regard this book as the most valuable treasure of my life.

(13) Trees are our best friends

Ans. In ancient time, people were generally dependent on forests to get food, wood, shelter and many herbs and shrubs. Forests not only provide these things but also protect the environment.

As we know, trees use carbon dioxide and provide oxygen which is necessary for human life and ecosystem. Trees take care of our planet's temperature and climate. They help to bring rain which is of paramount importance for the production of crops.

For our selfish activities of establishing factories, building, etc. we are destroying our rich forests. We cut them for land and do not plant trees, which is very dangerous for our environment as well as for future generations.

So, for the sake of future generations, we need to protect the forests and launch a forestation programme upto village level for plantation of trees. Awareness among students, people and society needs to be developed about importance of plantation because trees help us in many ways. They provide us food, wood and many herbs used for making medicines. Keeping in view the weather conditions, they provide variety of fruits like mango, apple, cherry, etc.

So, we can say that trees are our best friend and protect our environment from pollution which is harmful for us.

(14) Problems of Environmental Pollution

Ans. The term environment includes air, water, land, and the interrelation which exists among and between these basic elements and human being and other living being. Besides the physical and biological aspects, the environment embraces the social, economical, political, and cultural and several other aspects as well. Man's total environmental system includes not only the biosphere but also his interactions with natural and manmade surrounding. The term environmental degradation refer to the deterioration in physical components by anthropogenic process to such an extent that it could not be set right by homeostatic mechanism. It simply means overall lowering of environmental qualities because of adverse changes brought in by human activities in the basic structure of the component of environment to such an extent that these adverse changes adversely affect all biological organism in general and human societies in particular. The cause of environmental degradation include: (i) growth of population (ii) scientific and technological development at an accelerated pace (iii) ambitious developmental project aimed at fast economic development (iv) expanding industries, urban growth and agricultural development (v) unscientific utilisation of natural resources (vi) poverty (vii) affluence (viii) ignorance and lack of environment (ix) philosophical outlook of the society, etc.

Protection of environment presents a most fundamental challenge to the nation desire to industrialisation faster, to be self-sufficient in food, and too capable of fulfilling of certain basic needs of the growing population. Development can take place at the cost of the environment only upto a point. Development without concern for the environment can only be anti development and go on only at the cost of enormous human suffering, increased poverty and oppression. Law functions as an instrument for defining public policy through the enactment and implementation of a set of consistent authoritative and general rules. Environmental law is an instrument to protect and improve the environment and to control and prevent any act or omission polluting the environment. But in actuality the rigidity of structure and lack of adequate qualified personnel are there to determine the public interest by administration responsible for ineffectiveness of such laws.

(15) The person who has influenced you most in your life

Ans. Mahatama Gandhi or Mohandas Karamchand Gandhi was born into the Hindu family in 1869. He was the person who influenced my life in a crucial way. After reading his autobiography, I was very much impressed by him. His ideas of speaking truth changed my life. I found more strength and feel free after following his path. Here are some of his principles and ideologies, that have helped me to become a better and peace loving person.

Gandhi dedicated his life to the wider purpose of discovering truth, or Satya. He tried to achieve this by learning from his own mistakes and conducting experiments on himself.

Non-cooperation and peaceful resistance were Gandhi's "weapons" in the fight against injustice. Gandhi expanded his non-violence platform to include the swadeshi policy – the boycott of foreign-made goods, especially British goods. However, Gandhi was aware that this level of non-violence required incredible faith and courage, which he realised not everyone possessed. He therefore advised that everyone need not keep to non-violence, especially if it was used as a cover for cowardice.

To Gandhi, a vegetarian diet would not only satisfy the requirements of the body, it would also serve an economic purpose as meat was, and still is, generally more expensive than grains, vegetables, and fruits.

This decision was deeply influenced by the philosophy of Brahmacharya—spiritual and practical purity—largely associated with celibacy and asceticism. Gandhi saw brahmacharya as a means of going close to God and as a primary foundation for self-realisation. For Gandhi, brahmacharya meant "control of the senses in thought, word, and deed".

Gandhi earnestly believed that a person involved in social service should lead a simple life which he thought could lead by a Brahmachari. His simplicity began by renouncing the western lifestyle he was leading in South Africa. Gandhi spent one day of each week in silence. He believed that abstaining from speaking brought him peace. Gandhi was born a Hindu and practiced Hinduism all his life, deriving most of his principles from Hinduism. As a common Hindu, he believed all religions to be equal, and rejected all efforts to convert him to a different faith. He was an avid theologian and read extensively about all major religions. Gandhi believed that at the core of every religion was truth and love. He also questioned hypocrisy, malpractices and dogma in all religions and was a tireless social reformer.

I can never forget Bapu and his principles. Whenever I get time, I go to visit the Gandhi Sangrahalaya.

(16) Cyber Threat

Ans. Cyber threat in India is still not considered as a serious offence as it is very clearly reflected in our cyber laws. Cyber attacks like hacking, Phishing, Spamming, etc. are very common in our daily life and hardly do we hear any strict actions taken against such crimes. Despite the fact, that such attacks not only cause economic losses but put the entire National Security of a country at risk.

The various IT laws that have been enacted like IT Act 2000 and then the amendments thereafter are more of guidelines rather than deterrents. The Sony Cyber Attack highlights the vulnerability of the nations against such cyber crimes. Today the world is interconnected. All public services are supplied via the internet. Banking, Stock Market Trading, E-governance, etc. are all internet related. A country's economy can be totally sacrificed through such attacks.

CDAC, DRDO and various other organisations are doing a great job in keeping India safe and its networks via Nic, gov, etc. untouched by cyber threats. The country needs stronger laws with stringent punishments so that any sort of cyber crime is duly punished. New Government's plan of digitising India cannot be fruitful without secure cyber infrastructure. India should lead the global voice in terms of Cyber security and the nations should come together to protect one another against cyber attacks in the future. Internet is the most useful invention of this generation and actions should be taken to prevent its misuse by anti social elements.

(17) Hard Work is the key of success

Ans. Hard work is the real wealth of a man. No one can achieve success without any hard work. Hard work is the key to success as it always pays off. Hard work can turn sludge into gold. It starts from where we stop looking for alternatives. Hard work is the secret of success. Laziness and sluggishness makes one's life a bane and only hard work can turn it into boon. We can take a very simple example that if we do not study hard, we cannot clear the exam we are going for. A person can achieve his goal only with the help of hard work. Flyovers, roads, buildings, malls, etc. all are made by the labourers by working hard. A painter, writer, poet, etc. everyone get his reward on the basis of their hard work. Some people give more importance to their luck rather than working hard. And later on, when they fail, they blame their luck only which is very absurd. Luck can do nothing if a person himself is not willing and ready to work hard. Nature also works hard. Sun rises every morning and sets on its time every evening. Birds and animals work hard for getting their food. Plants and trees make food with the help of chlorophyll by the process of photosynthesis. Human is the best creature in the world. But a lazy person is a problem for himself too. A poor can gain wealth and become rich by working hard. Hard work is also helpful in reducing the problems of unemployment, poverty and failures in life. We can take the examples of the great personalities of our country. If Mahatma Gandhi and the other great leaders of our country had not worked hard for getting freedom for the country, then we might still be a slave.

(18) The Celebration of festivals in India

Ans. Indian Festivals are celebrated by varied cultures and through their special rituals, add to the colours of the Indian Heritage. Some festivals welcome the seasons of the year, the harvest, the rains, or the full moon. Others celebrate religious occasions, the birthdays of divine beings, saints and gurus (revered teachers) or the advent of the New Year. A number of these festivals are common to most parts of India. However, they may be called by different names in various parts of the country or may be celebrated in a different fashion.

Many festivals celebrate the various harvests; commemorate great historical figures and events, while many express devotion to the deities of different religions. Every celebration is centered around the rituals of prayer, seeking blessings, exchanging goodwill, decorating houses, wearing new clothes, music, dance and feasting. In India, every region and every religion has something to celebrate. The festivals reflect the vigour and lifestyle of its people. Vibrant colours, music and festivity make the country come alive throughout the year.

The emphasis laid on the different festivals differs in different parts of the country. For instance, Navaratri is celebrated with maximum fervour in West Bengal as compared to that in other parts of the country. Holi is celebrated with gusto in the north, and although it is also observed in the western and eastern parts of India, in the south it is almost unknown. There are also a few regional festivals like Pongal in Tamil Nadu; Onam in Kerala and the various other temple festivals devoted to the specific patron Gods and Goddesses of the temples, which are celebrated exclusively in those areas, which may be limited to one or a few villages. This galaxy of festivals that exist do contribute in inter-spicing Indian life with gaiety and colour as also in giving the country the distinction of having the maximum number of holidays.

(19) The pleasures of reading

Ans. Some people get pleasure from picnics and tours. Others like to discuss various topics and find pleasure in chatting. But the reading of books provides us with such pleasure as we do not get from any other activity. Great is the blessing of books!

Books are written by learned people. They contain the best experiences and thoughts of their writers. Literature is said to mirror society. Writers put in their books not only their own ideas and feelings, but also what they observe and find in society. The books of the past reflect the condition of the times in which they were written. By reading books written by great thinkers, we come in contact with their minds. Books enable us to know the best of different countries. So, if we want to keep abreast of the great minds of all ages, we must read books.

When we are alone, books are our best friends. They entertain us in our spare moments. Good novels, books on poetry and short stories, give great enjoyment. At times we become so absorbed in our books that we forget even our important engagements. Loneliness is peace for a reader.

If we are in cheerful mood, our joy is increased by reading. When we are in a depressed and dejected mood, books console and soothe our troubled minds. They provide us with the best advice and guidance in our difficulties. Indeed, books are our best friends as they help us in our need.

Books contain grains of wisdom. They give us sound moral advice. That is why all great men of our country have liked to read the Gita and the Ramayana. The example of Rama and Sita is cited, whenever we want to emphasise noble deeds and their results. We call a bad man by the name of Ravana. It is through the reading of books that we learn to love virtue and hate sin. The reading of good books develops and elevates our character.

Nowadays the world is changing fast. A man cannot remain untouched by the changes in his own country or in the world. One who wants to be respected in cultured society must keep himself well-informed. Good magazines, newspapers and other books provide us latest information. We get great satisfaction when we feel ourselves to be well-informed and capable of moving in any educated society. Reading of good books is the key to the store-house of pleasure.

It was the English author Bacon who said that reading makes a full man. No one can question the truth of this saying. But we cannot derive full advantage from reading, if our choice is not good. Some books are such that instead of doing any good, they harm the readers. Such books must be avoided. Cheaps books, not in cost but in contents, should not be read, even if they provide some amusement and entertainment. It is the reading of good books alone which bestows upon us the maximum benefit.

(20) Say 'no' to plastics

Ans. Science and technology have made the life a lot easier and comfortable for human beings. Lifestyle has improved, new medicines for diseases have been made, new ways of solving problems have been discovered, etc. The invention of plastic is one such discovery, which has influenced the human life immensely. A lot of things are made by using plastic. Things made of plastic are easy to carry, keep and wash. Bottles, utensils, containers, bags and a lot other things are made of plastics. However, it has made life a lot easier, but plastic also poses a great danger to the environment and human health.

Plastics do not biodegrade; they photodegrade, breaking down into smaller particles and microscopic bits in the oceans. These plastic bits and their chemical compounds find their way into the food chain.

Degrading plastics leach toxic chemicals such as bisphenol A into the seas. Smaller fish and crustaceans mistake the plastic debris for food are then eaten by larger and larger species.

There is an urgent need to educate society on the ill effects of plastic so that progressively we can reduce its usage and learn to use alternative products, which are eco-friendly and inculcate good practices of plastic disposal.

Dialogue Writing

Dialogue is a conversation between two people. In this we can write what we think and improvise our own ideas on any given topic.

EXAMPLES OF DIALOGUES

(1) Match fixing in cricket

Myself: Hello, Pawan, how are you and where were you?

Pawan: Hello, I am fine and due to my illness, I was on leave and I have joined today only, how are you?

Myself: I am also fine. Do you know that cricket nowadays is at its highest level of popularity and is at the top of all games, not only in India but also in the world?

Pawan: Yes, it is the most popular game in the world.

Myself: Pawan, the recent happening of match fixing incidents have damaged its popularity and have brought it a bad name.

Pawan: I have heard about the match fixing scandals coming up in the news nowadays. It is really a matter of shame. I was just surprised to listen to this news.

Myself: You might be knowing that top most cricketers of the team are involved in this scandal and they have been found guilty.

Pawan: Now there is sufficient evidence available against them.

Myself: I do not know, inspite of getting more than enough money, not only from cricket, but from advertisements also, how can our cricketers do this?

Pawan: Nowadays, the cricketers want to generate more money, whether it is from advertisements, match or match-fixing. They have become greedy.

Myself: Some people are of the opinion that cricket should be banned.

Pawan: It should not be banned but the players found guilty of match fixing should be punished or debarred forever from playing cricket.

Myself: Your suggestion is good but I think it should be banned because it is a waste of time and money, people are mad about cricket. They do not do any work during the matches. A lot of money is wasted, after all what is the use of cricket.

Pawan: If you think so, then everything should be banned, which is not useful. Basically, it is a source of entertainment.

(2) American Presidential Election (Year 2005)

Myself: Hello, Pawan, how are you and what are you reading in the newspaper? Do you know anything about the recent presidential election going to be held in America?

Pawan: You have asked a number of questions at a time. Anyway, yes, I know about the presidential election going to be held in America. As Bill Clinton is going to be retired and also Bush is more popular in comparison to his opponent.

Myself: Yes, you are right, but I think Bush will become the President. Amongst Indians also his recent visit made him more popular.

Pawan: As you are aware, elections are conducted just to establish a healthy and social set up. Moreover, America is a democratic country and they believe in democracy which means for the public, of the public and by the public.

Myself: Yes, indeed Americans are very particular of their rights. Even the presidential candidates come from the public to show their stand. They believe that they are not different from the public.

Pawan: For the post of President, a lawful, honest, good, great diplomat, good politician can be a right candidate.

Myself: But, Mr. Bush's statement reveals that he would follow the same foreign policy as far as India is concerned.

Pawan: But why Indian Government has changed its policy regarding Americans?

Myself: I know, India has very good relations with Russia and it has helped India a lot against America in the past. So, India is still inclined towards Russia.

Pawan: But there was a time when Russia and America were equivalent and these were known as two super powers in the world. These two super powers headed two groups of nations. These power blocks were maintaining balance in the world, now the situation has changed. So, policies on foreign affairs should be changed.

Myself: It is right. Since Russia no longer has the same power as America; still it is quite powerful.

Pawan: Now the situation has changed. Americans are also trying to establish better relations with India. We have to think over it twice.

Myself: OK. I think Bush has got better support and I am of the opinion that Bush will come as new President of America.

Pawan: Let us wait and watch the situation.

(3) Religious tolerance

Myself: Hi, Pawan, do you know that religious tolerance means to extend religious freedom to people of all religions, even though you disagree with their beliefs and/or practices?

Pawan: Yes, I know. In addition, India is a secular country and there are old people who still blame something in the past for any mis-happening. They are following their religion, beliefs and faiths blindly.

Myself: But I do not understand these religious struggles, fighting, riots and enmity among the followers of different religions.

Pawan: This will continue as there is no peace among the nations without peace among the religions, no peace among religions without dialogue between the religions and finally no dialogue between the religions without investigation of the foundation of the religions.

Myself: I appreciate your suggestion but I am of the opinion that public in general is not concerned at all with such things. They should have that much religious tolerance that they do not come in the way of other religions. There are number of Hindu and Muslim saints who have written about Ram and Krishna. Also some Muslims have got honourable positions in the history of Hindi literature. There are number of Hindi pundits who have written in Urdu and Farsi.

Pawan: That is all about religious tolerance. The best way is that everybody should follow good things of all the religions and should have equal regard for every religion.

EXERCISE

(1) You want to go abroad but your wife is against it.

Ans.

Myself: Hi Rama! A good news for you, I have been transferred to Australia from India. Get ready and be prepared for it.

Wife: What? I am not ready for it because Australia is a very hot country and it is very difficult for me to settle there.

Myself: Why? I know you can easily manage and also it is a golden opportunity for me. My boss has specially recommended my name for this transfer.

Wife: You know I am also working and it is very difficult for me to leave my job immediately.

Myself: You can get more jobs in Australia with higher salary and perks. It is good time for you also to show your skills.

Wife: Sorry, I am already getting good salary and perks in India. Moreover, all our relatives and friends are here in India whereas in Australia everybody will be stranger for me. It is very difficult for me to adjust in such a western and modern culture.

Myself: If you are not ready to go, then I have no other alternative but to request my boss to forgive me and send somebody else.

Wife: Thank you, dear.

(2) A friend is trying to convince another friend to take part in a play.

Ans.

Ram: Hello, Shyam. Why did you come so late to the college? Do you want to participate in our Independence Day function?

Shyam: Hello, yes I do want to participate but I do not know the activity in which I should take part.

Ram: Why don't you take part in our play 'Heer Ranjha'?

Shyam: Oh, no I don't have good dialogue delivery.

Ram: Please come with me. I know that you have already taken part in various competitions of the school and have won prizes also.

Shyam: Yes, it is right. However, I never participated in dramas and I am afraid what will happen if I forget my dialogues.

Ram: It will not happen. Have confidence in me. I know that you can really perform well and we will also practise a lot, so that you will not forget any dialogue during drama.

Shyam: OK. If you insist, I will think of taking part in it.

(3) A daughter wants to take up a job of a police-woman but the father raises objections. Each person must have at least three turns of dialogue.

Ans.

Meena: Good morning Papa. Why don't you give me permission to join the job of a police-woman. Nowadays, women are treated equivalent to men and can drive trucks, provide petrol on petrol pumps and also go on a space mission.

Father: I know, but I want you to perform well in some sophisticated and feminine job. Nowadays in police service, you have to perform duties in the night also and have odd working hours which is not safe for woman.

Meena: Papa, you have said that woman is not safe and even then you stop me to be in police. If I am in police and if we have many girls in police, we can do a lot for the protection of women.

Father: You will not get a proper match if you work in police.

Meena: Now that is not correct. Some of my friends have their parents in police force and they all belong to decent families. Please do not have negative opinion about them.

Father: OK, I will think and then give you the final answer.

(4) A father/mother, whose son/daughter has been caught cheating in the exams and the school principal.

Ans.

Myself: If you are not ready to go, then I have no other alternative but to request my boss to forgive me and send somebody else.

Mr. Ram : (Father) Sir, may I come in?

Principal: Yes, please come in and be seated.

Mr. Ram: My name is Ram and I am Ravi's father.

Principal: Mr. Ram, I have something very urgent and serious to discuss with you.

Mr. Ram: I know sir. You had asked me to come and meet you as my son has been caught cheating in the examination.

Principal: Well, I know your son. He is a very sincere student and was selected to represent the school in a debate. He has also obtained excellent marks and was listed in the top 10 students. But I think there is some problem with him this year.

Mr. Ram: Sir, I agree with you. Ravi has always performed well and has been respectful also.

Principal: Keeping in view the above, I had asked you to come and meet me. I do not believe in punishing the students blindly. I am strict but I think twice before arriving at any decision.

Mr. Ram: Sir, I am very grateful to you.

Principal: Mr. Ram, I have observed your son wandering here and there with some boys who are not sincere in studies. I think he has fallen into bad company. You can still save him by talking to him frankly. A talented boy like Ravi copying in the examination does not hold good. Please be friendly with him and if any kind of help you need from me, I am always with you.

Mr. Ram: Thank you very much for your cooperation, Sir.

(5) A mother trying to convince her child to watch less TV and read more books.

Ans.

Mother: Seema, you are not in your room, where are you?

Seema: Mom, I am in the drawing room watching T.V.

Mother : I think you are not in your room since morning. Are you watching T.V. since morning?

Seema: Yes, mom. I am watching a very interesting programme.

Mother: Well, watching T.V. for a continuous period is not good for health. You should also involve yourself in other useful activities.

Seema: Mummy, what are those activities? Can you tell me please?

Mother: Well, you can go out with your friends, study your books for sometimes and help me in my work. I think you should also concentrate on reading good books. It will help you in enhancing your knowledge and vocabulary.

Seema: Oh, mamma! It is very boring to read all the books that we have in our house.

Mother: You can buy new books of your choice and I will give you money.

Seema: O.K., I will, but let me see this programme now. It is really interesting and entertaining.

Mother: O.K. I will not interrupt you, but try to consider my advice seriously and devote your most of the time in reading more books. This will not only enhance your knowledge but also help in your preparation of MBA examination in future.

Seema: You are right mother. After watching this programme, I will switch off the T.V. and devote my time to reading books.

(6) Two people discussing their hobbies

Ans.

Ram: Shyam, Can I ask you one question?

Shyam: Why not?

Ram: As we are going to start some curricular activities in our college, I want to know about your hobbies.

Shyam: My hobbies are singing, reading, dancing, reading newspaper and taking part in competitions.

Ram: Oh, great. I never knew anything about your hobbies. I think you can be very much helpful in our activities. Do you know how to play western music and dance to it?

Shyam: Oh yes. I can play and even dance very well on Western music. I have spent two years in learning the music as well as dance and also participated in various stage shows.

Ram: Oh, great! Which type of competition are you planning to take part in?

Shyam: I am very much interested in taking part in quiz related to general knowledge. My hobby of reading has helped me a lot in taking part in such competitions.

Ram: I am of the opinion that you can help me and my friends very well in getting prepared for the quiz.

Shyam: Ram, you have not told me anything about your hobbies.

Ram: Well, my friend, my hobbies are singing songs, listening to music and travelling.

Shyam: Good, which kind of music do you like?

Ram: I like western music and also classical music.

Shyam: Please come to my house, I have a good collection of songs related to western music. Please listen.

Ram: Sure, I will.

Shyam: OK, bye bye see you soon.

Ram: OK, bye.

(7) Somebody who owns a pet convincing his friend to have one.

Ans.

Bobby: (to her friend) Romi, yesterday I waited for more than two hours at my residence for you, but you did not come. What is the matter?

Romi: I will definitely tell you, but first of all you have to promise me that you will not get angry with me.

Bobby: Oh, not at all. Now tell me the reason of your not coming.

Romi: Well! Actually I do not like dogs. Whenever I plan to come to your house, your dog Roxy comes to me and starts licking here and there. He makes my shirt, hands and legs dirty.

Bobby: Oh, come on Romi. Roxy likes you and shows his love in his own way by licking. You see, the animals are more faithful, obedient and affectionate than human beings.

Romi: You may be right but I don't like even to sit near a dog. I just hate them.

Bobby: I suggest you to think over your ideas in this regard. I suggest you to have a dog as your pet animal and soon you will start loving the dogs.

Romi: Sorry, I cannot even think of it.

Bobby: Don't be so rigid. As you are aware that nowadays human beings are not trustworthy. The dogs can prove to be good friends and can also help you in case you have any problem.

Romi: I do not like to spend time in feeding and cleaning him.

Bobby: Once the dogs are trained, they do not bother you for such petty things. I suggest you to think about what I have said.

Romi: Alright I will think over it.

Bobby: Ok, bye bye, see you soon.

Romi: Ok, bye.

(8) A young man who enjoys drinking and a man who is against this habit.

Ans.

Mr. Ram: Sir, I agree with you. Ravi has always performed well and has been respectful also.

Ramu: Hi, Ram. Please come and join our party on the eve of India's win against Pakistan in cricket match.

Ram: Ramu, sorry. You are drinking alcohol and wine, which is injurious to health.

Ramu: Come on. I am just celebrating with my friends as India has got a record victory in cricket test against Pakistan.

Ram: Ramu, I know, you just need one or the other pretext for drinking. Why don't you give up your bad habit? It is really harmful and injurious to health.

Ramu: You do not know what kind of enjoyment I am feeling after drinking. You take one peg and see.

Ram: There are many other ways of enjoying the event but you are just killing yourself. This will harm your lungs, your nervous system and your health too.

Ramu: Oh come on friend! There are many other things equally harmful in life but still we are using them. I suggest you to have a one glass of drink. Here! Have it, my friend! And enjoy.

Ram: I think you will never improve in your life. It is of no use discussing with you because you never want to improve. It is a slow poison which can create a lot of problems in future.

Ramu: Please take a glass of drink and see how much enjoyment you feel.

Ram: I think I am wasting my time with you. Please carry on, I am going. Follow my advice to give up this bad habit of drinking. Bye.

Ramu: Bye.

(9) Two friends arguing over what they would rather be – a sick millionaire or a healthy beggar.

Ans.

Ram: Hello, good morning, today I had a discussion with my friends in college about a very different kind of topic – What would I like to be – a sick millionaire or a healthy beggar.

Shyam: Good morning and what was your reply?

Ram: I told that I would prefer to be a sick millionaire rather than being a healthy beggar. At least I will have enough money to cure my disease.

Shyam: If I were in your place, I would prefer to be healthy beggar. I think health is the most important thing in life. We can buy almost everything except good health. Do you know that people spend a lot of money in order to have good health?

Ram: Yes, I know. However, I also know that without money, a person is considered worthless and he is cut off from the society, friends and even the pleasures of life.

Shyam: But what kind of pleasures you expect from a sick person?

Ram: A millionaire can afford to have the best treatment.

Shyam: Yes, he can afford to have the best treatment but can he buy long life and healthy body?

Ram: No, he cannot, but what will a healthy beggar do with good health and no money.

Shyam: Healthy beggar can enjoy a lot with his good health.

Ram: OK, I think you are right. Let us stop discussing further. I have to go because I remembered some work to be done by me. Bye Bye.

(10) Convince your father/mother that you should be allowed to go to play during your Board examinations.

Ans.

Rakesh: Good evening, mother I am going.

Mother: Rakesh, where are you going? Do you know that you have to take your Sr. Secondary School examination next week? Go inside and start preparing for that.

Rakesh: Mummy I am going out to play with my friends, which will refresh my mind.

Mother: If you are bored, you can sit with me and have a talk for a while. Your going out will waste a considerable time.

Rakesh: Oh, mom! I have already completed the revision of each subject and I am very much confident that I will secure good marks in my examinations. Kindly allow me to go out, I will come back within an hour or so.

Mother: Your father will also get angry with you and me also. What will I tell him when he will come back from office?

Rakesh: Please let me go, Mom. I cannot study the whole day. I need a break. It will help me further to study in a more better way. Please try to understand.

Mother: O.K. You can go out to play but remember not more than one hours and promise me that you will study seriously for getting good marks.

Rakesh: O.K. mother I will. Thanks.

(11) Two students talk to each other about the merits and demerits of distance education.

Ans.

Ram: Hello, where are you? I have seen you after a very long time and what are you doing nowadays?

Shyam: Hi, where are you too? I am studying in a regular college and doing B.Com(Hons.). What about you? I have heard that you have taken up a job in a public sector undertaking. Have you left your studies?

Ram: Not at all. I am working and doing MBA from IGNOU. The university provides me with an option to work along with my studies.

Shyam: I have heard that the open university degrees do not have any value and proper care is not taken to teach the students.

Ram: Your information is not correct. The degree from distance learning university stands equivalent to degree taken from the regular university and you can get a better job. There are some students who do not study well and they often spread such remarks that proper care is not being taken.

Shyam: What about the fee structure and arrangement of lecturers?

Ram: The fees is reasonable and you can make the payments in installments also. The lectures are generally arranged during the week and holidays to meet the requirement of working students.

Shyam: I think you have made a right choice.

Ram: OK bye, see you soon!

Shyam: OK bye.

(12) A father tries to convince his 10-year-old son that there is no such thing as ghosts.

Ans.

Son: Father good evening, I want to take my books from my study room for reading. Please accompany me.

Father: Why did you want me to accompany you? Is there any problem with you? You should go alone.

Son: Father, I am afraid of ghosts. One of my friends Ram says that ghosts are hidden in your house. They will harm us. Father, it is very dark in the room, please accompany me.

Father: Listen to me. Certainly, I can accompany you but then you will never come out of your fear and you will loose your confidence too. I will accompany you up to the corridor leading to the room and you go inside to take your books.

Son: OK father. (Both of them together go to the room. The father stands in the corridor and son goes inside the room and gets his books and rushes outside).

Father: Now, tell me. Did you find any ghost in the room?

Son: No, not this time. But may be when I go alone, next time.

Father: Look at me. Do you have faith in me?

Son: Yes, father.

Father: Then, keep on trying. Go alone even when you feel scared. You will never see any ghost. I promise.

Son: OK, father. I will definitely try.

(13) A doctor tries to persuade a patient that s/he needs a major operation to get cured.

Ans.

Doctor: Please take your seat and listen to what I say.

Patient: Yes, please. Is there anything serious with my health?

Doctor: Not now! But if you are not ready for operation then I cannot promise you that your health will be alright.

Patient: Advise me what should I do?

Doctor: I will explain it to you in detail. You see that there are many stones in your body. If they will not be removed, you will have problems of swelling in your body and pain in stomach about which you always complain to me. Generally, it is a minor operation but in your case it should be considered a major one since you have the problem since last 15 years.

Patient: I am scared when I think of operation.

Doctor: Have faith in me. It is really very essential to have an operation.

Patient: When do you suggest to operate on me?

Doctor: As early as possible. Rest depends on you.

Patient: Can it be performed next week.

Doctor: OK. I am ready to operate next week.

Patient: OK. I am ready for the operation.

(14) A daughter tries to persuade her mother that she should be allowed to study further and make a career for herself, rather than getting married without completing her education.

Ans.

Mother: Radha, do not go anywhere today because your father has invited some people to see you.

Radha: Mummy! I hope it is not for my marriage?

Mother: Of course, Radha, it is for your marriage only. Now you are in college we should think seriously about fixing your marriage. Try to understand.

Radha: Oh, please mummy! I want to complete my studies and make my career.

Mother: Radha, this is the right time otherwise good boys of decent families will be out of our reach. After all, a girl studies only till she gets married.

Radha: No, mummy! Now, time has changed. Now girls work even after marriage. They also get the best education.

Mother: My dear daughter, we have selected very mature family. You do not need to worry about education.

Radha: Oh mummy! It is not only for money that a girl prepares herself in life with the best education. Please let me complete my studies. You know, it is my dream to be highly educated.

Mother: OK I will try to have a talk with your father on the issue.

Radha: Thanks for giving consideration to my feelings.

(15) Two classmates discussing a Hindi film they have watched recently. Where one of them has liked it and the other one has not.

Ans.

Sunny: Have you seen the new film, 'Three Idiots'?

Shefali: Yes, I have seen last week.

Sunny: Did you like the film?

Shefali: Not at all. I did not enjoy the story. It was really a boring film and waste of money.

Sunny: Why did you dislike such a good film? It was highly entertaining film with melodious songs, which are very popular these days.

Shefali: Anyway songs were good but some of the incidents were loosely placed in the story without any sequence/ connection with the main story.

Sunny: My many other friends have seen the movie repeatedly and you are the only person who did not like it. A large number of people have also already appreciated the film.

Shefali: Well, my friend many a times, some films are appreciated due to presence of good actors, sometimes due to hit songs and sometimes due to good music, but the effect of such films cannot be long lasting. As there is nothing worth appreciating, it will be forgotten soon.

Sunny: I am not able to understand your logic behind it. OK. I am going now.

Note-Making

Note-making is a useful skill for the students. We can develop the skill with regular practice. It is an essential part of academic like.

Five Important Reasons to Make Notes

- Notes trigger memories of lecture/reading.
- Your notes are often a source of valuable clues for what information the instructor thinks most important (i.e. what will show up on the next test).
- Notes inscribe information kinesthetically.
- Taking notes helps you to concentrate in class.
- Notes create a resource for test preparation.
- Your notes often contain information that cannot be found elsewhere (i.e. in your textbook).

Guidelines for Note-Making

- Concentrate on the lecture or on the reading material.
- Make notes consistently.
- Make notes selectively. Do not try to write down every word. Remember that the average lecturer speaks approximately 125-140 words per minute, and the average note maker writes at a rate of about 25 words per minute.
- Use the Abbreviation and symbols.
- Translate ideas into your own words.
- Organise notes into some sort of logical form.
- Be brief. Write down only the major points and important information.
- Write legibly. Notes are useless if one cannot read them later!

Use of Abbreviations and Short Forms in Notes

It is often noticed that students try to make down every word the lecturers speak, they miss out important points while jotting down a lot of unimportant or irrelevant points. Therefore, use of abbreviations and short forms are very important in note-making, to save time and to avoid repetition. Commonly used standard abbreviations are listed below:

and so on	:	etc.
that is	:	*i.e.*
therefore	:	∴
because	:	∵
for example	:	*e.g.*
compare	:	*of.*
less than	:	<
more than or greater than	:	>
same as	:	=
not same as	:	≠
approximately or about	:	Ca @
increase or higher	:	↑
decrease or lower	:	↓

Apart from the above listed abbreviations, arrows are used to indicate cause, effect, changes into or can show relation of one point to another.

e.g. Smoking causes cancer can be written in notes as

Smoking → cancer.

A reverse arrow indicates 'caused by'.

e.g. cancer is caused by smoking can be written in notes as:

Cancer smoking.

Other words can be shortened by using a few letters instead of the whole word or with very long words one can write in the shortened form of the word with its ending indicated at top.

For example: Examination – examina", abbreviations – abbrev", developing – develop", important – imp"

Kilometre	:	km
Metre	:	m
Kilogram	:	kg
Year	:	yr
Second	:	sec
Hour	:	hr
Month	:	mth

Note: When you shorten a word, sometimes it is necessary to put a full-stop after the word.

Words can be shortened using only one or two letters or using your own short forms, *e.g.*

Blood pressure	:	B.P.
Continue	:	Cont.
Tri Nagar	:	T.N.
Advantage	:	advant.
Principal	:	Princi.

If you are using your own short forms then it is better to include the original word at the beginning with the short form you intend to use, in the brackets. Subsequently, you can use only the short form.

e.g. Shakespeare (Shk)

But only sensible abbreviations should be used, otherwise it can be misinterpreted.

EXERCISE

Q1. Read the following passage and make notes using the format of points.

Influence of Faiths and Languages on Education

There are two problems that cause great worry to our educationists – The problem of religious and moral destruction in the land of many faiths and the problems arising out of the large variety of languages.

Taking up the education of the children we see that they should be trained to live one another, to be kind and helpful to all, to be tender to the lower animals and to observe and think right. The task of teaching them how to read and write and to count and to calculate is important but it should not make us lose sight of the primary aim of moulding personality in the right way.

For this, it is necessary to call into aid culture, tradition and religion. But in our country we have, in the same school, to look after boys and girls born in different faiths and belonging to families that live diverse ways of life, easy path of evading the difficulty by attending solely to physical culture and intellectual education. We have to evolve a suitable technique and method for serving the spiritual needs of school children professing different faiths. We should thereby promote an atmosphere of mutual respect, a fuller understanding and helpful co-operation among the different communities in our society. Again we must remain one people and we have, therefore, to give basic training to our schools to speak and understand more languages than one and to appreciate and respect the different religions prevailing in India. It is not right for us in India to be overtaking the young mind. What is necessary must be done. And it is not in fact the great a burden.

Ans. Notes: Influence of Faiths and Languages on Education

(1) Worry of our educationists

(i) prob. of relig. And moral edn.

(ii) innum. faiths & variety of langs.

(2) Task of teaching

(i) moulding right personality

(ii) oving one another

(iii) being kind & helpful to all

(iv) tender to lower animals
(v) observing & thinking right

(3) Spiritual needs of school children
(i) teaching mutual respect
(ii) co-operation among diff. communities
(iii) speaking & understanding more langs. than one

Abbreviations used:

1. Religious	relig.
2. Problem	prob.
3. Education	edn.
4. Innumerable	innum.
5. And	&
6. Languages	langs
7. Different	diff.

Q2. Read the passage given below and make notes keeping in view the main ideas.

Corruption

Corruption makes government control ineffective and undermines the ability to govern. It serves as a constraint on all decision-makers, causes delays, affects efficiency and ultimately leads to crisis in public administration.

Bribes are so powerful as incentives that they determine the results of soccer games, cricket matches and the like. Corruption undercuts the rules of law and devastates economic and political development. It allows "polluters" to foul rivers, hospitals to extort patients. It can be environmentally and socially corrosive.

Corruption springs from the selfishness and desire for material gains which are a part of human nature. Greed and egoism replace the legitimate guest for betterment of one's condition. Wherever there is gold, there is greed. Corruption is endemic to human nature. A conscientious man has to rise above all this.

Bribes enable criminals to escape convention, who will haunt the society, breaking its moral fibre. It would thus allow subversion by one group to destroy the freedom of others.

Klitgaard claims that corruption is a political issue. There are cultural differences over what constitutes corruption. But there is unanimity that corruption is socially harmful.

African gift-giving is a bribe according to Western point of view. But it has been challenged by the Africans.

Corruption is said to be dangerous because it is infectious. One infected person will infect another. If a member in a family is corrupt, the fault lies with the family. If the system fails to proceed against this person, the fault lies with the system. Corruption has the tendency of corrupting the system. If people take of pay bribes and the system tolerates them, then more and more people will turn corrupt.

Ans.Notes: Corrptn.

(1) Corrptn. looses ability to govern by govt.
(2) It constraints all decisions get delayed or affected; their efficiency causes public admin. crisis.
(3) Bribes are one powerful tool of corrptn. which also influences result of our sports.
(4) Corrptn. not only felt in political arena but also feels in field of law. It leads all social, environmental probs.
(5) It generates from selfishness and desire of personal gain, greed and egoism which are part of human nature. Corrptn. helps the convicts, which allow the society to destroy the freedom of others.
(6) Klitgaard claims that corrptn. generates via politics, though different in diff. cultures but unanimity socially harmful.
(7) Corrptn. is like an infection which spreads from person to person and diseases the whole family.
(8) If system fails against corrptn., it is the fault of the system. If people bear the corrptn. then more people turn corrupt.

Abbreviations used:

1. Corruption	Corrptn.
2. Government	govt.
3. Administration	admin.
4. Problems	probs.
5. Different	diff.

Q3. Read the following passage and make notes using the format of points.

History

Western Australia was first settled in the 1820s by the British, chiefly to prevent the French from doing so. A temporary military outpost was set up on King George Sound, where the town of Albany now stands, in 1826. The first permanent settlement came with the founding of the Swan River Colony in 1829. The settlers were led by Captain (later Admiral) Sir James Stirling, the colony's first Lieutenant Governor, and among the settlers was Thomas Peel (c. 1795-1864), a cousin of the British statesman, Sir Robert Peel, Later, the settlement schemes of Edward Gibbon Wakefield were tried.

In many places, the soil was poor and the aboriginals fought against the settlers. From 1850 to 1868, British convicts were sent to the colony which was ruled from London through a local governor until 1891. By then, however, gold had been discovered, and more small farmers settled in the south. The population grew to about 50,000. Then in 1892-93 came the discoveries of the eastern goldfields of Coolgardie and Kalgoorlie. These attracted a great rush of prospectors chiefly from the eastern Australian colonies.

The miners, who wanted postal, railway and water services to be provided quickly, often criticised the government. Unlike most of the earlier settlers, they supported the federation (union) of the Australian colonies, and their influence helped to unite Western Australia with the other states to form the Commonwealth of Australia on 1 January 1901. Gradually farms spread and the sheep and cattle industries increased. The Trans-Australian railway linking Kalgoorlie with the eastern states was completed in 1917. The line has since been extended to Perth and expresses run daily from coast to coast.

The great worldwide depression of trade and business that began in 1929 brought much unemployment and poverty to Western Australia, as world prices of wool and wheat fell sharply. Some Western Australians felt that some of their troubles were the fault of the federal government, and for a while there was a move to separate from the Commonwealth of Australia. This movement died out as things improved.

The most famous Western Australian was John Forrest (1847 – 1918), who as 1st Baron Forrest of Bunbury was the first native-born Australian to be created a peer. He was premier (prime minister) of the state during the exciting 1890s and later an important member of the federal parliament. John Joseph Curtin (1885-1945), who was the Prime Minister of Australia during World War II, spent much of his life in Western Australia.

Ans.Notes: Hist.

(1) Brt. first settled in Wstn. Australia to avoid presence of French.
(2) First military set up outpost at King George Sound (now Albany).
(3) First permanent settlement at Swan River Colony led by Cap. (later Admiral) Sir James Stirling, Thomas Peel a cousin of British Statesman, Sir Robert Peel.
(4) Sent British convict, ruled under London by a local Governor.
(5) Gold were discd., population increased upto 50,000.
(6) Coolgardie and Kalgoorlie goldmines discovered & attract many colonies, civil govt. provided many basic postal, railways, water services.
(7) CW of Australia formed with help of such WA colonies, farm, industries spread.
(8) Railways link with eastn. states formed, extended to Perth, Express run coast to coast.
(9) Worldwide depression brought feeling of separation from CW of Australia but thing improved.

(10) John Forest, the most famous WA, 1st person for Bunbury, 1st native born as peer, premier of the state during 1890's, an important member of federal parliament.

(11) John Joseph Curtin, PM of Australia during WWII, spent much time at Wstn. Australia.

Abbreviations used:

1. History	Hist.
2. British	Brt.
3. Western	Wstn.
4. Captain	Cap.
5. Discovered	discd.
6. And	&
7. Government	govt.
8. Commonwealth	CW
9. Eastern	eastn.
10. Western Australian	WA
11. Prime Minister	PM
12. World War II	WWII

Q4. Read the passage given below and make notes keeping in view the main ideas:

The Source of All Foods

Without plants, animals (including human beings) would not be able to exist. This is because green plants have one special quality; they are able to live on inorganic substances (water, salts dissolve in water and air) and build them up into their bodies – whereas animals can only absorb food already manufactured by plants. This important process of making food is called photosynthesis (photo means "light" and synthesis means "building up"). During photosynthesis, carbon dioxide from the air and water from the soil in a more disordered state are combined to form the more ordered sugar molecules. This can only take place in living plant cells containing the green colouring matter called chlorophyll. The energy necessary for this process comes from sunlight.

The sugars made by the plant can be used in several ways. They can be built up into new living matter, with the result that the plant grows. They can be stored as starch for future use, as in seeds or potatoes. They can be broken down again into carbon, hydrogen and oxygen to set free energy for the plant. These sugars and starch made by plants are, in fact, the source of food for all animals as well as for the plants themselves. To take an example: bread is made from flour which is the ground-up seed of wheat; it contains starch and this is food to us, for it is digested and taken into the blood. Animals which live on other animals are another example: for instance, a cat eats mice and the mice live on parts of plants such as seed, sand, fruits. In every case, it is possible to trace such "food webs" back to plants. They are the original source of food.

Ans.Notes: The Source of All Foods

(1) Phtosys. – process of making food by plants with help of inorganic subst., animals does not.
(2) Phtosys. – H_2O+ CO_2 + sunlight + help of chlro. = sugar.
(3) Uses of sugar made by plants:
- building work for plant's body;
- store for future use, providing energy to plants and animals;
- food web: sugar-starch-seed-flour-bread; and
- food web: plant-fruit (seed)-mice-cat.

Abbreviations used:

1. Photosynthesis	Phtosys.
2. Substances	subst.
3. Combined	+
4. Water	H_2O
5. Carbon-di-oxide	CO_2
6. Chlorophyll	chlro.
7. To form	=

Q5. Read the passage given below and make notes keeping in view the main points:

India was partitioned along communal lines at the time of its Independence. Even today communalism continues to be a major problem. Progress is possible only when nation can unitedly march onwards. Divisive forces are only an obstacle. These, unfortunately are on the increase. Not enough has been done to check the menace of communalism. Most political parties are responsible for the sad state of affairs. Even the police and the administration are not fully faultless.

Greater spread of education can help us to fight communalism. People need to become more alert and less responsive to irresponsible politicians. The government also needs to be very strict with troublesome elements.

Ans.Notes:

(1) India partitioned along communal lines.
(2) Comm.: A major problem.
(3) Progress only possible when nation united.
(4) Diverse forces obstacles, on the increase.
(5) Need to check the comm.
(6) Pol. parties and adm. are responsible for the comm.
(7) Spread of edu. Is needed in this regard.
(8) People need to be alert and responsive against such oliticians.
(9) Strict govt. action needed in this regard.

Abbreviations used:

1. Problem	prob.
2. Communalism	comm.
3. Political	pol.
4. Administration	adm.
5. Education	edu.
6. Governmental	govt.

Q6. Read the passage given below and make notes keeping in view the main points:

The way our society is structured affects all human relationships. Outside the home, we have a system of power relationships: worker/employer, individual/state, etc. and most people feel powerless outside the home to a greater or lesser extent. People can feel particularly powerless if their specific situation is beyond their control: for example, if they are unemployed, scraping a living, working at unpleasant jobs at unpleasant hours or if they have to 'be' people they don't want to be (such as a man 'having' to be a breadwinner or a woman 'having' to be a housewife). The resultant stresses and strains need outlets.

There are many different kinds of outlets. We can use our anger or frustration by directing it constructively – into charging society. But many people drown their feelings in drink, for example, or go into a depression or perhaps lash out. Many of us are inclined, at least sometimes, to take out our frustration on people nearest us. The limitations of private family life can act like a hot-house, increasing frustration so that we lash out in our various ways.

The kind of destructive outlet that a woman uses may be physical – either against her husband or children – but often it is psychological (against her family or herself). If the violence is against the man, he still has the ultimate sanction: he can walk out. The kind of oppressive violence a woman can persistently use is more often directed towards her children – because they cannot walk out. It is interesting that while the law has protected children for some years, it is still equivocal in the protection it gives to battered women. Commonly, women turn violent feelings inwards: twice as many woman as men suffer from depression. Women who live in deprived areas, who don't go to work, are not surprisingly, the most vulnerable to depression.

As far as men are concerned, they have been brought up to use their firsts – and even encouraged to do so. It is not surprising, therefore, that a man's outlet can, in its extreme form, involve physical violence against his wife and family. Many women do not have the ultimate sanction: we cannot easily leave home. Men – even the most oppressed men – have a semblance of legal and economic power in areas such as housing, employment, education, child care, fertility control. Women are, in comparison, relatively powerless.

Ans. Notes:

(1) Society structure affects the human reltnshp.
(2) Powerful reltnshp. – outside the home, e.g. worker employer, etc.
(3) Some people feel powerless outside the home as situation outside their control, e.g. unemployed, etc. which results in stress and strain.
(4) Outlet of anger or frustration into const. form though people choose destctv. way, let down themselves.
(5) Many of us ousted the frustration on our beloved that increases tension in family.
(6) The female destruction outlet in phys. or psycho. against her family. Husband simply walks out but children do not.
(7) Woman suffered depsn. twice as man with so many reasons.
(8) Men took the depsn. for encrgnt.
(9) Men have more legal and ecol. power to control than the female.

Abbreviations used:

1. Relationship	reltnshp.
2. Example	e.g.
3. Etcetera	etc.
4. Constructive	const.
5. Destructive	destctv.
6. Physical	phys.
7. Psychological	psycho.
8. Depression	depsn.
9. Encouragement	encrgnt.
10. Economical	ecol.

Q7. Read the passage given below and make notes keeping in view the main ideas:

Evolution

As countries developed their industries, mines were sunk for coal, and cuttings and tunnels were made for the railways. Fossil animals and plants were dug up, which included plants and animals that were no longer to be found. These discoveries led to the conclusion that living things must have existed and must also have been changing from one form to another for millions of years. This theory is called evolution because one form evolves, or develops, out of another. The idea was very fiercely opposed at first, especially by people who took the biblical story of Adam and Eve to be true in every detail, and who did not like the idea of people having evolved from animals.

The first theory, put forward by a Frenchman, Jean Lamarck, in 1809, was that the changes in any animal or plant which led to its becoming another kind of animal or plant were brought about by alterations in its surroundings; in other words, that acquire characteristics could be transmitted from parents to offspring.

However, in 1859, Charles Darwin published his book "The Origin of Species". He and Alfred Russel Wallace, both English naturalists, had separately come to the conclusion that evolution occurred by a process of selection. Darwin's ideas were supported by the biologist Thomas Henry Huxley.

Heredity

In every generation of an organism or living thing, there is a range of variation in all possible characteristics. This is because of the random assortment of chromosomes in the formation of sex cells. Those individuals which are best equipped to survive in a particular environment, survive and breed. More of their particular characteristics are then passed on to the next generation.

The work of Lamarck and Darwin led scientists to study both heredity, the passing on of characteristics from one generation to another and environment, the surroundings in which they live. In 1865, an Austrian monk named Johann Gregor Mendel showed how the height and other characteristics of different varieties of peas were passed on to their seedlings. Mendel published his findings in 1866 but little notice was taken of them at the time. When microscopes had been improved enough to study living cells, it was noticed that inside the nucleus there were thread-like bodies. These are called chromosomes. When the cell divided, the chromosomes behaved in a way which agreed with Mendel's laws and suggested that these were the carriers of hereditary characteristics. Viewed closely through a microscope, the chromosomes look like strings of beads. It is the beads, or genes, which hold the hereditary factors.

The 20th century has been the development of biochemistry. Biochemists have discovered the stages in which the body acts on the complex chemicals it contains, in order to renew itself. The agents needed for each state in this reaction are called enzymes and if an enzyme is missing, that particular link in the chain reaction cannot take place. The controlling factor which produces the right enzyme for a cell is the DNA (deoxyribonucleic acid) present in the nucleus. Scientists have discovered both the structure of DNA and the way in which it controls the build-up of enzymes.

Biological studies today include microbiology, the study of microscopic organisms, molecular biology, the study of molecules in biology and marine biology, the study of life in the oceans. In many of these fields, biologists are interested in the relation between living things and their surroundings – the economy of an area – and especially the effects of man on his environment. The threat of man's activities to the existence of other living things is now understood more clearly.

Ans.Notes: Evol.

(1) Dev. of countries and industries.
(2) Mines were sunk for coal.
(3) Tunnels were made for railways.
(4) Fossils of animals and plants were dug up.
(5) Conclude existence of HB.
(6) Th. of evol.
(7) Oppose idea of theory of Adam and Eve.
(8) Oppose idea of not like evol. of man from animals.
(9) Lamarck (1809), Frenchman.
(10) Theory of acq. character in offsp. through their parents.
(11) Darwin (1859) with Alfred Russel, Englishman,
(12) Th. of natural selection – only best survived.

Heredity

(1) Th. of change of character in gen. due to presence of chromosomes.
(2) Pea exp. by Mendal proved the character acq. due to presence of chromosome later proved by microscope.
(3) Bioch. Dis. chain link process conducted with help of enzymes.
(4) DNA produces right enzymes for cell.
(5) Discovery of DNA helps to meet threat on man's act. more clearly.

Abbreviations used:

1. Development	dev.
2. Human Beings	HB
3. Theory	th.
4. Evolution	evol.
5. Acquired	acq.
6. Offspring	offsp.
7. Generation	gen.
8. Experiment	exp.
9. Biochemist	bioch.
10. Activities	act.

Report Writing

A report is a form of communication in which some information is conveyed, usually in writing to someone. The report should be easy to understand for the receiver. The report can be of many kinds, e.g.

Reporting news, scientific articles, business, sports, interviews, experience, etc.

The Report can be divided in three main parts

- **The introduction:** The introduction states the main purpose and topic of the report.
- **The Main body:** The main body contains the actual detail and organised account of the topic.
- **Conclusion:** And the conclusion is usually a summary of the report.

Points to Remember

- Language should be simple and easy to understand instead of ambiguous language.
- The words should not convey different meaning.
- Avoid writing long sentences, and repetition of words. You may give a head line or a title as it is done in the newspaper.

TYPES OF REPORTS

(1) Accidental Reports/Event Reports

Many events happen everyday. Accidents, natural disasters or sports events like cricket matches or football matches or riots, etc. are all incidents which you may experience or know in your daily life. You may have to write the report of an accident to determine the causes and to suggest measures for prevention.

Accidental Reports:

- state the nature of and exact time date and place of accident.
- indicate the cause of accident. If there are different opinions on the cause you may cite one or two, which you feel are feasible.
- give details of the persons dead or injured and damage to property.
- next list the relief measures – whether they were effective or not.
- suggest remedies or solution to prevent such accidents.

Note: Usually in major railway or other transport accidents or fires, you may introduce a quote by the minister or authority concerned regarding the cause and the action taken.

The above points will be clear to you from the report on a major fire accident given in the model reports at the end of this chapter.

Apart from accident reports, you may be asked to report on events such as strikes or riots in your town. Such reports will also follow the same pattern as the accident report in giving the time, place and date, cause and subsequently the actions taken by authorities. Your report should list casualties if any. Given below is an example of a report on a riot.

You may give a headline or a title as is done in newspaper reports.

Example:

Riot in the city

Six Killed in Firing – Army Called Out

South Delhi experienced one of the worst cases or communal rioting on 15 June 1990, necessitating the employment of armed forces.

Trouble started when, miscreants threw stones and tried to disrupt a religious procession near Malviya Nagar Market at around eleven in the morning. There was much confusion and stampeding as people in the procession started retaliating. Many unruly scenes of violence were reported by dazed shopkeepers and residents of the area.

As news of the violence spread, DTC buses were forced off the roads in many areas of South Delhi and shops downed their shutters in protest. Standard passengers looking frantically for means of conveyance, added to the general confusion.

The police and army were called out at once. In many areas in Chiragh Delhi and Kalkaji, police and the protesting mobs clashed.

Police are armed forces used tear gas to disperse the unruly mobs and the procession. Six persons are believed to have been killed in the police shoot-outs at Malviya Nagar and Chiragh Delhi, thought the actual number is put at much higher by eye-witness. Scores of minor casualties have also been reported.

Most schools immediately made arrangements to inform parents that their children were held up at the school. Later arrangements were made by police to escort school buses with children, safely to their homes. Taxis and rickshaws had a field day as buses were off the road.

The President, the Prime Minister and all the leading Cabinet Ministers have condemned the unruly violence. The Prime Minister has ordered a committee to be set up immediately to inquire into the incident. Announcing an *ex-gratia* payment of fifty thousand rupee to the next of kin of the deceased, the Prime Minister has warned anti-social elements, who would like to disrupt the unity and communal harmony of the country of stern action. He also assured the people, that no effort would be spared to bring the criminals. Meanwhile police has declared an indefinite curfew in parts of South Delhi.

Note: The student will notice from the above report that the introductory paragraph mentions the date and place, while the second paragraph immediately states how the rioting started and pinpoints the exact place and time. The report includes the effect the riot had on people and how the police tackled it. Lastly, the action taken by the Government stated.

(2) Reports on Meetings and Speeches

In the course of your life, you may be required to attend many meetings. As a student, you may attend the meeting of the University Student's

Association or later in life, you may attend important board meetings. Every organisation or association holds meetings to discuss important issues concerning it. It may be your job to prepare a report of the meeting you have attended. In the course of the meeting, speeches may be made by important officials. In this section, we will first deal with writing reports on meetings and then discuss reporting speeches.

Reports of Meetings: The essential points to remember are:

- State the name of the organisation at the beginning (The report should tell who is holding the meeting).
- The venue (place) and time of the meeting are important points which have to be mentioned, just as you did while reporting events.
- State the agenda – *i.e.* the purpose and the programme or the items listed for discussion in the day's meeting. (*e.g.* the agenda of a meeting of the University Student's Association may list items such as exams postponement, reduction of college fees, action being taken by the association to redress injustice to some students and the campaign for university elections.)
- You may then give a brief history of the organisation.
- Coming to the points on the agenda, in your report you need not follow the order of the items taken up in the meeting. Rather you should discuss the important issue first. You can quote exact words in case some important resolution is passed.
- You can include arguments provided for and against a certain resolution.
- While names of participants are to be given, you need not report all the speeches made during the meeting. Pick out only the important speeches or rather portions of speech, which are interesting and of particular relevance.
- Meeting reports of business houses often include statistics, which can be represented through tables or charts.

Example:

Traffic Problems and Solutions

The state centre and the Gujarat Institute of Civil Engineers and Architects organised a meeting to discuss 'Growth of Vehicles, Traffic Problems, and Engineering Solutions' at Ahmedabad on 27 April 1989. Presided over by the outgoing chairman of the GICE, the meeting was well attended by eminent civil engineers, consultants, senior municipal corporation and traffic managers from state transport undertakings.

The meeting discussed major problems relating to planning of parking places, enforcement of traffic rules, encroachment on parking places, mass transport through railways, creating public awareness, industries, sponsoring traffic projects, traffic patrolling and public discipline and education.

The chairman Mr. G. Shah, in his inaugural address emphasised the need for civil engineers to take up the challenge of constructing new suspension bridges over the Sabarmati, in place of the old, derelict and traffic hazard bridges. Appealing to private industries, he said that leading business houses could contribute much in terms of funds for creating traffic island and parking lots.

Mr. M.K. Desai, the President of the Union of Traffic Policemen felt that the major thrust was to be aimed at educating people on traffic rules and inculcating discipline among them. He felt stiffer penalties and threat of imprisonment would go a long way in checking traffic offences. Mr. Kulkarni, the Director of State Transport Undertaking, made a spirited defence and highlighted the difficulties under which the undertaking operated, in reply to charges leveled by Mr. M.K. Desai that state transport buses with their shoddy maintenance upkeep were a major traffic hazard.

Finally, it was proposed to consolidate the report already made in this direction as far back as 1960 by various seminars, conferences and study papers. The meeting decided to form study groups for:

- Mass Transportation to be headed by Shri Brahmabhatt, Senior Town Planner, Government of Gujarat;
- Planning the parking place to be headed by Mr. Kulkarni and Public Awareness and Education to be headed by Shri H. Patel, who represented the institution.

Shri Brahmabhatt made the closing address and thanked all participants for interesting discussions presented and hoped that the study groups formed would successfully fulfil their tasks before the next meeting to be held six months later.

Reporting a Speech: This is set of rules which will help you in writing good speech reports:

- Introductory passage must identify speaker, venue, time and occasion of the speech.
- Write the title, if the speech has any.
- Do not write down the entire speech.
- Intersperse direct quotations with paragraph which paraphrase the main points of the speech.
- It may be helpful to take down notes or use a tape recorder, while listening to the speech.
- Organise the points and identify the main point of the speech.
- Begin your report of the speech around the main point you have identified.

- Arrange your points in the order of importance.
- It need not necessary to be in the same order which the speaker had used.

In case there is more than one speech in your report, the most important speech, usually by the most important speaker should be given first. You can then mention opinions expressed by others.

Example:

Need for value-based Education

Speaking on the occasion of the 50th convocation of A.B. University held on 30 September 1989, at the University senate hall, the chief guest Dr. H.S. Rao stressed the necessity for value based education.

An eminent writer and litterateur, his witty style held the audience in rapt attention for more than half an hour.

In his speech, Dr. Rao deplored the criminalisation of education. He was especially concerned about instance of mass copying, violent incidents and intimidation of invigilators in examination centres. Questioning the students on their real aim of acquiring education, he said, "India will soon be a nation of uneducated literates". Education, he felt had not been able to inculcate the right ideals in the students who valued the degree certificate more than the knowledge that they failed to gain in their years at college.

The ancient Gurukul system of education has a lot to offer students in terms of community life and in teaching them values of amity, friendship and co-operation. The lack of these values, he felt was the main cause of the alarming incidents of violence in the country. He urged the students "Work for a better and stronger India" for "the power of youth can subdue mountains and achieve the impossible".

Earlier in the speech, he thanked the Vice-Chancellor for bestowing on him the honour of chief guest. Recollecting his student's days, Dr. Rao confessed that while he had never been an outstanding student, he was always an honest and sincere one. It was this, which stood him in good stead in life, he said.

Congratulating, all those who got their degree certificates and especially the medal winners, the remarked that their real test would be in the actual field of life. Dr. H.S. Rao was also pleased to note the increasing number of women candidates in the medal tally.

Finally, he again thanked the Vice-Chancellor and the students for hearing him out patiently and wished the students the 'Very Best in Life.'

(3) Interview Report

The interviews discussed here will not be the job interview types. Rather you have to report interviews with important people, who have made a mark in some field. Others would therefore like to know more about them, their opinions and achievements.

Interviews require some planning. You need to take a prior appointment with the person you want to interview. Secondly, you should collect some facts about their life so that you can plan a series of questions and how you would like to proceed with the interview. However, the questions are to be your guidelines only. It is always better to let the interviewee continue his talk and questions will automatically arise out of spontaneous conversation. It is necessary to establish a good rapport. Your difficult questions should be posed in the middle. After the interviewee is at ease, he is less likely to take offence at a critical question. Even if you are using a tape recorder, it is better to jot down notes of your comments or observation of the interviewee's personality. Never overstay the time given to you, unless the interviewee is also keen to continue. Before you end the interview, check your guidelines to see whether you have left out any question of importance and clarify all doubts.

Two Ways of Reporting Interview: Once you have completed the interview and have the points before you, you can report the interview in two ways:

- If your interview is merely for information and is brief, you can adopt the **question and answer form**. However, introduce an explanatory passage about the person in the beginning. Here you can also add the opinion you have formed of the person through the interview. This paragraph will act as a link to the actual question and answer which follows.
- If the interview is lengthy and you would like to convey more of your opinion, it is better to alternate your comments with direct quotation from the interview. This method is better than the merely question-answer format, which can sometimes make dull reading.

In both cases, provide an appropriate title. We give below reports of interviews in both the styles:

Example 1: Interview with a Sports Personality

"Get Them Out of Defeat Syndrome!"

Sitting among the empty stands of the Hockey Association Ground in Bangalore Bikram Singh, the Captain of the gold winning Olympic hockey team of yesteryears, spoke on the disturbing trend of decline in Indian hockey. Presently Director of sports in the A.B. University, he is responsible for the setting up of one of the most professional training centres, which has given us some of the most promising hockey players in past years. He was an outstanding centre-half, rated among the greatest in the history of the game. An astute captain, he led India to some of its greatest victories. In this forthright interview, he condemns the administrators and selectors for the dismal showing of our hockey team.

Excerpts:

Q. What are your views on the debacle of the Indian team?
A. To be frank, it is most humiliating that country which had won Gold in eight Olympics and taught the world the game of hockey should be fumbling in this manner. But success cannot be had without hard work. We failed to work hard and hence the dismal showing.

Q. Do you think that one of the major causes of failure has been the inability of our boys to adjust to astro-turf?
A. I don't think so. The basic skills are the same. In fact playing on grass, which we did in our time was tougher as playing surfaces were different in Europe. Playing on astro-turf is much easier – there are no unexpected bounces. I think physical fitness is an area which has been neglected and has caused our failure.

Q. What do you think of the selectors and administrators?
A. Much of what ails Indian hockey is the bureaucratic set up of the Indian Hockey Federation. The selectors who talk of foreign coaches and training camps are people who have never held a hockey stick. India has enough coaches to produce a winner ... perhaps we don't give them a chance.

Q. Who was your inspiration?
A. Who else but the greatest hockey player of all time – Dhyan Chand. He was the most versatile and perfect player who ever lived. His technique of using the wrist while hitting scoring was unique. It is a pity that there are no films of the matches played during those days and thus the incredible technical skill and expertise of Dhyan Chand is lost.

In the above example, we used the question-answer format along with inductor paragraph which gives you some details about the person. Let us now go on to the example of a report where dialogue and narrative are intermingled:

Example 2: Interview with a Classical Dancer/Musician

5 June Delhi: "The classical form of dance is gaining popularity" Hema Malini the Bharat Natyam maestro dancer and famous Hindi movie actress said that people were getting fatigued with the unsystematic steps of the popular form. Mrs. Hema Malini answered when asked by the question in press club after a dance programme organised by Hindustan Times news paper. She said that she has got an appreciable applause from audience wherever she has performed. This appreciation has only grown with time and there has been no dearth of newcomers to this art form. She said that the meaningful dance with an aesthetic sense always touched the audience and was able to express many things that

cannot be said through any other medium. She appreciated the newly emerging keen interest of the corporate sector in the art form has been very encouraging to the new artist and several old maestros have come back to the stage who once seemed to have been lost in a situation of neglect to the art form. She encouraged her daughters to learn such art of dance and music. The foreigners are attracted a lot towards the classical dances as they find the soul touch in Indian classical dances. She proudly said that the Indian classical dance shows at foreign places are fully packed.

(4) Survey Reports

Survey reports can be of various kinds. A market survey would include finding out about the sales of a particular product – the demand it has, the price range which consumers favour, etc. More detailed survey reports could include reports of land or soil survey, to determine whether an agricultural project could be undertaken there or survey of a river – its flood pattern, etc. to determine the construction of a dam. Such geological or other industrial surveys require very long reports often published in book form. It follows an elaborate pattern with a preface, content table, list of illustration, summary, introduction, discussion, recommendations, etc. Finally list of Reference, Bibliography, Appendix, and Glossary are given.

How to write a Survey Report?

(1) Survey reports are produced in response to a request for information. The instructions which tell you what you are required to do are called 'Term of Reference.' The terms of reference will help you plan the scope of your survey.

(2) You have to fix the objective of your report, *i.e.* what it intends to convey and to whom?

(3) The next step is to collect the data. You can do so by personal interviews where not only what the person speaks, but your personal observation of the people, will be important. Interviews are helpful if you need to collect information from only a few people. If a large number of people are involved in the survey, you can make use of questionnaires. Questionnaires should be clear and precise as clarifications are not possible unlike in an interview, where you can explain a question better, if the person does not understand.

(4) We have noted in the introductory paragraph, that long survey reports follow elaborate patterns. However shorter reports may be written along the following pattern:

   (a) Mention the Terms of Reference.
   (b) Describe the procedure – the method used.
   (c) Report the findings.
   (d) Recommendations and conclusion.

An example of such a report is given below:

Example:

Report of the survey done by the Learner's Association of Delhi on the Study Habits of Students of IGNOU University.

(1) Terms of Reference: The 'Learner's Association of Delhi' decided to do a survey on the study habits of the students of IGNOU University. The decision was taken on 21 March 1989 at a General Body Meeting. Accordingly, a Survey Committee was set up to investigate the study habits of degree students at the University. The committee was given two months to complete the study.

(2) Procedure: The Survey Committee drew up a questionnaire comprising 25 objective questions related to students attitudes towards studies and examinations. Five hundred copies of the questionnaire were distributed among the students, with the request that they would be returned to the Secretary of the Survey Committee within 15 days.

180 students returned the copies of the questionnaire duly filled in, out of these 40 came from girl students.

(3) Findings:

(a) 52 per cent of the 180 students who returned the questionnaire duly filled in admitted that they never studied regularly except when examinations were near.

(b) 20 per cent of the students replied that they study for only 10-15 days before the examinations.

(c) More than 60 per cent of the students replied that they needed reference book to help them with the exam preparation like GPH Book.

(d) 40 per cent of the students said that they had joined IGNOU only to get a degree.

(4) Recommendations: The Survey Committee recommends the holdings of regular tests and assignments. The marks obtained in these assignments must be considered in the determination of credits awarded in the final university examinations.

It further recommends that the marks obtained in the assignments to be mentioned in the statement of marks issued by the University.

(5) Scientific Experiments: Scientific experiments have to be reported with accuracy. You can write reports of experiments as follows:

(a) State the aim of the experiment, *i.e.* why the experiment is being performed.

(b) Apparatus or material used.

(c) Describe the procedure, *i.e.* how the experiment was done.

(d) Note down your observations. Observations form very important parts. You have to report them accurately. Big scientific experiments require the noting down of many results, which may often have to be tabulated. On these observed results may depend the failure or success of an experiment.

(e) Conclusion of the report will state the results of your experiment and what it proved or disproved. Sometimes you may have to interpret and analyse the results.

(f) Illustrations, diagrams, graphs, etc. are important parts of a report on experiments.

(g) Language used should be clear and accurate, since you will be dealing with scientific facts. Avoid too much technical jargon, unless the report is for circulation among experts.

Given below is an example of a report on a very simple chemistry experiment:

Aim: To test whether (H_2SO_4) Sulphuric acid and Sodium Carbonate are acids or alkalis.

Apparatus: Two test tubes with test tube holders.

Materials: Red litmus paper, a strip of blue litmus paper and a little sulphuric acid and sodium carbonate.

Theory: Red litmus turns blue when dipped in alkalis, while blue litmus turns red in acids.

Procedure:

- Take two test tubes.
- Fill one test tube with H_2SO_4.
- Fill the other test tube with sodium carbonate.
- Take the strip of red litmus and insert it in the first test tube which contains H_2SO_4.
- Then insert red litmus paper in the second test tube, which contains sodium carbonate.
- Note that the red litmus in the first test tube does not show any colour change.
- Now remove the red litmus and insert blue litmus paper in the first test tube with H_2SO_4.
- Repeat the procedure, putting blue litmus paper in the second test tube too.
- Note there is no colour change in the blue litmus inserted in the second test tube.

Observations:

- Red litmus does not change colour in H_2SO_4.
- Red litmus turns blue when inserted into sodium carbonate.
- Blue litmus changes to red when dipped in H_2SO_4.
- Blue litmus does not change colour when dipped in sodium carbonate.

Conclusion:

- As red litmus turned blue in sodium carbonate, sodium carbonate is an alkali.
- As blue litmus turned red in H_2SO_4, it is an acid.

EXERCISE

(1) The production from the factories has suddenly decreased sharply. You have been sent to investigate the matter. Report your findings to your Manager.

Ans. Report on sudden decrease of production

Dear Sir,

I had been appointed by you to investigate the matter of sudden fall in production in factory in month of May 2005. I have investigated the matter and am submitting my report on finding of reason of such fall. The sudden fall of production is a matter of great concern for us as it affected our supply order badly. The main reason of sudden shortfall in production was due to the failure of generator installed for unit no. 3 in the factory. In the month of May, the demand for electricity increased due to increase in the temperature which increased the burden of workload on generator and it failed. The non performance of generator badly affected the work of unit no. 3. The carelessness of electricity department of our staff increases the woe as they did not repair it on time. The repair had not been done properly by the staff which damages it regularly. The whole system of factory was badly affected due to non functioning of unit no. 3 as it is the biggest and main controlling unit of the factory. In absence of support from unit no. 3, the other unit decided to decrease the pace of their production, which resulted in sudden fall in production. Now the generator has been repaired but we need to be alert to manage such an accident.

XYZ

(2) A tragic incident

Ans. Delhi 6 March, yesterday foggy night witnessed an accident between a car and a bus near the Pitampura flyover in city area. The collision was so sudden that the loud noise diverted the attention of the people in the surrounding area also. According to an eye witness the speed of the car was so high and the driver of the car tried to rush out but lost the control over the car and collided with the bus. Four people in car and thirteen in bus had severally brushed between the bus and car and got injured. The driver of the car was found drunk and was arrested on the spot. The people in the crowd suggested that the injured should be rushed to the hospital, but nobody was ready to take the initiative. After a while, a man offered his car and took them to the hospital. Later, the ambulance had reached on the spot and rushed the injured to the hospital. The police station was not far away from the accident site and it reached there within minutes. It took the statement of some eye witness. The relatives of the victim were informed by the police they were rushed towards the hospital. The police also booked a case of rash and negligent driving against the driver of the car.

(3) You are the Deputy Director of Medical and Health Services. You visited a hospital in Rajouri Garden, Delhi. You found that the beds were not in adequate number, the stocks of medicines were limited, even the life-saving drugs were not available. The wards were not clean. Add some more details and write a report about your visit.

Ans. Visiting to Rajouri Garden Hospital report

Dear Sir,

I am submitting the report of inspection conducted by me on 5 June 2012 to the Rajouri Garden Govt. Hospital. I reached the hospital at 10 am in the morning with my staff. I had seen so many irregularities in the functioning of hospital. In the store room, the stock of medicine shown by their register did not properly match. There was shortage of stock, than what was actually shown by the register. There were no proper arrangements for distribution of medicines to the patient. Most of the life saving drugs needed in emergency was not available. In the wards, the beds were not in adequate number to admit all the patients. The wards were not clean and hygienic at all. In the canteen of the hospital, garbage fell on the floor. Flies and mosquitoes were hovering on tables. The people were not served hygienic food. The emergency department is also not in proper shape. Doctors were absent on usual time of hospital without any explanation. I hope that you will take proper action in this regard, as this is a serious matter. After all, health is priority for all.

XYZ

(Deputy Director of Medical and Health Services)

(4) You are the traffic policeman at a busy traffic crossing of your city. Write a report about the traffic trends and problems in commuting, to your Inspector.

Ans.

Dear Sir,

There has been a increase in the number of vehicles on the roads, which in turn leads to traffic problems in city. It is observed that the people do not obey the rules of traffic. Shortage of traffic policemen is one of the biggest reasons behind the crumbling of the traffic management leading to less of precious lives. The people do not care to cross the red light crossing on most of the red light as there are no policeman posted on duty at most of crossings. The illegal parking at the main road of the city centre congested the road to be used by other vehicles. The roads are narrow for heavy traffic and the lanes inside the Connaught Place are ban for the heavy vehicles but most of the truck drivers entered in these lanes and ignored the laws. Two wheelers driver do not wear helmet while driving. Most of car owners do not follow the safety norms. They do not wear the seat belt while driving the car. The important reason behind these problems are, people do not fear to pay the fine on caught, as the fine are very small in amount, most of the people in this city belong to high society they make it a point to disobey the law as a fashion. The corrupt policeman in department motivates the law breaker. The condition is really pathetic and is deteriorating day by day. A complete system needs to be established and rules to be made. Once everyone starts following them strictly, the city will become very organised and away from this chaotic situation.

XYZ

(Traffic Policeman)

(5) Recent India-Pakistan match

Ans. 19 March 2012, Mirpur: A match between India and Pakistan was played at Shere Bangla National Stadium. The Indian batting monster has woken up, well and truly.

Pakistan won toss and elected to bat first. Mohammad Hafeez and Nasir Jamshed came to batting first and Praveen Kumar from India came to bowling. After first over, score were 5 without any loss of Pakistan. Pakistan team played well in this match. After batting of Pakistan, total score were 329/6 at end of 50 overs. This was a great score given by Pakistan to Indian team.

From Indian team, Gautam Gambhir and Sachin Tendulkar came first for batting and Muhammad Hafeez came for bowling. Gambhir was out on second ball of first over. India's first over's score were 3/1.

The whole ground was full of audience. It was an honourable challenge for Indian batsman. India was batting very carefully. Younis took a smart catch at first slip of Sachin. He scored only 52 runs off 48.

Indian batsman showed a grand batting and won the match. Virat Kohli (183 off 148 balls) was hero of that match. Rohit Sharma (68 off 83 balls) also played good. With this win, India stayed in the hunt for a final in the Asia Cup 2012.

When Tendulkar and Kohli came together at 0-1, things looked really tough. The Pakistan bowlers were breathing fire, the field was in, and the crowd was strongly behind the Men in Green.

But, the master craftsman and the young aggressor were judicious. There were no undue risks taken, it seemed they knew that it was just a matter of staying at the wicket and the runs would come.

The unbelievable wrist-work of Kohli was again a treat for the eyes while Tendulkar seemed to be free of all the shackles of the world after his 100th hundred.

(6) You are in-charge of the hospital canteen. A fire had broken out in the canteen. Report the event to the Superintendent of the hospital.

Ans._Report on fire in hospital canteen

Dear Sir,

I would like to submit this report on the fire in hospital canteen on 15th of November 2004. I got the information of fire in the evening of 15th of November at around 5 pm when some employee came to me to report the incident of fire in canteen. I rushed towards the accident site with those employees and found that kitchen of the canteen was under the flame of the fire and the staff of the canteen tried to pacify the fire with fire extinguisher and water. The safety system of fire was not working properly. I immediately rushed back to my office and called the fire tenders. When I reached again on the fire spot I found that the fire was touching the sky. Within 15 minutes, the fire tender had arrived on the spot and started their action to pacify the fire. It took another 15 minutes to completely control the fire. There was no casualty as the entire team escaped safely before the fire got stronger. But a loss of kitchen and equipment is expected to be around '1,00,000/- as it needed whole refurnishing. It will take 2-3 weeks to refurnish the whole kitchen. Presently, it partly runs by storeroom. I am attaching the list of articles lost in this fire tragedy needed to be repaired and damaged for which the claim of insurance already filled by me.

XYZ

(In charge of Canteen)

(7) You are a newspaper reporter working for the News Today. You have been assigned the job of reporting on the experiences of Delhi people using the Metro. You interview about 25 persons of all ages and write a report for the newspaper. Mention the problems, if any, that the commuters face during travel.

Ans. Report on people's experience in METRO

Thousands of people everyday travel by metro. There are several people who are satisfied by it and other who wants more accessories in it. Today I interviewed about 25 person of all ages and sex who travelled by metro. Most of them are satisfied by its services. They praised it for lessening of the traffic problem of Delhi. Many of them prefer the metro rather to any other medium of conveyance because it saves lots of time in travelling from one part to another part of Delhi. In their usual rides by car it takes 2 hr to reach the Connaught place by Dwarka but metro takes only 45 minutes. Another reason is its comfort. The problem of excessive crowd in buses attracted most of the commuters. Especially the girls prefer its rides due to avoid the crowd and ill abuses in buses. While most of commuters are happy with its rides some complaint about its fares which is too high for going to nearby areas. Secondly not all the metro stations are connected with supplementary feeder buses. The hopes of the people of Delhi are very high with metro.

(8) Interview with a film actress/sportswoman

Ans. Delhi, 20 March: Aishwarya Rai the actress of the Hindi films was in the capital for being declared the best actress of the year and she had come here for receiving the award. She said today that she always like to work in the good cinema either it Hindi movies or any other regional one.

The actress who got her fame through films like Iruvar, Mohabbattein, Hum Dil De Chuke Sanam, Devdas, etc. also worked in many art films like Raincoat. She said that Art films have been different from the mainstream cinema, got a kind of satisfaction in the works, and needed more attention than in the popular cinema. Aishwarya who recently worked in many foreign films has earned fame for Indian cinema.

Aishwarya said that she was not averse to popular cinema though and if she gets a good role she would work in them also. She said that the name of her forth coming film has not yet been decided. She said to work with Mr. Amitabh Bachchan in Mohabbattein is like a dream come true for her. She did not reply to the question that who was her best hero of the film industry.

(9) Imaginary Parliament proceedings during Confidence/ No confidence motion

Ans. Parliament is the highest decision-maker body in our country which controls the govt's function. The govt. of our country is responsible towards the parliament. The prime minister and his cabinet are answerable towards the parliament. They do all their work of govt after getting approval of parliament. If parliament disapproves any of the proposals of govt that deems that govt. lost its confidence in parliament and should be resigned. The proper way to check the support of the govt in parliament is confidence or no confidence motion. If the govt wins the confidence motion or defeats the no confidence motion in the house of Lok Sabha that means the Govt has the Trust of parliament. Today the govt. decided to check its trust in parliament for coming budget session. The minister of parliament affair on behalf of govt presents a memorandum of confidence motion on Lok Sabha. After the usual work the speaker allowed to vote on such issue the minister of govt defended their work by answering the arguments of opposition after one hour discussion the speaker allowed to vote the motion. All the members of the house cast their secret vote. After counting the vote, the speaker declared that the govt. wins the trust vote by 34 votes.

(10) Celebration of Deepawali in your town/city

Ans. Delhi, 12 October: Yesterday, Deepawali was celebrated with great fun in the town. All went well amidst the 'diyas' and 'crackers', and 'flowers'. Crackers went on bothering the old people even after the deadline of 10 o' clock of night as it was set by the administration for a peaceful celebration and considering the demands of the senior Citizen. The sweet sellers played the important role as they were awfully busy the whole day. In our locality, the people make a list of some people who took responsibility of whole preparation of deepawali in locality.

The markets were open and busy till midnight after which the shops went on getting a colourful decoration. But the cracker sellers were selling their goods till 9 o'clock. Panditji of our area declared the time of pujan about 7 o' clock. After that, the people visited each other's home with packs of sweets. Shopkeepers worshipped the goddess of riches, Laxmi and distributed 'prasad' to all and everyone that came by. In night all the children with their families collected together at colony's park and fire the crackers.

(11) An experiment of physics/chemistry performed by you at school/college level.

Ans. The national talent hunt programme launched by the state government to search the new talent in field of science. All the school prepared well for this talent hunt. I also took part in this competition on behalf of my school. Our school team thought a new idea of generating the bio fuel as the country badly feels the invention of homemade fuel as the continuation of gulf war increase the burden of balance of payment on our country. The process of forming bio fuel from some herbs it was demonstrated successfully by our school team in annual science experimentation function at the school. There were many other students who participated in the function. Each one was allotted a different kind of experiment that was to be demonstrated.

We set out with arranging the equipments on the table in the specified member. The experiment took almost 50 minutes concept, which was a sign of full efficient working of experiment procedure. We all were very much excited as the education minister was the chief guest of the workshop. We performed well as the guest appeared quite impressed and asked so many questions in this regard. Our team won the excellence award of the tournament.

(12) You are a newspaper reporter working for the Delhi Times. You have been assigned the job of reporting on the rampant thieving of car stereos and other accessories in the Kutub Colony. On interviewing the residents, you discover that the colony has poorly lit roads, infrequent police patrol and scarcity of guards. Add some more details and submit the report to the editor.

Ans. Report on rampant thieving in Kutub Colony

Dear Sir,

As per your instructions I have interviewed the resident of Kutub Colony where the frequent complaint of thefts are received. Theft and burglary is common in the colony as in previous fortnight more than 7 theft cases were registered by the resident. The thieves have broken the lock of car in the night and steal the stereo and valuable accessories of the car. The president of the resident welfare association blamed the inadequate police patrol in the area. Most of the resident blamed it on the scarcity of security guard in the area and the street lights which do not lighted up in night. Most of the street lights do not function. MCD take no proper action to repair them despite several complaint lodges in this regard. The irony of the colony is that the police station a hardly 500 metre away from the colony. Now the resident welfare association of the colony decided to raise the issue with the senior officer of the police on 20 December.

XYZ

(Newspaper Reporter)

(13) You are the Secretary of the Residents' Welfare Association of the Kutub Colony. Your association has organised a cleanliness drive for a week. Write a report for the Association Newsletter, saying how you motivated all the residents to participate actively in the drive. Also says how you managed to get the municipal authorities to remove the garbage dump from the area. Add some more details to the report.

Ans. Report on cleanliness drive in Kutub Colony

Dear Sir,

I would like to report to you about motivation to all the residents to participate actively in the cleanliness drive. As per the decision of the association held on 15 December, we decided to start the cleanliness programme in the colony from Sunday. All the resident of the society gave their contribution in this cleanliness drive. On Sunday morning, we had come out in streets of colony and started sweeping there. I had found some garbage near the main gate of the Colony. So I waited for a while to see whether there was any other kind of problem. I had reported the in-charge of MCD but they did not give me any positive response. So I had hired a garbage truck to collect the garbage in colony. Many people were participating in it. We all sorted a motivation campaign for finishing the garbage of the locality. I got very positive response from this motivational campaign. Some people had visited the colony and said that they feel very good because of cleanliness drive in the locality. It is working. Some resident came to me and said that there was a lot of care needed in this direction.

XYZ
(Secretary)
Resident Welfare Association

(14) You are an NSS student in B.A. first year studying in a college of Delhi University. You attended 3-day literacy camp in the slum area of Raghubir Nagar near your college. Write a report on your experiences of teaching the slum children, to be published in the college magazine.

Ans. Experience of teaching the slum students

On 4 June 2006: The NSS unit of our college organised a three day camp at Raghubir Nagar, Delhi. It was started from 4th of June and ended on 6th of June. I with 20 other student of my college under the supervision of Mr. C.M. Jha, the head of NSS unit of our college attended the seminar. There were about 250 students of different colleges of Delhi took part in it. The basic theme of the camp was Literacy among the slum children. The speaker of various colleges asserted their views on this issue. One thing was common in all the presentation that they all rendered co-operation of student in this mission. We decided a slogan 'Each One Teach One' to start the mission of teaching slum students. Some of the student had proposed to form a forum and prepared a list of volunteer who were interested to help in this mission. We made a list of about 120 students who took an oath to teach at least one person in a year in life. This was a very valuable function for me as a student.

(15) You are the Secretary of the students' Union of your college. The principle of your college has asked you to interview different sections of the student population and find out if they are facing any problems regarding availability of books and journals and adequate space for reading in the library. You are also supposed to suggest ways in which more facilities can be provided to the students. Write a report and submit it to the principal.

Ans. Report on problems of students regarding books

Dear Sir,

As per your instructions, I'm submitting the report on the problems of students on the issue of books. As I interviewed many students in various section of college regarding their problems of library and books. Most of them are not satisfied with the services provided by the staff of library. The new students of the college in first year faced more problems in this regard. As they are not much familiar with the college, they find it difficult to search the books in library as no proper catalogue of books are maintained by the library staff. The books are not properly placed in their respective racks. Also some of the student's complaint of issue of only two books at a time. When at least five subjects are studied by the student in a semester it is difficult for them to choose the two books. Some student of final year also complaint about the lack of study space in library in the examination days as the crowd in library is increased so much as most of them do not get space to study. They requested you to look after the problems of library and do something in this regard at the earliest.

Thanking you
XYZ
(Secretary, Student Union College)

Letter/E-mail Writing

Q1. Write a letter to your friend and his wife thanking them for their hospitality while you stayed with them in Mumbai during the Xmas break last. Say how much you appreciate the way they took care to make your stay a wonderful experience.

Ans.
To
Akhil Sharma
House No. 347/4 C
Thane, Mumbai

Dear Akhil,

It was a great pleasure to spend my holidays with you and your family during the Christmas break. At first, my family was quite apprehensive and also they were hesitating to join you, but your wife Natasha's and your daughter's cordial nature enabled to make us comfortable. We enjoyed the sights seeing in Mumbai. We felt that we are living in our home only. I am highly grateful for your kind hospitality. I strongly feel that I am blessed to have such loving, kind and considerate friends. Kindly join us with your family in Kangra H.P. We are looking forward for your stay during summer vacations.

Hope to see you soon!

Your friend
Naveen

Q2. Imagine that you have received an appointment letter from GullyBaba Publishing House (P) Ltd. Write a letter of acceptance to.

Ans. GullyBaba Publishing House (P) Ltd.
Tri Nagar, Delhi-110035

Subject: Acceptance of appointment letter.

Dear Mr. Anand,

I have received the appointment letter. I am very pleased to accept the position of Manager with GullyBaba Publishing House (P) Ltd. Thank you for the opportunity. I am eager to make a positive contribution to the company and to work with everyone on the GullyBaba Publishing House Team.

As we discussed, my starting salary will be '35,000 and health and life insurance benefits will be provided after 90 days of employment.

I look forward to starting employment on 1 July 2017. If there is any additional information or paperwork you need prior to then, please let me know.

Thank you.
Yours Sincerely
Rohit Sharma

Q3. Assuming that you work for a company that sells art products (paintings/musical instruments/cds). Imagine that you have been asked to visit an African country– Nigeria or Kenya – to survey and send back a report for the export of your company's products. Write the report in about 250 words.

Ans.
Gold Paintings Limited
23 Connaught Place
Delhi

The Chairman
Gold Painting Ltd.
Connaught Place
Delhi

Dear Sir,

I had been asked to visit the head office of St. John group of companies in Kenya as they wanted a huge variety of our company's products. I visited their office on 15 July and observed that the company has a very good reputation. They have a very fair dealing with their clients. Most of the employees are Indians and our company will also gain profit and reputation by dealing with these people.

Yours truly
Sahil Kumar

Q4. Imagine that you were interviewed by 'The Times of India", and selected for employment mean while you got a better assignment elsewhere. Write a letter refusing the former offer.

Ans.
The Editor
Times of India, Delhi
Date: 7 June 2016

Dear Mr. Pathak,

Thank you very much for offering me the opportunity to work at Times of India. Unfortunately, I will not be accepting the position as it does not fit the path I am taking to achieve my career goals.

Once again, I'd like to express my gratitude for the offer and my regrets that it didn't work out. You have my best wishes in finding someone suitable for the position.

Signature
Rhea Verma

Q5. Write a letter to your friend describing either a historic monument or a place of scenic beauty.

Ans.
23 Saraswati Vihar
Delhi
Date: 23 September 2016
Dear Rohit,

Hello! How are you? During my Child's holidays, I took a package tour and went to Malaysia. It was a neat and beautiful place. People are very disciplined and they strictly abide the rules and regulations formed by the law and order. The best attraction was the twin towers. One could spectate the whole scenic beauty of the people on the top of the towers. We also made a trip to sunway lagoon. The rides and games were awesome. I strongly suggest that you should also plan your vacation in Malaysia.

Hope to see you soon!

Your Friend
Raj

Q6. Imagine you are Alisha – a tourist. Draft a letter/e-mail to the manager of a hotel confirming the reservation of the accommodation in their hotel.

Ans.

Date: 23/11/15
Mr. A.H. Thomas
Manager
Andaman Beach Resort
Corbyn's Cove, Port Blair.

Dear Mr. Thomas
Thank you very much for your letter of Nov 7, booking our accommodation in your hotel as per our requirements. As desired by you, I am enclosing a draft of ₹33,600/- an advance payment of tariff for the accommodation. I must also thank you for sending me information brochures giving more details about the facilities available at your hotel.

Looking forward to having an exciting holiday in Port Blair and a comfortable stay in your hotel.
Thanking you

Yours sincerely
Alisha
F 9/3, Vasant Lok
New Delhi

Q7. Your company, India Garments, wants to buy good quality Chinese silk from a Chinese company. Write an email to the business head of the Chinese company stating your purpose.

Ans.

To: chinesesilk@company.net.in
Cc:

Subject: Information about the variety of silks

Dear Madam/Sir,
We have heard a lot about the good quality of silks manufactured by you. We deal in making and selling silk dresses and we are based in New Delhi, India. As such, we require high quality silk fabrics for our products. Could you please send us information about the variety of silks manufactured by you and their corresponding prices as soon as possible? Please let us know about freight, custom and other charges (if any), as such charges may be applicable to transnational business orders involving two countries. This will enable us to place our order with you.

We look forward to hearing from you and to the beginning of a new relationship. In case you wish to verify our credential, please contact the referees given below. One of them is a company with whom you have already share a business relationship and who had recommended your name to us.

Thank you!

With regards,

India Garments
2524/A; Okhla Industrial Area,
Delhi, India
Ph. 27XXXXXX

Q8. You are K. Shankaran, the Chief Account Officer. Write a letter to the bank manager of Bank of India informing him about the delay in collection of cheques.

Ans.

203, Kushal bazaar,
Nehru Place
New Delhi -110 019

24 May 2016

The Manager,
Bank of India
Nehru Place
New Delhi - 110019

Sub: Letter for delay in collection of cheques

Dear Sir,

We deposited the following two cheques in your Bank on May 9, 2016, to be credited to our current account no. 0015 001700 CP after collection.

(1) Cheque No. 345670 dated 2.3.2016 drawn on State Bank of India, New Delhi, for ₹5,000/-

(2) Cheque No. 5431798 dated 5.4.2016 drawn on New Bank of India, New Delhi, for ₹6,900/-

Going through the statement received from you, we find that these cheques have not yet been credited. We shall be grateful if you could look into the matter and do the needful as soon as possible.

Yours faithfully
K. Shankaran
(Chief Account Officer)

Q9. You and five of your friends have decided to visit Port Blair, the capital of Andaman and Nicobar Islands. After looking at the various kinds of accommodation available on Port Blair, you have decided to spend a week in December this year at Andaman Beach Resort, Corbyn's Cove, Port Blair. Here is the phone message left by you at the hotel:

Message from : Arun Srivastava, F9/3Vasant Lok, New Delhi. Date and Time : 5 November 11:30 a.m. Mr. Srivastava wants to book three double rooms with A/C and attached bath for a group of six persons from 12:00 noon of Dec. 24 to 12 noon of Dec. 31. The group would prefer rooms facing the sea. Please quote price including the breakfast.

Imagine you are the Manager of the hotel Andaman Beach Resort. Write a letter/email confirming reservation of the accommodation.

Ans.

Andaman Beach Resort
Corbyn's Cove, Port Blair
Tel. 6321463
Date: 5th Nov, 2016

Mr. Arun Srivastava

F 9/3, Vasant Lok
New Delhi

Dear Mr. Srivastava

Thank you very much for your telephonic message. I am writing to you to say that we can reserve three double rooms with A/c from Dec. 24 (12:00 noon) – Dec. 31 (12:00 noon.) All the three rooms have a sea view and are on the second floor of the resort.

The cost of each room would be ₹3200/-per night including taxes and service charges. Breakfast for each person would cost ₹150/- extra.

I would be grateful if you could confirm this booking by email by the end of this month, along with a draft of ₹33,600/- as 50% advance payment of tariff for the accommodation.

I must thank you for taking interest in our resort. We look forward to welcoming you and your group on Dec. 24 and assure you of all attention and care.

I enclose two brochures describing our resort and its facilities. If you have any questions, we would be pleased to answer them.

Sincerely
(A.H. Thomas)
Manager

Q10. You are Vijay Bhargava, live in 269 Tri Nagar, New Delhi-110035. Write a letter in response to an advertisement, which appeared in The Hindustan Times on 1 March 2016 for the post of Account Assistant preferably with degree in commerce and knowledge of typing.

Ans.

269, Connaught Place,
Delhi-110001

Subject: Application for the post of Account Assistant

Respected Sir/Madam,
I am writing to apply for the position as Account Assistant. I have completed my B.Com from IGNOU. I have total three year of experience in specific field.

I understand that working for your organisation requires a candidate who is team oriented and is able to deal with people in various departments. I am confident that I possess these skills, which will help me to perform the job efficiently and effectively. I believe that my qualification is an ideal match for this position, and I am confident I would be able to make a valuable contribution to your organisation.

I have developed a unique range of inter-disciplinary skills that would add value to your organisation. I am looking to meet with you to discuss how my background and qualifications can work for your organisation. I appreciate your consideration and can be contacted on mobile at +91-9350849407, or by email at jobs@gullybaba.com.

I enclose my resume as a first step in exploring the possibilities of employment with your company.

Looking forward to receive your positive reply.

Thanking you,
Yours truly,
Vijay Bhargava

Q11. Imagine that you are Rohan, staying in a government hostel, you feel extremely homesick. Write a letter to your parent explaining that how much you are missing and remembering them. Also state about your study progress and examination.

Ans.

Jijamata Govt. Hostel
15,Nehru Park,
Aurangabad-431002

20 September 2016

Dear father,

Since long I have not received your letter or any phone call. These days I feel homesick. If I were a bird, I would have been with you at present. I am eager to meet mother, little Sony and you. I miss you a lot. My first term exam is about to be held in the next month. I have to prepare for that but my homesickness takes me away from study. You need not worry. Just send a letter and family photograph along with additional one thousand rupees to buy Alarm watch. Our teacher of English is a kind and disciplined person. Under his guidance, I am improving myself. My roommates at hostel are studious and of helping nature. Convey my regards to mother. Remember me to Raju, Ahmad and Christopher.

Yours Loving Son
Rohan

Q12. On the occasion of a 'Mother's Day' write a letter to your mother thanking her for the valuable thing you have learnt from her.

Ans. Gujarati Govt. Hostel
15, Nehru Park,
Aurangabad 43002
October 22, 2016

Dear mother,

Celebration of 'Mother's Day' made me think about you. At hostel, I really miss you. I remember you and the thing you taught me. You inspired me to go ahead and kiss the world .You made me take interest in reading newspaper that made my awareness about the world. You taught me to respect subordinates too. Your teaching enabled me to face the challenges of life. I am really grateful for the thing you have taught me. Thanks a lot.
Wish you very happy Mother's Day.
Your loving son
xyz

Speech Writing

A speech is meant to convey one's thoughts or opinions, share information with or spread awareness among a large number of people. A good speech has clarity of thought and expression, accuracy of facts and an unbiased view of issues.

Format:

- Beginning : A Pre-speech note
  : Salutation

		: Occasion of speech
		: Announcement of topic
•	Development of topic	: Reference to newspapers statistics, effects and results, arguments, etc.
•	Winding up	: Summing up of all points
•	Conclusion	: Conclude with a hope or an appeal or a warning
		: End with a 'Thank You'

Some Key Points to Remember:

- It is very important to hold the attention of the audience. Therefore, keep the speech to the point and appealing.
- Start the speech with an interesting bit of information, a question or a quotation.
- Convey your opinions and views in an organised and coherent manner.
- Develop each point properly and then move on to the next one.
- Provide examples, statistics and facts that are properly researched and authentic.
- Interact with the audience by posing questions and including some humour, if it is appropriate.
- End with an emphasis on your point of view and personal inferences so that the audience thinks about what you have expressed.
- Always thank the audience for listening to you before leaving the stage.

EXERCISE

Q1. Today is women's day and you are asked to deliver a speech on changing role of women in 21st century acknowledging their significant contribution in changing face of modern era. Your speech should not exceed the limit of 120-150 words.

Ans. ROLE OF WOMEN

Respected Principal, Teachers and My Dear Friends,

I am delighted to have this golden opportunity of expressing my views on the ROLE OF WOMEN on the eve of "WOMAN'S DAY".

In the past, women were considered inferior to man. Today, women are as good as men in every aspect. They have proved their worth. Name any field of progress wherein they have not left their mark? They are known for their sincerity, sensibility, hard work and timely wit. They have never failed in using them in time of need. Women like Barkha Dutt and Sonia Gandhi have excelled in their respective task. Being woman myself, I feel tremendous power in myself and see no reason to lag behind. I am proud to be a woman. We know that modern world cannot afford to leave women as they have time and again made the world realise their strong presence.

I acknowledge the vital role the women play for the emancipation of the society and their immense contribution in shaping and creating a strong nation with their spirit of dedication, devotion and duty.

Thank you

Q2. Write a speech in about 150–200 words on 'Environmental Pollution', which you have to deliver during the morning assembly in your school.

Ans. Respected principal and teachers and my dear friends,

Today I am going to speak on the topic 'Environmental Pollution', which is a serious problem that the whole world is facing today. The tremendous increase in population is the root cause of all kinds of pollution. More people on this earth means more waste material being created. Another factor is the advancement in science and technology. It has made our lives very comfortable but has also given rise to a variety of problems that are harming the environment.

Pollution comes in various forms. Air pollution is caused by the smoke from factories, the exhaust fumes from vehicles and the burning of garbage containing chemical materials. Water pollution is caused when toxic waste materials are disposed off into seas and rivers. Soil pollution is again the result of incorrect methods of waste disposal. Radioactive waves from electronic objects and non-biodegradable material like plastics also contaminate the air and the soil. With modernisation, we have reached a stage where the enormous noise caused by industrial and transport activities has become a health hazard.

Even though it may not be possible for mankind to eliminate environmental pollution totally, the hazards can be minimised by adopting alternate methods and following certain rules. We must remember that by protecting the environment, we are protecting ourselves.

Thank you

Q3. You are Aarti/Aman. You are to give a speech in the school morning assembly on 'Peer pressure'. Write the speech in about 120 words using the hints given below.

- **taking decisions–tough job–peer influence activities and life.**
- **take to smoking and drinking under peer pressure.**
- **not always bad–you may be a sports person, better in academics**

- **take up–of fear–of left alone**
- **learn to say 'No'**
- **take help from teachers or parents**

Ans. PEER PRESSURE

Good Morning respected Principal, Teachers and Students.

Today, I want to say few words on 'Peer Pressure' in front of you all.

As we grow older, decision making becomes tougher and tougher as most questions do not have an answer in Yes or No. These may be questions like should I try a cigarette? Should I drink with my friends? Making independent decisions is very tough but what makes it tougher is the involvement of other people. People of our age or peers try and influence our activities and life. This is where, peer pressure creeps in.

Peers no doubt are an important part of one's life. Thus, it is inevitable to avoid their influence, as it is basic human nature to listen to people around and act accordingly. But it is largely seen that peer pressure has proved out to be dangerous for the children. Many a times children take up smoking or drinking under the veil of peer pressure. Not at all times peer pressure is negative. At times it can be positive too. They might help you be a better student or a sports person, or an enthusiastic book reader.

Children give in to peer pressure as the worst feeling is of being left out. Thus, to be liked by all and not to be an object of ridicule they give in easily. "Everybody is doing it" makes them feel they are right. But, remember, to walk away with peer pressure is not all that difficult. You just need to use your head and not heart. Learn to say "No" and make independent decisions. Take parents' or teachers' advice and accordingly move ahead in your life to go far on the road to success.

Thank you

Q4. You have lately read the account of many cases of violent behaviour by school children. Some instances have been quite injurious and harmful to the victims. You are shocked by these accounts and decide to share your views with your schoolmates. Prepare a speech for the morning assembly on the topic 'Growing violence in children: Causes and cures'.

Ans. Honourable principal, respected teachers and my dear friends, I would like to share my views on the growing violence among children these days, which is proving to be rather detrimental to the children's progress.

Lack of an appropriate environment and good parental care, and pressure of peers are some of the factors that are responsible for giving rise to negative emotions in children. Feelings of neglect and immense pressure cause anger and dissatisfaction in these youngsters. The growing exposure to crime films and thrillers too raises the levels of aggression in them. Moreover, the rush of consumerism has aroused a child's desire to possess whatever he sees in the advertisements on the television. And in case of non-fulfilment of these desires and wants, there is cause for resentment and frustration

Television shows like WWF and violent scenes in movies etc lead the innocent children to imitate them. The negative characters in movies become their role models whom they want to ape in order to appear 'cool'.

Parents, teachers and social reformers should inculcate the right values in children through persuasion and instruction. Being the torch-beaness of the future, children need to be guided well and shown the correct path in life. Let us hope for a better future with the children of today becoming sensible and sensitive citizens of tomorrow.

Thank you

Q5. You are Aruna Negi. You are very disturbed about the various instances of dowry deaths and cases of harassment reported in the newspapers. Write a speech that you would like to deliver highlighting the evils of the dowry system and suggest what could be done to eradicate it from our society.

Ans. Dear friends, we all have at some time or the other read or heard about the negative impact of the dowry system in our country. India got its freedom more than sixty years ago but we have not been freed from the shackles of this heinous system. Incredibly, brave battles have been fought on this land, great discoveries and inventions have been made in this country, but unfortunately little has been done to fight the dowry system.

A victim of dowry abuse is subject to physical harassment and mental trauma. Apathy towards such cases is not only a sign of moral weakness but it also indicates that we are willing to accept and continue with a tradition that we all condemn.

Young people like you and I can make a difference, if we decide to do so. Navneet Kaur of Karnal and Neha Sharma of Noida showed immense courage when they refused to get victimised by the greedy families seeking huge amounts as dowry. They have set examples for others to follow. Even the boys sitting here could help in bringing an end to a tradition that has compelied many a father to run into heavy debts. After all, a future groom could be the father of a daughter tomorrow. Nothing much can be achieved by the mere formation of laws. The laws need to be implemented and the victims have to be brave enough to raise their voices.

I strongly suggest that girls should study well, establish a place for themselves in society and say NO to dowry. Remember, only we can help ourselves in this case and if the young men support us, our generation will triumph over an 'enemy' that our predecessors tried but failed to conquer.

Thank you

Debate Writing (Argumentative Writing)

A debate is a formal contest of argumentation in which two opposing teams defend and attack a given proposition. It is a persuasive manner of speaking with the aim of converting the view of another person, or an audience, to your own point of view. In this speech, the speaker speaks either for or against the issue being discussed.

Format:

- **Salutation :** Address the jury and the audience properly
- **Introduction :** Begin with a quotation, question or increasing statistics
- **Starting the stand :** Make your stand very clear from the very beginning
- **Main points :** Highlight the main points very emphatically
- **Develop points :** Substantiate them with relevant examples, statistics, etc
- **Conclusion :** State your own opinion or view in the concluding lines to emphasise your stand on the issue.

Points to remember:

- Open by addressing the audience with 'Respected chairperson, members of the jury, and dear friends', or begin with a simple 'Good morning, ladies and gentlemen'.
- Begin the first paragraph by making your stand clear, that is, mention 'the motion tabled before the house is ...' and state whether you're speaking 'strongly in favour of'... or 'firmly against...' the issue.
- Develop 3–4 good points in support of your stand and negate at least two points of your opponent.
- Try to give a strong example with your best point.
- Language structures used should be specific to a debate.
- At least one point could be built up by asking a series of questions for more effective presentation. For example, instead of making a statement such as 'class room teaching methods even today are often mundane and boring...', it would be more effective if the point was conveyed thus– 'In today's technology-driven world, may I ask why classroom teaching methods are still so mundane and boring?'
- Conclude with your strongest point and reiterate your stand once again (use a quotation if possible).

EXERCISE

Q1. On the National Debate Forum, the topic given to the students is 'Should college students or even higher secondary students be given unlimited freedom?' Write a debate for or against the topic in about 200–250 words.

Ans. Good morning, ladies and gentlemen, Teenage proclaims itself near adulthood. So shouldn't a teenager be allowed to probe the mysteries of the world all on his/her own? The modern environment and educational facilities surely enable that. However, I strongly feel that some kind of guidance is necessary for their young and impressionable minds.

It is true that the modern world offers a variety of opportunities for all age groups in all the fields of knowledge, and everything is accessible at the click of a button. But, with one click on the wrong button, one could get access to harmful knowledge. Therefore, there needs to be some kind of control over the kind of freedom a teenager enjoys.

One could argue that aren't teenagers capable of deciphering the good from the bad as they are on the threshold of adulthood? I agree with this thought but too much curiosity can lead to added confusion, and even chaos. Some kind of parental guidance should be exercised on teenagers regarding the kind of movies to be watched, the books to be read, friends to have, etc.

Some of us may strongly protest as to why can't we be on our own and enjoy life. But the truth is that the world consists of both good and bad things and teenagers are not in a position to differentiate between the grey areas amidst good and bad. So the parents' guidance to a certain extent is essential.

Therefore, I think that while creative urges and the inquisitiveness of teenagers about the goings-on in the world should not be suppressed with too much parental interference, teenagers, on their part should not insist on complete freedom to make their choices in life.

Thank you

Q2. You are Ashutosh/Anamika Malik. You have to speak in a debate against the motion, 'We do not need Mathematics'. Prepare a speech of about 150–200 words.

Ans. Good morning, ladies and gentlemen, I, Ashutosh/Anamika, strongly oppose the motion that 'We do not need Mathematics'. Does my knowledgeable opponent believe that Mathematics means only working on complex mathematical models? Or that it is an activity indulged in only by those with a lot of time on their hands? Or that it is of no use to those who, apparently, have better things to do?

On the contrary, Mathematics has always been—and will remain—a part of our lives. I should like to draw attention to the fact that almost everything we do— from buying a bar of chocolate to reaching the movie hall on time—involves Mathematics. At a cricket or a football match, what is score-keeping but the arithmetical form of Mathematics? While building a house, right from the planning stage, we need Mathematics in its various forms, such as arithmetic, algebra, geometry and trigonometry. We need Mathematics to keep track of our day-to-day expenses too.

I therefore firmly reject the view that we do not need Mathematics. In my opinion Mathematics is an important field of study in modern life. Thank you.

Q3. Write a debate on the topic "Should schools have uniform?" in against the moment.

Ans. Respected Principal, teachers and dear friends, I speak against the motion on Should schools have uniforms? I will prove that students do not require uniforms. Firstly, the word 'uniform' means 'without any difference'. Yet, education today caters uniquely to individual learners who are accepted as different. Since we are not clones of each other, why should we dress identically? Uniforms can even symbolise a total lack of imagination. Education is supposed to set the imagination free, yet students do not even design the uniforms they wear. Next, identity and team spirit are not caused by the uniform but the people who wear them. Friendship, too, is not based on superficial details. Do students make friends on the basis of the uniform or because they share similar interests, likes and dislikes? Thirdly, uniforms cost a lot of money. Better bargains are available at sales where you can buy even branded products at cheaper rates. Uniforms come at a fixed rate and are usually quite expensive. Again, the safety of students depends on the law and order prevalent in society. A uniform cannot save a student in an accident caused by rash driving. A careful teacher keeps a student safe in a school excursion, not the uniform. Lastly, I will end by firmly asserting that a uniform suggests unimaginative and repressive discipline, whereas no uniform suggests inborn responsibility and creativity in schools.

Q4. Write a debate on the topic "Is there any educative value of travelling?" in about 200-250 words.

Ans. Good morning, ladies and gentlemen, I, Anushka, strongly favours the motion that there is an educative value of travelling. Travelling plays a very vital role in education. It is often enjoyed by people as hobby and some plan to go out of their houses as soon as they get some time. Generally, people go out to enjoy and have fun. Particularly, during vacations, people are travelling and visiting new places. Some people are very keen to visit new places and meet new people. Basically, travelling provides us enjoyment, information and education about the new places around us. Travelling provides us opportunities to know about new places whereas some historical places give us the awareness of our rich heritage. There are number of places from where a lot of can be learnt about the people in the past, their art, culture and ability to work. We can learn and enjoy the geographic location of places and different kinds of climatic conditions. We also get exposure to life. We meet different types of people and see variety of products.

From travelling we know that how to make adjustments in different conditions. We cannot expect to get all types of facilities we are getting at our home, as we are far away from our house. We learn how to live with minimum facilities at low cost. As we meet different kinds of people we become more social. Sometimes, lifelong relations are developed with such people.

In this way, we can say that travelling has many advantages. Travelling provides us not only good memorable moments but also entertains us. Travelling makes a man bold and provides him expose. Travelling also develops confidence in the man, as he has to interact with different people and different cultures.

Q5. Today every person is busy, whether we see a kid, a mother or a father or any other man. But old people are very free in this regard. They do not have any work. Still they are considered to be vulnerable. Problems seem to persist them more as compared to young people. Is it really true? To what extent are you satisfied? Write a debate in about 250 words.

Ans. Good evening, ladies and gentlemen, I, Reema, strongly favours the motion that old people do have certain problems in their lives. In fact, the most pitiable people in our country are the old people. It is seen that mostly they are neglected in the family. With age, they are considered a liability. Nobody in the family takes good care of them. It is also seen that they are treated as unwanted. In the past, in India's joint family system, its tradition of respect for the old people, and its general structure of senior ownership of property provided people over sixty with an honourable place in society and in their families. But with a combination of industrial growth, urbanisation, and Western influences, these systems are rapidly breaking down, leaving many of India's old people without forms of support. Many of these people, especially the poorer classes, have also retired from jobs that lacked retirement benefits, leaving them without either financial support or the extended family's protection.

It is also seen that there are some old-age homes where old people are thrown away by their own family members without any reason.

Such people are continuing to live their life without any purpose. They live in their memories. They are not even able to criticise openly about their family members. This type of situation is generally found in some rich families. It is really surprising that some prosperous families also send away the aged people to old-age homes. Members of family need to understand the old people learn from their experiences and appreciate their efforts.

Old people suffer a variety of problems, ranging from boredom and a sense of abandonment and loneliness which can indirectly lead to illness and lack of healthcare, loss of working ability, sense of inferiority and generation gap. Hence the problems of the aged people are more than that of young generation. Their image does not present a healthy picture of our society. We cannot consider ourselves educated till the rights of the old people are not well recognised by understanding them sympathetically, encouraging them to make further contribution to the society, affirm their contribution, respect them and give them love and care.

Q6. Write a debate in favour of the motion "Is peaceful coexistence the only solution to the conflicts of the modern world?"

Ans. Good morning all of you, I, Purvi, strongly favours the motion that peaceful coexistence is the only solution to the conflicts of the modern world. Nowadays, life of the people has become very fast. People want all sorts of convenience at the earliest and do not want to do more labour than expected.

They create problems for their neighbours, relatives, friends and others for their own happiness. It creates conflict amongst them. Day by day, everybody is becoming very selfish. We are building our own castle on the graves of the others.

It hits the others in many ways, either it may be emotional or economical. Generally, people have no time and sympathy for their family and friends. A long time relationship may be breaking due to a little childish matter and we are not ready for compromise even in a trivial matter.

If we respect others, live in a peaceful manner and are ready to compromise in small matters with our family, friends, relatives and neighbours then there will be no conflict with anybody. We have to develop the policy of *Live And Let Live.* Then we will never have any problem or conflict with others.

Whenever people come to us for help, we must help them and also encourage them to face their problems in a very easy manner. Then only we will get reciprocal response and all will live like our own family and the world will become brotherly for all.

Therefore, the peaceful coexistence is the only and most important solution to the conflicts of the modern world.

Biography

A biography is a true story of a person's life written by another person. Writing a biography not only requires polished and developed writing skills, but it also requires intricate the analysis of that person about whom we are going to write.

In a biographical essay, you write about the life and personality of a person who actually lived. A biographical essay should have the following characteristics:

- a real-life subject;
- a thesis statement that states a specific idea about that person's life and achievements;
- an account of one or more major events in the subject's life; and
- a description of the subject's key character traits.

Important tips to write a biographical sketch:

- Written in third person
- Significant and impressive points be included
- Special awards or recognitions be mentioned
- Be descriptive

Main points to be included:

- Name and age
- Main personality traits
- Special interests
- Education and training
- Special contribution or research, if any
- Why people like him/her

EXERCISE (Sample Biographical essays)

Q1. Write a biographical essay on George Washington.

Ans. George Washington: A Quite American Hero

When George Washington was a boy, he liked to make up his own sayings. "Lean not on anyone" was one of them. As he grew older, a strong sense of self-reliance and responsibility—to his family, his soldiers, and his country —shaped Washington's character. It gave him a quiet strength that helped him direct the course of our nation.

Washington grew up on his family's Virginia plantation. As a young man, he decided to learn a trade as a land surveyor. George Washington was only sixteen years old when he set out on his first surveying expedition. Sleeping outdoors and hunting for his food made the teenager more mature. This maturity and sense of responsibility were the perfect qualities for a military leader.

Seven years later, Washington was already a colonel commanding Virginia's colonial troops. At six feet two inches tall, he was a forceful leader who inspired his men to defend the colony's 350-mile western frontier.

In 1775, Washington's leadership was called upon one more time. The Second Continental Congress named him commander in chief of the army. From 1775 to 1783 his strength helped his soldiers overcome many problems. Washington's troops didn't have enough supplies, and many soldiers deserted. The men suffered horribly during the bitterly cold winter at Valley Forge.

After Washington's death, Thomas Jefferson said about the leader, "His integrity was most pure, his justice the most inflexible I have ever known." Without this quiet American hero, with his strong sense of responsibility, our nation's early history would have been very different.

Q2. On the basis of given hints on the biography of John F. Eaton (1886-1967), write a biographical sketch on him.

- **1886 Born in Boston, Massachusetts**
- **1911 Earned Bachelor's Degree from Massachusetts Institute of Technology in electrochemistry**
- **1911 Enrolled in Harvard Graduate School as a philosophy and psychology student**
- **1912 Went to Germany to study for his PhD examination.**
- **1915 Earned Doctorate from Harvard after his dissertation studying retroactive inhibition**
- **1915 Began teaching at Northwestern University**
- **1916 Married Susan Thompson at Boston, Massachusetts**
- **1918 Began teaching at University of California Berkeley**
- **1942 Published numerous papers about psychology**
- **1959 Received an honorary LL.D. degree from the University of California**
- **1967 Died January 19th**

Ans. John F. Eaton was an American psychologist who made significant contributions to the studies of learning and motivation. Eaton was born in Boston, Massachusetts in 1886. He remained there as he grew up and was educated in public schools. He lived in a family of "upper middle" socioeconomic status and had a father who was the president of a manufacturing company. His brother, Robert, was five years older than he was and both he and Robert were expected to go into the family business.

He and his brother decided to seek academic careers, against their family's wishes. Both went on to attend the Massachusetts Institute of Technology. Robert pursued a career in academics, ultimately becoming a world-renowned theoretical chemist and physicist, and John initially sought a bachelor's degree in electrochemistry. Eaton changed the course of his career during his senior year. He decided to become a philosopher. After graduation in 1911, he attended summer school and took a course in philosophy and psychology. He concluded that he wasn't quite smart enough for philosophy and that psychology was more to his liking.

That coming fall, Eaton enrolled at the Harvard Graduate School as a philosophy and psychology graduate student. At that time, the disciplines were a combined department. After his first year as a graduate student, he went to Germany to study for his PhD examination in German (at that time all PhD examinations were conducted in French, German, or Russian).

He received his doctorate in 1915. Eaton became an instructor at Northwestern University and taught for three years after receiving his doctoral degree. He described himself as being self-conscious, inarticulate, and fearful of his classes.

Eaton went on to become an instructor at the University of California in Berkeley in the fall of 1918 where he remained for the rest of his life. He married Susan Thompson; they had 3 children, Joseph, Susan and Grace. Read GPH books and score excellent marks.

Q3. With the help of the given clues, write a bio sketch of Subhash Chandra Bose in not more than 80-100 words:

Name: Subhash Chandra Bose; Netaji

Contribution: Immense, Freedom Fighter

Born: January 23, 1897 in Cuttack, Orissa.

Career: Civil Services

Achievements: Joined struggle; established Indian National Army

Motto: Give me blood and I will give you freedom

Setback: Retreat after the defeat of Japan and Germany.

Death: Air crash over Taipei, Taiwan (Formosa) on August 18, 1945

Ans. Subhash Chandra Bose, affectionately called Netaji, was born on January 23, 1897 in Cuttack, Orissa. He was one of the most prominent leaders of Indian freedom struggle. Deeply moved by the Jallianwala Bagh massaore, he gave up a promising career in the Civil Service to join the Freedom Movement. He founded the Indian National Army to overthrow British Empire from India. His famous motto was "Give me blood and i will give you freedom". However, defeat of Japan and Germany in the Second World War forced INA to retreat and it could not achieve its objective. Subhash Chandra Bose was reportedly killed in an air crash over Taipei, Taiwan (Formosa) on August 18, 1945.

Q4. Use the notes in the following box to write a bio-sketch of about 80 words.

VIJENDRA SINGH

- **Born October 29, 1985 in Haryana**
- **Spent early days in village - practised boxing in Bhiwani Boxing Club**
- **Picked up by coach Jagdish Singh - won national championships**
- **Participated in 2004 Athens Summer Olympics, 2006 Commonwealth Games, 2006 Asian Games**
- **2008 Beijing Olympics, defeated Carlos Gongora of Equador to win first ever Olympic medal (bronze) for Indian boxer.**

2009 awarded Rajiv Gandhi Khel Ratna Award - India's highest sporting honour.

Ans. Vijendra Singh, born on October 29, 1985, in Haryana, spent his early life in a village. He practiced boxing in Bhiwani Boxing Club. Coach Jagdish Singh became his trainer and he won many national championships. He participated in 2004 Olympics at Athens, 2006 Commonwealth and 2006 Asian Games. In 2008 Beijing Olympic, he became the first Indian boxer to win a bronze medal. In 2009, he was awarded the Rajiv Gandhi Khel Ratna Award, the highest Indian sporting honour.

Q5. Based on the following given hints, write a bio-sketch on Sachin Tendulkar in about 250 words:

ALSO KNOWN AS	:	**Sachin Ramesh Tendulkar**
FAMOUS AS	:	**Indian Cricketer**
BORN ON	:	**24 April, 1973**
AGE	:	**43 Years**
BORN IN	:	**Mumbai, India**
FATHER	:	**Ramesh Tendulkar**
MOTHER	:	**Rajni Tendulkar**
SPOUSE/PARTNER	:	**Anjali**
CHILDREN	:	**Sara and Arjun**
AWARDS	:	**Arjuna Award (1994), Wisden Cricketer of the Year (1997), Rajiv Gandhi Khel Ratna (1998), Bharat Ratna (2013)**

Ans. Sachin Tendulkar was a former Indian cricketer who made his test debut against Pakistan as a 16 year old. In his homeland, India, Sachin is more than just a popular sportsperson; he is an institution in himself. He is not just loved and respected, but revered. Called the "God of Cricket" by his fans, Sachin has ruled the game for well over two decades—a very rare feat for a sportsperson.

He was born as the youngest of four siblings to Ramesh Tendulkar, a Marathi novelist and Rajni, who worked in the insurance industry. He was named after his father's favorite music director, Sachin Dev Burman. As a young boy, he was a bully. His older brother encouraged him to play cricket in order to divert his attention from fights and got him enrolled at the academy of the coach, Ramakant Achrekar. He went to Sharadashram Vidyamandir High School at the advice of Achrekar as the school had a rich cricketing tradition. He shone as a star cricketer playing for his school and soon people were predicting that he would one day become a famous player. Along with his friend Vinod Kambli, he was involved in a record 664-run partnership in an inter school match against St. Xavier's High School in 1988.

Sachin Tendulkar embarked on his domestic first-class career in 1988 playing for Mumbai and scored a century on his very first match. He ended the season as the highest run scorer. His form faltered after the World Cup and he went through a lean phase. He retired from all forms of cricket in November 2013 and was given a very emotional farewell by his fans.

He met Anjali, a doctor, in 1990 and dated her for five years before tying the knot in 1995. The couple has two children. His son Arjun is also a budding cricketer.

Tendulkar received the Arjuna Award in 1994 for his outstanding sporting achievement, the Rajiv Gandhi Khel Ratna award in 1997, India's highest sporting honour, and the Padma Shri and Padma Vibhushan awards in 1999 and 2008, respectively, India's fourth and second highest civilian awards. After a few hours of his final match on 16 November 2013, the Prime Minister's Office announced the decision to award him the Bharat Ratna, India's highest civilian award. At 40 years of age, this famous sportsperson became the youngest ever to receive the Bharat Ratna.

Question Papers

Foundation Course in English: BEGF-101
Sample Paper-I

Note: Answer all questions.

Q1. Read the following passage and answer the questions that follow:

Roughly speaking, one may divide the history of dance into two periods: [a] from 2nd century BC to 9th century AD, and [b] 10th century to the 18th century AD. In the first period, tradition, as formulated by the Natyasastra, was strictly adhered to dance, drama and music couldn't be disassociated from one another. The available evidence suggests that the sculptors who produced the remarkable specimens of art in Sanchi, Mathura, Amravati and finally at Ellora, were well versed in the Natyasastra tradition. They or their masters have purposefully sought to depict some of the poses described in the Natyasastra especially the *Charis*. During this period, we also find that not much stylisation had been achieved because the outward bend of the thigh and knees had not become a stereotyped convention.

From the Sanskrit literature of the classical period, especially the *Kavya* and the *Nataka*, we gather that the poets and dramatists were equally well versed in the technical intricacies of dance. The tradition continues in literature beyond the 10th century AD until the writings of Rajasekhara. His Karpuramanjari is not only a dramatic tradition in Sanskrit but also a theatrical tradition. By Karpuramanjari's time, it is evident that the pure drama form had given place to the musical form. The growth of the musical is important because it was this which generally determined dance and drama forms of the regional culture in the later medieval period. Medieval temples also provide ample evidence that

sculptors had considerable technical knowledge of the art of dance. The Brihasdeswara temple in Tanjore was built in 11th century. It was here that *Karnas* were first illustrated. The Oriyan temples of Parameswara and Rajarani belonged to the period from 9th to 11th century. The *charis* (movement) and *sthanas* (position) described in the Natyasastra are elaborately depicted in the sculptures on the outer walls of these temples. Each temple portrays a variety of dance poses and movements which are accurate illustrations of either the original style or of texts which were followed by regional artists.

The dance continued to be divided into *Natya* and *Nrittya* on the one hand and to *Tandava* and *Lasya* on the other. Although, they continued to follow broad principles, many distinctive regional styles evolved and each region ultimately developed a native vocabulary. This led to the formulation of different classical styles in India. The beginning of the contemporary classical styles, whether, Bharatanatyam, Kathakali, Manipuri, Odissi, Kuchipudi or Kathak, can be traced back to the developments in the medieval period, roughly dating from 1300 to 1800 AD.

The British system of education didn't recognise the "arts" as a subject of educational curricula. The generations which went to the schools and colleges founded by the British in India in the 19th century were, thus, isolated from the art traditions of the country. The recent revival of interest in dance, developed as a sign of national pride in the glorious, indigenous art and culture helped the development and popularity of our dance styles. The storehouse was so rich and the layers of dust so weak that the sincere artist had only to dig a little to discover its essential luminosity. The digging continues and each time one delves deeper, a greater treasure is discovered.

(a) Answer the following questions:

(i) What are the two periods that dance can be divided into?

Ans. The two periods of dance are: (a) from 2nd century BC to 9th century AD, and (b) 10th century to the 18th century AD.

(ii) Why is the growth of music important to the dance form?

Ans. The growth of the music is important to the dance form because it was this which generally determined dance and drama forms of the regional culture in the later medieval period.

(iii) Give examples to prove that temples showed ample knowledge of the dance form.

Ans. The Oriyan temples of Parameswara and Rajarani belonged to the period from 9th to 11th century. The *charis* (movement) and *sthanas* (position) described in the Natyasastra are elaborately depicted in the sculptures on the outer walls of these temples. Each temple portrays a variety of dance poses and movements which are accurate illustrations of either the original style or of texts which were followed by regional artists.

(iv) What were the main divisions of the dance form?

Ans. The dance continued to be divided into *Natya* and *Nrittya* on the one hand and to *Tandava* and *Lasya* on the other. Although, they continued to follow broad principles, many distinctive regional styles evolved and each region ultimately developed a native vocabulary.

(v) What happened to the dance form during the British period?

Ans. The generations which went to the schools and colleges founded by the British in India in the 19th century were thus isolated from the art traditions of the country.

(b) Find words similar in meaning from the passage:

(i) Followed (para 1)

Ans. Adhered

(ii) Show (para 1)

Ans. Depict

(iii) Clear (para 2)

Ans. Accurate

(iv) Finally (para 3)

Ans. Ultimately

(v) Separated (para 4)

Ans. Isolated

Q2. Do as directed:

(a) It is important to work hard and show commitment. (Convert into an interrogative form of sentence)

Ans. Is it important to work hard and show commitment?

(b) If________ student is interested in becoming a leader, he should identify_________ qualities of some well-known leaders. (Insert an appropriate article in each blank)

Ans. a, the

(c) Breeding aims at_________ (increase) the yield of animals and _________ (improve) the desirable qualities of the produce. (Fill in the blanks with the correct verb forms)

Ans. increasing, improving

(d) I can never remember birthdays, I always __________ look them up. You __________ note them in your diary. (Fill in the blanks with must or have to)

Ans. have to, must

(e) I had to return early. There was no one at home to receive the guests. (Combine the two sentences using an appropriate conjunction)

Ans. because

Q3. Fill the correct form of verb in the given blanks:

(i) I like __________ (listen) to music when I am tired.

Ans. listening

(ii) While she was in that country she spent all her days __________ (sightsee)the imperial cities.

Ans. sightseeing

(iii) When I saw his performance, I couldn't help __________ (laugh).

Ans. laughing

(iv) He gave up __________ (smoke) many years ago.

Ans. smoking

(v) I hate __________ (sleep) in the dark.

Ans. sleeping

Q4. Write an essay in about 200 words on any one of the given topics:

(a) Cleanliness is a virtue to be cultivated.

Ans. Cleanliness is next to Godliness is the common proverb which promotes us to maintain cleanliness in our daily lives to get the feeling of well being. It highlights the importance of cleanliness in our lives and teaches us to follow the clean habits all through the life. Cleanliness is not only to keep ownself clean physically but it means to keep both physically and mentally clean by maintaining personal hygiene and bringing positive thoughts. Cleanliness is the way to godliness which means maintaining cleanliness and thinking good bring a person more near to the god. Being clean is very important for getting a good health and living moral life.

A clean and well dressed person indicates good personality and good character with impressive habits. Good character of a person is assessed by the clean dress and good manners. Cleanliness of body and mind improves the self-respect of any person. Cleanliness of the body, mind and soul lead towards the godliness which ultimately bring feeling of physically, mentally and socially well being person. A person needs to maintain cleanliness in daily life, need to follow a strict discipline and certain principles in the life. People who become clean are generally religious and god-fearing in nature and never feel hate or jealous to others. The book you can most believe—GPH book.

(b) Some forms of investment are sure to bring in returns.

Ans. Return on educational investment measures typically quantify the relation between investments made by students in order to participate in higher education, such as tuition payments and foregone net salaries and the increase in students' net earning power. While such measures may not always be explicitly labeled as productivity metrics, they do address the shortcomings of a previous two measures by considering a true educational output–an increase in students' net caring power.

A return on educational investment measure, in this case, would suggest an improvement in productivity, but in fact, value would merely have been shifted from the public to students. Second, return on educational investments measures focused on students' earning power disregard non-economic educational outputs. While these are obviously difficult to quantify, it would be hard to argue that they are entirely irrelevant. After all, the tremendous public subsidies spent on higher education are often justified, at least to some extent, by the expectation that students leave institutions of higher education as moral and active citizens, an educational output that is not captured by typical return on educational investment measures.

The public reaps benefits from higher educational through an increase in income tax revenues, for example, a fact that is neglected by return on educational investment measures that focus only on the student' perspective. And while tuition discounts may improve the return to students, they might also require governments to spend more on public subsidies for higher education.

(c) Movie making is a creative art.

Ans. Movie making is a creative art since it includes many aspects that include thinking creatively, like choreography and directing a scene. The quality of the film is improved with the help of special effects, costumes, decorations and of course, the performance of actors. On the other hand, the films addressed to a mass-market audience are supposed to be less aesthetic. Many critics say that art films are more serious and independent. They are intended for the definite niche market. One of the biggest arts in movie making is the script or the base storyline because the storywriter has to deeply think what people will like and appreciate. The role of dialogues cannot be overestimated, because protagonists present their deep ideas and feelings in complex and sophisticated sharp dialogues and monologues. Acting is another creative activity included in movie making. If an actor is not creative than s/he if not fit for being cast in movie. Moreover, a director is one of the most creative person included in movie making since he needs to look into the movie as an audience as well as a movie maker. We also should look that not all actors and directors get enough appreciations since they are not very much creative.

Q5. Write a dialogue of about 150 words on any one of the following situations:

As a member of the school alumni, you – Karan Thapar, are very keen to help the school in some way or the other. You meet your school Principal in this regard and have a talk with her about this issue.

Ans.

Karan Thapar : Excuse me, sir! May I come in?
Principal : Yes come in.
Karan Thapar : Good morning, sir.
Principal : Good morning, sit down.
Karan Thapar : It's alright sir.
Principal : First, sit down.
Karan Thapar : Thank you, sir.
Principal : Good to see you again in the college.
Karan Thapar : I am also feeling delighted.
Principal : So, what are you doing these days?
Karan Thapar : I am working in Municipal Corporation Department.
Principal : Good. So, why are you here?
Karan Thapar : I want to contribute in the progress my school.
Principal : I am feeling glad to hear this. How?
Karan Thapar : I want to donate some amount of money for the school's construction work.
Principal : Yes, you can do it.
Karan Thapar : Can I give you a check?
Principal : Yes, of course.
Karan Thapar : Ok, Sir.
Principal : Thank you Karan for this help.
Karan Thapar : It is my honour, Sir.

Or

You wish to go on a holiday to Kerala. Talk to your travel agent and make relevant enquiries.

Ans.

You : Hello, travel agent? Good Morning.
Agent : Good Morning! What do you want?
You : I want to ask about the famous spots in Kerala.
Agent : When you are planning to leave?
You : When my exams will get over, i.e. on March 31.
Agent : That is summer season, Right?

You	:	Yes, you are right.
Agent	:	You can visit the cool Allepy Back waters, Munnar – a hill station, Wayanand, Thekkady Cool waters, etc.
You	:	Can I collect a brochure by 12: 30 PM?
Agent	:	Why not, certainly.
You	:	Thank you, bye.
Agent	:	Bye, see you at 12 : 30 PM.

☺☺☺

Foundation Course in English: BEGF-101
Sample Paper-II

Note: Answer all questions.

Q1. **Read the following passage and answer the questions that follow:**

Vimala Devi prefers being addressed as the mother of Sarita rather than people calling Sarita, her daughter. "Who wouldn't like to be known as the mother of a brave heart girl? For me, it's immense honour to have given birth to a girl who has carved a niche for herself against all odds," says the doting mother. Media glare is not new to Vimala Devi. Her daughter's courageous fight against her physical disabilities has invited immense media attention for the family in recent times, with praises emanating from all quarters. But despite all the high profile meetings — from President of India to higher army officials and bureaucrats — Vimala still remembers the fateful day when her daughter, Sarita, was electrocuted by a 11,000 watt high tension wire. The doctors had to amputate Sarita's hands and the right leg. Though heart broken, Vimala recollected her nerves and instilled courage in Santa along with raising her other children. The most important fact was Vimala encouraged Sarita to continue with her studies and learn writing skills with the toes of her left foot.

Today, Sarita is not only self reliant and can manage all her daily activities but is also perfect in handling delicate strokes of paint and brush while being equally proficient in things like stitching, embroidery, etc. She has also twice been awarded with President's Medal 'Bal Shree', besides other awards.

"The world came down for us after Sarita's electrocution in 1995. But I mustered courage and resolved that my

daughter would not be second to anyone", said the proud mother.

"I started encouraging her to do small things like picking up a utensil for me or trying to write holding her pencil with her foot. She finally started her studies in 1999, Vimala added, "Today we feel proud when she gets various awards. She confidently appeared in the board examinations too," said the mother with a glint in her eyes.

(The Times of India, Allahabad–Monday, May 11, 2009)

(a) Answer the questions that follow:

(i) Give an appropriate title to the passage.

Ans. The title of the passage can be 'Courage against odds'.

(ii) Why does Vimala Devi prefer being addressed as the mother of Sarita rather than people calling Sarita, her daughter?

Ans. Vimala Devi prefers to be called the mother of Sarita beacuse Sarita is a brave girl whose courage has set an example for others.

(iii) Vimala Devi and her daughter have received a lot of media attention. State the reason for this attention.

Ans. Vimala Devi and her daughter have received media attention because Sarita has bravely fought against her physical disabilities and Vimala Devi has supported her whole-heartedly.

(iv) Briefly describe the tragedy in which Sarita lost most of her limbs.

Ans. Sarita was electrocuted by 11,000 watt high tension wire in 1995. As a result, doctors had to amputate her hands and sight leg.

(v) "My daughter would not be second to anyone" Vimala Devi had resolved. What efforts did she make to ensure this?

Ans. Vimala Devi did not want her daughter's disability to become a hurdle in her career. Vimala Devi taught her daughter to be courageous. She encouraged Sarita to continue her studies and learn writing skills with the toes of her left foot.

(b) Say whether the statements given below are *true* or *false*.

(i) When Sarita's arms and right leg were imputated, Vimala Devi's world crashed around her. She didn't know what to do with a helpless child.

Ans. False

(ii) The passage conveys the message that the impossible becomes possible when you live with courage and determination.

Ans. True

(c) Pick out words from paragraph 2 which mean the same as 'gathered her wits/courage'.

Ans. Recollected her nerves.

Q2. Do as directed:

(a) My favorite fruit is mango. (Change into the interrogative form).

Ans. Is mango your favourite fruit?

(b) I_________(think/thought) we should go for a walk in the evening.

Ans. think

(c) Father_________(Ring/rang) up for the ambulance when mother fell ill.

Ans. rang

(d) Rama is self-reliant. She can manage all her work. (Use a connection to join the sentences).

Ans. Rama is self-reliant who can manage all her work.

(e) The clothes are lying in a bucket. I want you to wash them. (Combine using the adjectival clause).

Ans. The clothes are lying in a bucket **that** I want you to wash.

(f) All our plans were shattered by the land grabbers. (Rewrite using active voice).

Ans. The land grabbers shattered all our plans.

(g) After______________(complete) the job assigned to him, Ravi__________(leave) the city. (Use suitable forms of the verbs).

Ans. After **completing** the job assigned to him, Ravi **left** the city.

Q3. Change the following sentences into indirect speech:

(i) 'Are you a clever boy?' the stranger asked Harry.

Ans. The stranger asked Harry if whether he was a clever boy.

(ii) 'Do you believe in God?' the little girl asked me.

Ans. The little girl asked me if I believed in God.

(iii) 'Do you know the answer?' the teacher asked the boy.

Ans. The teacher asked the boy if he knew the answer.

(iv) 'Did you come here yesterday?' the man asked the boy.

Ans. The man asked the boy if he had gone there yesterday.

(v) 'Have you ever been to a zoo?' Mr. Smith asked me.

Ans. Mr. Smith asked me if I had ever been to a zoo.

Q4. Write an essay in about 200 words on any one of the following topics:

(a) Education for All

Ans. Education is one of the most important elements for a developing nation like India, which leads to a literate population. This literate population is the backbone of any country. There is a significant relationship between education and development. It is such a ship that takes to the port of success. If we climb this ship, we can easily cross the sea of troubles and difficulties and make our life meaningful. We all know India is the second most populated country of the world after China. Its huge population is considered as a liability rather than an asset. Making investments in the form of education can make this huge population a valuable asset. Thus, it is education, which makes our living meaningful. Hence, it is very important to educate all the citizens of our country. Education facilities are very much present in urban areas. Most people in cities and towns send their children to schools. Under Sarva Shiksha Abhiyan, children under the age of 14 are provided free education. Rural areas require more attention. Thus, more schools and colleges need to be set up in the rural areas. Government should try to promote more awareness among the people about the importance of education and how it enlightens their lives. Above all, we as responsible and educated citizens of our country need to join hands and make efforts to educate our fellow countrymen and turn them into valuable assets, important for the nation's progress. Thus, it is very important for each one to realise that education is the tree, which bears the fruits of success. So, '*Each One Teach One*'.

(b) A United Country Remains Strong

Ans. As the United Nations opens its 68th General Assembly session, publics around the world continue to have a positive impression of the international organisation. Through the Better World Campaign and the United Nations Association of the United States of America, a strong, effective and fully funded United Nations has been supported. As the single largest network of American supporters of the UN, the public has been educated about the UN's work, mobilise media to communicate UN efforts, and help ensure the US government pays its dues to the UN on time and in full. Because a strong UN is the world's most effective voice for international co-operation on behalf of peace, development, global health, the environment and human rights. As just a few examples, a robust US – UN relationship means that peacekeeping efforts can continue serving American interests overseas, building security both at home and abroad. It also means that entities like the World Health Organisation can continue protecting against many of the world's most pervasive, deadly and yet often preventable diseases. And it means that the education, livelihood, and rights of women and girls around the globe can be safeguarded, creating a more equitable future for women and girls everywhere. The main aim of GPH book is to provide knowledge as well as good marks in exam.

(c) Protecting the Girl Child

Ans. The birth of a daughter in the house has been compared with the advent of Goddess Laxmi, the Goddess of wealth and Goddess Saraswati, the Goddess of Knowledge and Wisdom. No ceremony was considered to be complete in absence of women. The belief was that "No home is complete without a woman." India is a "Male Dominated Society" hence women are the receiving end. They are always will treated and ill-treated at every step. As a matter of fact, a girl child is under constant, vigil initially by the parents, then her husband and finally her own children. She is never allowed to dwell and survive freely. Worst of all she is often killed before being born while in mother's womb itself. This is fetus killing or infanticide. This is the gross downfall of humanity, morality and the human values. The situation has drastically worsened these days. Women suffer badly, infanticide have become widespread. Parents don't send daughters for schooling thinking that the daughter is going to be a kitchen confined housewife. There was, hence, decline in female literacy and her position in the society. This practice is lasting till today and the killing of foetus after the sex determination is fearlessly continued. The crime of female foetus aborting is widespread not only in rural areas but in urban areas too. In most Indian families, a daughter is viewed as a liability, and she is conditioned to believe that she is inferior and subordinate to men. Sons are idolised and celebrated. In fact, gender has been the most statistically significant determinant of malnutrition among young children and malnutrition is a frequent direct or underlying cause of death among girls below age 5. Of the 15 million baby girls born in India each year, nearly 25 per cent will not live to see their 15th birthday. It is really a pity that a girl child in a country like India is not given dignity and respect that she truly deserves. An atrocious fact is that even in urban areas it is being done to a large extent. Due to these circumstances, one day would come when there wouldn't be any female child left over. Thus, there is a great need to protect girl child.

Q5. Write a dialogue in about 150 words on any one of the following situations:

Sudhir and Ravi are waiting at a bus stop. They are discussing the poor service and problems commuters face daily while going to college or for a work. They discuss that the government must find a solution to this problem.

Ans.

Sudhir	:	Ravi, Can I ask you one question?
Ravi	:	Why not?
Sudhir	:	The government transport service is getting poor day-by-day.
Ravi	:	You are right. I am totally agree with you.
Sudhir	:	We are waiting for the bus from 45 minutes, the problem of late bus services is increasing day-by-day.

Ravi : Yeah! Everyday we have to wait for more than half-an-hour. Most of the students and employees, who are being punctual at their timings, getting late due to the delay in bus service.

Sudhir : Yes, these people are at a huge loss.

Ravi : For being punctual, the bus driver should come at time. Otherwise, only government can tackle this situation effectively by taking some steps.

Sudhir : We should go to the concerned department for this problem.

Ravi : Yes, you are right.

Or

Sunita has read a newspaper article on the good work an NGO is doing to create awareness about the environment. She tells Priya about the work being done by the organisation. Priya feels that it is a good step. She thinks that every citizen of the country must participate in this work.

Ans.

Sunita : Hi Priya, how are you?

Priya : I am fine. What about you?

Sunita : I am also fine. Have you read the newspaper?

Priya : Not yet. Is there something special in today's paper?

Sunita : Yes, an NGO is performing great works to create environmental awareness.

Priya : Very good, this is amazing. But which NGO?

Sunita : NGO Godavari. A 9-km cycle rally, tree plantation and lectures on environmental awareness were started by Godavari.

Priya : It's amazing. This kind of work will surely help in preventing our environment from degradation.

Sunita : You are right; they interact with washerwomen, asking them not to wash clothes on the river banks, and many more.

Priya : Its been great! I want to participate in this work.

Sunita	:	Yes, in fact I am also thinking the same.
Priya	:	Ok, then we both are meeting in the evening and go for the membership to participate.
Sunita	:	Yes dear, we will.

☺☺☺

"It doesn't matter who you are, where you come from. The ability to triumph begins with you – always".

-Oprah Winfrey

Foundation Course in English: BEGF-101
December-2016

Note: *Answer all the questions.*

Q1. Read the following passage and answer the questions following it:

Pongal, O Pongal, "the cry reverberates through the air and a feeling of contentment combined with the spirit of thanksgiving marks the onset of this South Indian festival called Pongal or Makar Sankranti Which is one of the most important ones in the region.

Pongal is among the best-known, and certainly one of the major festivals in the State of Tamil Nadu. The three or four-day festival which takes place in January, celebrates the harvest, and in particular the rice crop. It is said to be an ancient form of thanksgiving and is believed to come from Dravidian practices almost untouched by Aryan influences.

The first day of the celebrations is known as Bhogi Pongal which is set aside for preparations. Homes are washed and decorated. Doorways are painted with vermilion and sandalwood paste and colourful garlands of leaves and flowers adorn the outside of almost every home. The courtyard is decorated with designs in chalk powder, intricate or simple, but always beautiful. Everyone dresses in new clothes and a happy glow of anticipation surrounds the participants.

The second day, or the Surya Pongal, as it is known, is dedicated to the Sun God. It is on this day that the most important ceremony of the four-day festivities takes place. A new metal or earthen pot is filled with milk and set to boil. To this milk is added the freshly harvested rice, specially saved for the day, and sugarcane juice and

turmeric. This special rice pudding is what is known as Pongal and the festival has been named after it.

The third day of the festival is called the Mathu Pongal or the Pongal of the cattle. In the morning, the animals are herded into the village pool and bathed. They are then decorated and the rice preparations made the previous day are offered to them. This is also a time when the sister prays for the longevity and happiness of her brother. Five different kinds of rice are cooked in as many different colours, and from each of these, in a symbolic gesture, a rice ball is made and fed to five types of birds and animals.

The last day called Kunnam, is a day reserved for the outdoors. This is a day of outings, picnics and outdoor sports. Today, however, the last two days are combined, making the festival a three-day affair.

(a) Describe the feeling associated with Pongal.

Ans. The feeling associated with Pongal is a feeling of contentment combined with the spirit of thanksgiving. It is said to be an ancient form of thanksgiving and is believed to come from Dravidian practices almost untouched by Aryan influences.

(b) Which is the most important day in the four-day celebrations? Describe in your own words what happens on that day.

Ans. Surya Pongal, or the second day, is the most important day. This day is dedicated to the Sun God. A new metal or earthen pot is filled with milk and set to boil. To this milk is added the freshly harvested rice, specially saved for the day, and sugarcane juice and turmeric. This special rice pudding is known as Pongal.

(c) State whether the following statements based on the passage are true or false. Correct the false statements.

(i) Pongal has how been reduced to a three-day festival.

Ans. True

(ii) Bhogi Pongal is marked as a day of preparations.

Ans. True

(iii) On Mathu Pongal rice preparations are freshly made and offered to cattle.

Ans. False

(iv) On Kunnam, a sister prays for the longevity and happiness of her brother.

Ans. False

(v) The festival is named after the Sun God.

Ans. False

Q2. (a) Use the following words from the passage into sentences of your own:

(i) combined

Ans. Groups of teachers combined to tackle a variety of problems.

(ii) adorn

Ans. Pictures and prints adorned his walls.

(iii) anticipation

Ans. Her eyes sparkled with anticipation.

(iv) longevity

Ans. The greater longevity of women compared with men.

(v) symbolic

Ans. *The dove is symbolic of peace.*

(b) Give opposites of the following words from the passage:

(i) contentment

Ans. Discontentment

(ii) ancient

Ans. Recent

(iii) intricate

Ans. Simple

(iv) colourful

Ans. Colourless

(v) outdoor

Ans. Indoor

Q3. (a) Use the phrasal verbs given below to complete the passage:

took turns, turned out, turned off, turned down, turned on

(i) Shortly after the writer had sent her story to the magazine, she received a letter telling her that her work has been________.

Ans. turned down

(ii) Hearing this, she ________ the television set, __________ the air-conditioner, and began to write another story.

For three days she __________ between writing and eating and wrote another story which _________ to be so good that it was readily accepted.

Ans. turned off, turned on, took turns, turn out

(b) Fill in the blanks with the correct forms of the verbs given in brackets:

(i) In U.K. today, the number of working women________ (reach) nearly 50% of the working population.

Ans. has reached

(ii) In the 1950s and early 1960s, very few women ________ (go) out to work.

Ans. went

(iii) Today the situation ________ (change) a lot.

Ans. has changed

(iv) In the 1970s, new laws ________ (make) employers offer women and men equal pay and conditions.

Ans. made

(v) Several changes in the present law ________ (give) women today better conditions than before.

Ans. has given

Q4. You wish to go on a trip to an animal sanctuary and desire to stay in the midst of the forest. Ring up your travel agent and tell him the following:

- **The place you wish to go to**
- **Hotel/guest house you would like to stay in**
- **Dates of the trip**
- **Members of the family accompanying you**

Keeping all these points in mind, write a telephone conversation between you and the travel agent.

Ans. TA: Good Morning. Aries Travels. How can I help you?

Me: Good Morning. I want to go Keoladeo National Park, Rajasthan. Can you book train tickets and a room in hotel?

TA: Yes Sir, Please wait while I check.

Me: Ok. Oh and I would prefer to stay in the midst of the park.

TA: Sure Sir. How many people you want go and what is the date of your departure?

Me: Me and my wife and we would like to leave on 13th of February.

TA: Ok Sir. There are seat available in Rajdhani. May I have the details of the passengers, please?

Me: Certainly. My name is Ravi Saxena and age is 27 years and my wife is Swati Saxena and she is 24 years old.

TA: Ok. And now tell me Sir, how many days you want to stay in hotel?

Me: We would like to stay two days and three nights.

TA: There is a hotel 'Nature View' in midst of forest.

Me: That's good. Book one room.

TA: Sure sir. You can come tomorrow and collect your tickets.

Me: Thank you.

TA: You are welcome. Have a good day Sir.

Q5. Write an essay in about 200 words on any one of the following:

(a) Your personal contribution to saving and preserving the environment

Ans. A healthy environment is necessary for human and animal life to survive. Drinkable water, breathable air, and edible food are some of the resources that are necessary for life to continue. Yet at the same time, people cannot maintain a desirable standard of living without the consumption of natural resources, which causes damage to the environment. In addition, using natural resources reduces their availability, which can lead to shortages of building and manufacturing materials, food, and water. Human activity that is harmful to the environment can cause public health crises, render areas uninhabitable, and otherwise reduce standards of living on a societal or global scale. When people protect the environment, they are protecting themselves and their future as well.

Personally I do certain things to save and preserve the environment. I have planted many plants in my garden. I do watering daily in my garden. I always use compact fluorescent light bulbs. These bulbs are more expensive, but they last much longer and they save energy. I donate my old clothes or things I want to get rid of. If they are still usable, I give them to someone who needs them. When I don't use a house device, I turn it off. I save lot of money as well as electricity. We all know driving is one of the biggest causes of pollution. So I always try to walk or use my cycle. I always watch leaky faucets, which can cause a significant increase in the water bill. I always try to recover rain water. This water can be used for different purposes.

(b) A cultural festival that you particularly enjoy

Ans. India is famous for a lot of things around the world from yoga to its diversity from its travel destinations to its rich past but one thing that this country is better at doing than most is celebrating festivals, lots of festivals. A country with diverse religious and cultural backgrounds India as a nation gets to celebrate festivals of different types, tastes and colors and that is what makes festivities in this country so special to experience.

I particularly enjoy Deepawali. The festival of festivals, Deepawali is one of the most widely celebrated cultural festivals in India, marked across communities and regions.

At night, buildings are illuminated with earthen lamps, candle-sticks and electric bulbs. The city presents a bright and colourful sight. Sweets and toys shops are tastefully decorated to attract the passers-by. The bazaars and-streets are overcrowded. People buy sweets for their own families and also send them as presents to their friends and relatives. Children explode crackers. At night, Goddess Laxmi, the goddess of wealth, is worshiped in the form of earthen images and silver rupee. People believe that on this day, Goddess Laxmi enters only those houses which are neat and tidy. People offer prayers for their own health, wealth and prosperity. They let the light on so that Goddess Laxmi may find no difficulty in finding her way in and smile upon them. Deepwali celebrations are best seen in the northern parts of the country such as UP, Rajasthan, Punjab and Delhi.

(c) Caring for and respecting the elderly

Ans. Elderly people need someone who has love for them, to get proper care. People, who don't want to be with them, just mistreat and neglect them. The elderly people need someone who loves their job. They don't need a person who hates coming to work. We should give the elderly respect, privacy and good assistance.

Today, in society we see many people hate elderly. They don't given much time or respect. But we should respect an elderly needs and wants, because they don't have much time left to live. The body of an elderly needs a great amount of attention. Their dentures, body and diet is important. Their dentures and mouth need cleaning daily, to stop bacteria and germs. Their bodies need proper cleansing, because their skin is old and sensitive. The food we feed them could depend on their life. Elderly can eat certain things, but some foods they eat can affect their health.

Privacy is very important. That time is used for dressing, bathing and other personal hygiene's. The elderly can use someone is full of energy. That could help assist them. Young men and women are good for the job. They are full of energy, and all their limbs are fresh. Older people might be good for the job, because some have patients. Someone close to the elder's age could understand what is necessary, and what is not necessary. People, who don't have patients or the time, should not do this. They do half their job. Some might half clean the elder or just neglect all their needs. Bad assistance and neglect could cause an elder to die.

(d) Your favourite cuisine (food)

Ans. Among the numerous kinds of food, my favourite is pizza. It tastes really fabulous. Most kids even adults, love to eat pizza. Pizza originated from Italy and was a basic part of the Italian diet. In fact, the world's first pizzeria opened in Naples, Italy in 1738.

Through the centuries, pizzas have revolutionised from just plain dough and tomato sauce into 4-in-1 pizzas. That means you can choose four different flavours and only pay for one pizza. In other words, you don't have to order four pizzas. Isn't that amazing?

I like to have pizzas straight from the oven when they are still soft in the middle and crispy at the sides. I love to eat the crispy crust most. Furthermore, the heavenly aroma always tantalises my nostrils whenever it is freshly out from the oven. It never fails to make me feel hungry even if I have just had a heavy meal.

When I bite into the pizza, I can feel the explosion of flavours in my mouth. It is cheesy and there are mushrooms, diced vegetables, tomato sauce with deluxe cheese inside. I would never grow tired of eating pizzas. Absolutcly nothing could stop me from eating the tasty pizza till my very last breath.

☺☺☺

Foundation Course in English: BEGF-101
June-2017

Note: *Answer all the questions.*

Q1. **Read the following passage and answer the questions that follow:**

Sports Create Goodwill

by George Orwell

I am amazed when people say that sport creates goodwill between nations, and that if people of the world could meet one another at football of cricket, they would have no inclination to meet on the battlefield. In reality, however , sporting contests lead to orgies of hatred. Nearly all sports today are competitive and you do the utmost to win. Rarely are there occasions when you play simply for the fun and exercise; but as soon as the question of prestige arises, as soon as you feel that you and some larger unit will be disgraced if you lose, the most savage combative instincts are aroused. Anyone who has played in a school football match knows this. At the international level, sport is mimic warfare. But the significant thing is not the behaviour of the players, but the attitude of the spectators, and behind them the nations who seriously believe that running. jumping of kicking a ball are tests of national virtue. Even a leisurely game like cricket demanding grace rather than strength can cause ill will.

Fiercer passions prevail during football matches. At the first big football match in Spain, spectators threw bottles. tins and whatever else they could lay hands on, at the opposite side's players. As soon as strong feelings of rivalry are aroused, the nation of playing according to the rules vanishes. People want to see one side win and the other humiliated. Even when the spectators don't

intervene physically they try to influence the game by 'rattling the opposing players with boos, insults and noise. Serious sport has nothing to do with fair. It is bound up with hatred, jealousy, boastfulness, disregard of the rules and sadistic pleasure in witnessing violence. In other words, it is war minus the shooting.

(A) (a) When do sports become savagely combative?

Ans. The sports become savagely combative when the person playing sport feel that she/he and some larger unit will disgraced if she/he lose.

(b) What does the author mean by 'mimic' warfare in the context of the passage?

Ans. In the context of passage, the author refers 'mimic warfare' to the attitude of the spectators, and behind them the nations who seriously believe that running, jumping or kicking a ball are tests of national virtue.

(c) What example of violence in the field does Orwell use to prove his point

Ans. The example of violence in the field Orwell uses to prove his point is the fiercer passions prevail during the football match in Spain.

(d) How do spectators behave? Why?

Ans. Spectators behave fiercely towards the opposite side players with boos, insults and noise.

(e) What is the stand of the author in this passage? Do you agree or disagree with him? Support your answer with examples.

Ans. The author wants spectators as well as players to play sport for fun, and yes, I'm agree with him sports are for entertainment. These are not a mimic Warfare. Either we lose or win, there should not be any feeling of rivalry. It should be played simply for fun, entertainment and to exercise. For example, cricket match between India and Pakistan is considered as an international War, which should not be happened. Match (cricket) between any 2 nations should be entertained by the spectators as well as players.

(f) What does the author mean by the phrase "it is war minus the shooting"?

Ans. Sport is bound up with hatred, jealousy, boastfulness, disregard of the rules and sadistic pleasure in witnessing violence. Therefore, the author says, it is war minus the shooting.

(g) Do you agree with the title of the passage? Why/Why not? Give reasons to support your answer.

Ans. Yes, I am agree with the title of the passage because today all sports are competitive and people do the almost to him. Rarely are there occasions when people play simply for the fun and exercise; but as soon as the question of prestige arises, as soon as they feel that they and some larger unit will be disgraced if they lose, the most savage combative instincts are aroused.

(B) Make sentences with the following words:

(a) Goodwill

Ans. The scheme is dependent on good will between the two sides.

(b) Prestige

Ans. The organisation has recently gained considerable prestige.

(c) Disgraced

Ans. Mohan has disgraced the family name.

(d) Humiliated

Ans. You humiliated me in front of the whole school.

Q2. Do as directed:

(a) Fill in the blank with the appropriate linking word:

The Guptas live far from the city centre, __________ they don't get many visitors.

Ans. therefore

(b) Fill in the blanks with the appropriate forms of the verbs given in brackets:

(i) The Principal _________ (finish) his round of the school and is returning to his office.

Ans. has finished

(ii) I________ (think) of inviting all my close friends for dinner.

Ans. think

(c) Fill in the blanks with appropriate preposition:

(i) She was ________ a loss for words.

Ans. in

(ii) I have gone ________ this book carefully.

Ans. through

(iii) I am _______ a fix, please help me.

Ans. in

(d) Fill in the blanks with appropriate modals:

(i) Who________ you like to speak to?

Ans. would

(ii) you ________ clarify this with your boss first.

Ans. must

(e) Fill in the blanks with the appropriate option given in brackets:

(i) It has been raining_______ early morning. (for, from, since)

Ans. since

(ii) This is ________ street I live in. (a,an,the)

Ans. the

Q3. A friend is leaving the country to study abroad. Write a dialogue where you discuss with another friend how best to give him/her a farewell party and a present.

Ans.

Yashmi: Hi Priya! How's you?

Priya: Hello Yashmi, I'm fine, you say how's you?

Yashmi: I'm fine too. Do you know Purvi is going abroad for her higher studies?

Priya: Yes, I know. Therefore only I called you to meet and have some preparations for her farewell party and present, together.

Yashmi: Right. I was thinking the same. First of all we will have her favourite dishes in lunch.

Priya: Yeah! She is very fond of those lovely homemade cookies. Include that one also and a butter scotch cake.

Yashmi: Besides this, I'll order five movie tickets.

Priya: Five..? We are only three.

Yashmi: Two for her parents.

Priya: Ohh! That's amazing.

Yashmi: Yes. But what about her present?

Priya: We will give her a big photoframe collage having our childhood and other pictures.

Yashmi: Great. Now, we should leave and do preparations.

Priya: Yeah! Meet you in the party. Bye.

Yashmi: Bye.

Q4. Write an essay in about 200 words on any one of the following:

(a) Human beings have treated animals badly

Ans. "The greatness of a nation is judged by the way it treats its animals", said Mahatma Gandhi once as he was leading India through the country's fight for independence from the colonial rulers. Though killing or torturing humans is considered to be a crime instantaneously, many amongst us perhaps pay mute witnesses to incidences of animal cruelty happening all around us. Human beings have treated animals badly. The fact is that laws do exist in this country of ours for protection of cruelty towards animals. The main laws are The Prevention of Cruelty to Animals Act, 1960 and the Wildlife Protection Act, 1972. However, few people and even fewer policemen and lawyers are aware of these laws and in the wake of human ignorance on these laws, animals are helpless and fall victims to needs and deeds of humans.

Overloading donkeys with bricks, exhausting the elephant and camels with overriding in a mela or at a tourist spot, whipping the horse and the bullock pulling the tonga or the cart, stuffing the cages with chickens in your local meat shop, transporting cattle and livestock one on top of the other in trucks while being taken to slaughter houses or even treating your pet with neglect- not providing him food or water or chaining him in the sun, killing, maiming beating an animal and so on, each of these acts is an act of animal cruelty under either Section 11 or Section 12 of the Prevention of Cruelty to Animals Act, 1960 (PCA Act, 1960).

Animals are also living beings, then why humans ill-treat them. There is no right to mistreat that dumb beings. We should behave with them properly.

(b) Games you played in childhood

Ans. I spent my childhood in an urban area that was full of natural graces and wonders. The vast green fields, rivers, hill, the blue sky and the playmates of my childhoods were my best part of my lively and magical childhood. I used to play lots of games in my childhood and among them blind-man's-buff was one of my most favourite.

This game required minimum 4-5 kids to play. Initially, one kid would be selected to be blindfolded and his/her eyes would be tied up so that s/he can't see anything. A big circle would be drawn and no one is allowed to go out of this circle. The blind folded kid would try to catch someone while others would try to protect themselves but would not be able to go outside the circle. If the blindfolded kid can touch someone and can say his/her name, the blindfolded kid would get free and the other one who was touched would be blindfolded this time. This was the basic rule of the game and we used to play this game according to this rule.

I mostly played this game with my cousins, neighbouring kids and classmates. I was then around 4-5 years old and the other kids whom I used to play with were around the same age. This was a game I played in my childhood and I enjoyed this game as a kid very much.

(c) The festival you enjoy

Ans. Refer to December-2016, Q.No.- 5 (b)

(d) Adventure sports that you may have participated in

Ans. The adventure sport that I had participated was mountain climbing, which was an exhilarating, rewarding and life changing experience for me. Although climbing a mountain can be one of life's greatest accomplishments, it is more than panoramic views, the satisfaction of reaching the summit, or a true wilderness experience. Mountain climbing is a great challenge that involves risk, danger and hardship. Mountain climbing is not for everyone, although some can find it irresistible, as well as frustrating and sometimes even deadly. There are qualities to mountain climbing that bring inspiration and joy in a pursuit that is more than a pastime or a sport; it is a passion and sometimes a compulsion. A distant view of a mountain may speak of adventure, but the mountains only hint at the joys and hardship that await the climber. Climbing a mountain takes much preparation, knowledge and skill. The mountain climbing environment is indifferent to human needs and not everyone is willing to pay the price or able to survive the hardship in exchange for the physical and spiritual rewards the experience can provide.

There are many different types of climbing. There is hiking on the lower elevation mountains, traditional climbing on the moderate elevation mountains, scaling rock walls of mountains, climbing through snow and ice, climbing glaciers and alpine trekking. Hiking includes various terrains such as rock, dirt, brush, talus and scree, which is loose rock fragments from the crumbling mountain, snow and streams. As the elevation gets higher, it becomes necessary to use additional equipment for the climb such as an ax, ropes, a harness, runners and carabiners. When climbing glaciers or climbing in the ice and snow, it becomes necessary to use crampons and gaiters.

Foundation Course in English: BEGF-101
December-2017

Note: *Answer all the questions.*

Q1. Read the passage given below and answer the questions that follow:

The dictionary defines luck as good fortune, events in life that cannot be controlled and seem to happen by chance. There are often too many people who explain their failures and ascribe them to ill luck. "Lady luck did not favour me." "I ran into major bad luck." "I am one of the unlucky ones around not to have landed a promotion" and several other statements like that. The idea in a defeatist mind is merely to pin the blame on bad luck instead of working out the real reasons behind the failure. Luck is a very small component of any outcome and has little say. But, on the contrary, the factor has been wrongly understood as a miraculous property that will bring about success against all odds, including indolence and apathy.

The prerequisites of success are actually sound vision, diligence,being passionate about goals, striving to build lasting relationships, enduring efforts at self-improvement, self-discipline and taking risks without them being quixotic. Beyond that, all that remains is luck. Edison had defined genius thus : one percent inspiration, 99 percent perspiration. It is now a cliché but there is nothing else that captures the spirit of the theme as this does. People who seemingly are the world's envy and possess much of the world's wealth, were not merely lucky. These are the people who have worked hard at arriving where they are currently and have kept it that way. The successful people work hard to put themselves into a position where good fortune can find them.

(a) Read the following statements and state which are *true* and which are *false:*

(i) Good luck is something that does not happen by chance.

(ii) **Most of the people do not blame their luck for their failure.**

(iii) **Blaming one's luck is the product of a defeatist mind.**

(iv) **According to the writer, luck does not play much part in one's success.**

(v) **Hard work is not a prerequisite of success.**

(b) **Answer the questions given below:**

(i) **What is the writer's perspective about luck?**

(ii) **Why does the writer not sympathise with people who face failures in their lives?**

(iii) **Explain the phrase, 'a defeatist mind'.**

(iv) **Mention any four requirements of success.**

(v) **Give a suitable title to the passage.**

Q2. Do as directed:

(a) **"Mukesh has cooked tasty food today," said Shweta. (Change into indirect speech)**

(b) **The doctor examined the patient. (Change the voice)**

(c) **As soon as I reached the school gate, the bell rang. (Rewrite the sentence using "No sooner ...")**

(d) **Ishaan is arriving ________ Chicago tomorrow________ 2 o'clock. (Use appropriate prepositions)**

(e) **I have ________ account in _______ State Bank of India. (Use appropriate articles)**

Q3. Correct the following sentences:

(a) **Animals had tails for different reasons.**

(b) **The tails serves them as a flyswat, a rudder and even to defend themselves.**

(c) **Crocodiles use there tails to protect themselves.**

(d) **Monkeys, at time, use their long tails to wind around branches to climb up and down the trees.**

(e) **A hippopotamus use its tail in a very interesting way.**

Q4. Write an essay in about 200 words on any one of the following topics:

(a) **The importance of water conservation**

(b) **Why I like the place where I live**

(c) **Walking is the best exercise**

(d) **The importance of being smartly dressed**

Q5. Write a dialogue in about 150 words on *one* of the following situations:

(a) **Arjun listens to music while studying. His mother says that music disturbs and does not let one concentrate on studies.**

(b) **Pooja wastes a lot of time on messaging through the mobile. Her father says that she should limit her messaging time to just one hour a day.**

Foundation Course in English: BEGF-101
June-2018

Note: *Answer all the questions.*

Q1. Read the passage given below and answer the questions that follow:

When William the Conqueror landed in England, the first thing he did was to stumble and fall down. A gasp went through his army at this omen of disaster. William, however, rose to his feet, crying: "I am so determined to conquer this land that, behold, I've seized it with both my hands!" At that moment a great shout of renewed confidence went up from every throat. William's army went on that day to win one of history's greatest battles. Failure comes only when we accept it as failure. Instead of telling ourselves, "I've failed!," we should say, "I haven't yet succeeded." A military leader would be foolish to forge ahead in the mere hope that his soldiers will follow him. He must address them; stir them to have faith in him and in his enterprise. So must we do with our disorderly subconscious mind. It isn't enough to ignore its bad habits and conflicting messages. We must inspire it to link hands with our conscious resolutions. A strong affirmation of will has the power to do this.

Troops whose grievances go unaddressed may eventually become rebellious. So it is with the subconscious. We can't afford to ignore it. Nor do we need to be led by it, helplessly. We can command it if we face it squarely and honestly.

A General doesn't need to know each and every soldier in his ranks. What he must do is put out the kind of energy they'll respect and obey. The same thing is true for us in our relation to the subconscious mind.

(a) Read the following statements and say which statements are True and which are False:

(i) William the Conqueror fell down from grace.

(ii) People shouted when William fell down.

(iii) William's army won the battle that day.

(iv) It is not necessary to motivate the soldiers to follow their leader.

(v) Troops become rebellious when their grievances are not attended to.

Ans. (i) True, (ii) False, (iii) True, (iv) False, (v) True

(b) Answer the following questions:

(i) Why did the army gasp at the fall of William the Conqueror?

Ans. The army gasped at the fall of William the conqueror because they don't want to see their leader to fall like that and to feel hurt. They want their leader to be confident and with leadership skills.

They gasped as they were shocked by the fallen down of their leader.

(ii) What was the factor which led William's army to success?

Ans. The main factor was mainly the leadership skills of William which help in motivating and boosting the troops with full confidence.

William changed the drastic scene of his fall down to a motivating one, which helps to fill up the troops with confidence and a desire of win.

(iii) "Failure comes only when we accept it as failure." Discuss the statement in light of the passage.

Ans. The statement, "Failure comes only when we accept, it as failure" is true. When you face any failure, then face it and try to take it as a challenge. Like in the sturing of passage, William changed the drastic scene of his fall down to boosting his troops with confidence. If you accept your failure then it will surely let you down. But if you face and try to change it, then you will win it.

(iv) What should a military leader do to make his soldiers follow him?

Ans. Military leader try to lead his soldiers and try to motivate them time to time and make them to win the war which helps in interesting results.

They should pass good leadership skills then only they will get positive out of their soldiers.

(v) Give a suitable title to the passage.

Ans. Anatomy of success and failure.

Q2. Do as directed:

(a) "Ishaan is going to school from tomorrow," said Ashok. (Change into indirect speech)

Ans. Ashok said that Ishaan was going to school from the next day.

(b) Utensils are cleaned by Rajvati. (Change the voice)

Ans. Rajvati cleans the utensils.

(c) He hired a taxi. He was getting late. (Combine the above sentences by using an appropriate linker)

Ans. He hired a taxi because he was getting late.

(d) Some people believe that Holi gets its name ______ Holika who was the sister ____ the demon king Hiranyakashyap. (Use appropriate prepositions to fill in the blanks)

Ans. from, of

(e) Holi is ____ very old Indian festival celebrated on full moon day in ___ month of March. (Use appropriate articles) (Use opppropriate prepositions to fill in the blanks)

Ans. a, the

Q3. Correct the following sentences:

(a) I prefer tea than coffee.

Ans. I prefer tea over coffee.

(b) Pooja is not knowing when her exams are commencing.

Ans. Pooja does not know when her exams are commencing.

(c) Neither my father nor my mother were present at the party.

Ans. Neither my father nor my mother was present at the party.

(d) Police has not caught the thief as now.

Ans. Police has not caught the thief yet.

(e) If you will not pay the money, the contract will be cancelled.

Ans. If you will not pay the money, then the contract will be cancelled.

Q4. Write an essay in about 200 words on any one of the following topics:

(a) Importance of effective communication skills

Ans. Communication is a part and parcel of everyone's life. All individuals need to communicate to share their knowledge and information with others. However, the degree of its effectiveness depends upon everyone's personal communication skills. The better are our communication skills, the better a person understands us.

The purposes of communication could be many but the most important part is to understand how to communicate effectively.

Communication is a two way process and therefore requires complete understanding among the communicators. This requirement can be fulfilled with effective communication skills.

The general forms of communication are oral or verbal communication and written communication. Effective communication skills are now an essential professional requirement and are considered vital to convert your performance into success. Whether it be your professional life or your personal discourses, communication plays an indispensable role in all walks of life.

In any form of business, communication is an internal as well as an external affair. The success of the business rests upon communication. To be a good communicator, we need to be a good speaker and a patient listener too.

The factors that play a vital role in effective oral communication skills are voice, body language, appearance and gestures made by the communicator. Not only the content but also the way the content is transferred is important.

Further, written communication also needs to be very accurate to make sure that message is understood correctly. The factors that should be considered in written communication are completeness, briefness, proper selection of words and clarity of thoughts to make the message easy to understand.

Effective communication skills also boost the moral of the individual and motivate him to work better. These skills not only make him a good professional but also promise to provide him a growth oriented career.

(b) The film that I have watched more than once

Ans. The movie I saw about half a dozen times or more in theater or on TV is Avatar. Even last Sunday, I saw it with my family. I saw it in 3D every time except one, when I didn't get ticket of this 3D film. This is one of the most entertaining and best film I ever watched. It is a 2009 American epic science fiction film directed, written, produced and co-edited by James Cameron at al. The reason I watched this movie many times is just because the film employs a new generation of special effects, and it is simply a sensational entertainment too. The film has the most vivid and convincing creation of a fantasy world, which ever seen in the history of moving pictures. It was amazing and simultaneously, fascinating me to watch this movie in 3D with the traditional film elements such as story, character, etc. Therefore, I enjoyed watching this movie very much.

(c) The importance of a healthy diet

Ans. A healthy diet is a diet that helps to maintain or improve overall health. A healthy diet provides the body with essential nutrition: fluid, macronutrients, micronutrients and adequate calories.

The requirements for a healthy diet can be met from a variety of plant-based and animal-based foods, although a non-animal source of vitamin B_{12} is needed for those following a vegan diet. A healthy diet supports energy needs and provides for human nutrition without exposure to toxicity or excessive weight gain from consuming more calories than the body requires. A healthy diet, in addition to exercise, may lower disease risks, such as obesity, heart disease, type 2 diabetes, hypertension and cancer.

Various nutrition guides are published by medical and governmental institutions to educate individuals on what they should eat to promote health. Nutrition facts labels are also mandatory in some countries to allow consumers to choose between foods based on the components relevant to health.

The idea of dietary therapy (using dietary choices to maintain health and improve poor health) is quite old and thus has both modern scientific forms (medical nutrition therapy) and prescientific forms (such as dietary therapy in traditional Chinese medicine).

A healthy diet contains a variety of different foods so that the body can get the nutrients it requires to function properly.

(d) Advantages and disadvantages of the joint family system.

Ans. Refer to Chapter-3, Q.No.-5

Q5. Write a dialogue in about 150 words on one of the following situations:

(a) Shweta wants to go to the mall, whereas Vicky wants to go to the local market.

Ans. Vicky: Hello! Shweta.

Shweta: Hello! Vicky. It is a beautiful day. Isn't it?

Vicky: Oh! yes, it is very pleasant. That's because it rained hard all last night. By the way, where are you going?

Shweta: I'm going to the mall to purchase some casual clothes. I always do shopping from there. Where do you do your shopping?

Vicky: I'm not particular about. I buy things from any shop nearby. And, therefore, I came to the local market to buy some grocery items and a saree for my mother.

Shweta: That's great! But there are a lot of advantages at the mall. You can walk around, choose your things leisurely and enjoy your shopping. All things are displayed on shelves with their prices marked. All new products can be seen at a glance. It is a self-service store.

Vicky: Do you do a lot of shopping?

Shweta: Yes, I do. Mine is a large family and thus naturally, I have to buy a lot of things.

Vicky: But mine is very small and I don't have much to buy.

Shweta: Even then, it is better to buy from a mall. They sell only first quality things. All the items are packed, sealed, labeled and displayed.

Vicky: Do you go to the mall often?

Shweta: It is not far from my house. I go there at least twice a week. I usually go with my mother. Today she is very busy and couldn't come with me. You can join me, if you want.

Vicky: Ok, but can I find some grocery items there?

Shweta: Yes. A mall has all daily purpose things. Even you can bought a saree for your mother too.

(b) Manu wants to go to a foreign country for a vacation while his wife Anu wants to go to Kerala.

Ans. Same as above Question.

Foundation Course in English: BEGF-101
December-2018

Note: *Answer all the questions.*

Q1. **Read the passage given below and answer the questions that follow:**

Behold every parent's worst nightmare: the six-year-old TV addict. He watches in the morning before he goes off to school, plops himself in front of the set as soon as he gets home in the afternoon and gets another does to calm down before he goes to bed at night. His teacher says he is restless and combative in class. What's more, he's having trouble reading.

Does this creature really exist or is he just a paranoid video-age vision? The question is gaining urgency as the medium barges ever more aggressively into children's lives. Except for school and the family, no institution plays a bigger role in shaping American children. Today, TV is being blamed for just about everything: from a decrease in attention span to an increase in street crime. Cartoons are attacked for their violence and sitcoms for their foul language. Critics and consumer groups like Action for Children's Television have kept up a steady drumbeat of calls for reform.

Some efforts are being made towards these problems by trying to limit commercial time in children's programming and making it compulsory for channels to air more educational kids' fare. Yet the central issue remains: the fact that children watch a ton of TV. Almost daily, parents grapple with a fundamental, overriding question: What is TV viewing doing to kids, and what can be done about it? Guided by TV, today's kids are exposed to more information about the world around them than any other generation in history. But are they smarter for it? Many teachers and psychologists argue that TV is

largely to blame for the decline in reading skills and school performance.

(a) (i) Give an appropriate title to the passage.

(ii) What steps are being taken to solve the problem of negative impact of TV viewing on children?

(iii) How, according to the author, is children's school performance affected by exposure to TV?

(iv) What does the author mean when he/she says, "The question is gaining urgency as the medium barges ever more aggressively into children's lives"?

(v) On the basis of your reading of the passage, what according to you, is the most important question for which an answer needs to be found?

(b) State whether the statements given below are true or false:

(i) TV plays a bigger role than school and the family in shaping American children.

(ii) From the passage it is not clear whether children who get a lot of information from TV become smarter and more intelligent.

(c) Pick out a word/phrase from the passage which means the same as - 'enter by force'.

Q2. Do as directed:

(a) The book of poems is lying on the table. It was written by the famous poet 'William Blake'. (Combine the above sentences into one sentence using ... 'which'...)

(b) I reached the market. I came to know that it .... (close). (Write the correct verb form)

(c) Scientists say that several earthquakes occur in Delhi every year. (Rewrite as an interrogative sentence)

(d) My book will be published in 2018 by ABC Publishers. (Change the voice)

(e) "Do not forget to carry your umbrella. It is raining heavily," said mother to Anjali. (Rewrite using indirect speech)

(f) Harsh ran to his friends. He told them he had won a prize for his artwork. (Join using a conjunction)

Q3. Correct the following sentences. There could be more than one mistake in each sentence.

(a) I wants to go to my friend house.

(b) Do you remembers the day you got your result?

(c) All of us should learn to becoming independent thinkers.

(d) Sunita told her friend that she feeling restless after a heavy meals.

(e) Each speaker was allowing five minutes to speak, after which other speakers was allowed to ask questions.

Q4. Write an essay in about 200 words on any one of the following topics:

(a) A day in the life of a college student

(b) The importance of healthy eating

(c) Life in the 21st century

(d) An adventurous holiday

Q5. Write a dialogue in about 150 words on any one of the following situations:

As part of your college studies you took up a project on 'leisure activities of youth'. You were asked to conduct a survey of 5 colonies in your neighbourhood to find out about hobbies of young people and to find out how they spend their leisure hours. Your friend Surabhi asks you questions about your project. She wants to know who you interviewed, how you did your survey and the result of the survey.

Or

A well-known hospital in your town has started a regular health-check camp for the economically weaker sections of society, free of cost. In 6 months' time the project has received tremendous response-especially from old people and young mothers. You are Anil, a doctor working at the hospital. A newspaper journalist wants to know details about the project and how many people have benefitted from it.

Foundation Course in English: BEGF-101
June-2019

Note: *Answer all the questions.*

Q1. Read the passage given below and answer the questions that follow:

Many psychologists lay great emphasis on the process of socialisation and its role in moral development. In Sigmund Freud's conception, for example, the young child's inappropriate impulses and desires can be controlled only through the process of socialisation. Here the word 'socialisation' refers to the way peers, adults and society in general, condition the child to conform to their rules. But, as you can imagine, things are nowhere near as simple as 'taking in the external rules and acting according to them'. Young people, if and when they attend to the moral values expressed by adults, do not always accept them! Hostility, anger and rejection are common, even when a young person is outwardly obedient.

What does research tell us that could help us in our work? Although most studies involve parents and their children, the same principles apply to any adult interacting with young people. Psychologists Joan Grusec and Jacqueline Goodnow, for example, have focused on discipline encounters, trying to discover what works and what does not. They have discovered several factors that influence interalisation, having in do with the situation, the adults's characteristics, and the student's temperament. For example, adult statements, may sometimes be irrelevant, such as when they say, "This is not the first time you've done this' or 'And another thing you always do is.....'. Whatever the situation, ultimately two things must happen for a value to be internalised:

(a) The child's perception of the adult's viewpoint must be accurate and (b) she must accept, not reject it.

(a) (i) Give an appropriate title to the passage,

Ans. Process of socialisation.

(ii) What do you understand by socialisation?

Ans. The word 'socialisation' refers to the way peers, adults and society in general, condition the child to conform to their rules.

(iii) Why is socialisation essential in the development of children?

Ans. The young child's inappropriate impulses and desires can be controlled only through the process of socialisation.

(iv) How does one know that a child, who seems to be obedient, does not actually accept the moral ideas expressed by adults?

Ans. Young people, if and when they attend to the moral values expressed by adults, do not always accept them! Hostility, anger and rejection are common, even when a young person is outwardly obedient.

(v) What factors are important in the socialisation process, according to psychologists Joan Grusec and Jacqueline Goodnow's studies?

Ans. They have discovered several factors that influence interalisation, having in do with the situation, the adult's characteristics, and the student's temperament.

(b) Say whether the statement given below are True Or False:

(i) 'Socialisation' is the process whereby the child learns through interaction with adults, teachers and other children to follow rules.

Ans. True

(ii) When a child shows that she is the following moral values taught by adults its means she accepts them.

Ans. True

(c) Pick out a word/phrase from the passage which means the same as —'a person's nature which permanently affects their behaviour'.

Ans. Temperament

Q2. Do as directed:

(a) The book of mystery stories is lying on the table. (Change into an interrogative sentence)

Ans. Is the book of mystery stories lying on the table.

(b) I reached home. I found a big lock on the door.

(Combine the above sentences into one sentence using .... 'when')

Ans. When I reached home, I found a big lock on the door.

(c) Rati .... (compose) a new song for the college festival.

(Write the correct verb form)

Ans. Composed

(d) The traffic policemen stopped the truck for over speeding. (Change the voice)

Ans. The truck is stopped by the traffic policemen for over speeding.

(e) "Do not forget to carry your project report. It is kept on your writing table", said mother to Anuj.

Rewrite in the indirect speech)

Ans. Mother told Anuj not to forget to carry his project report kept on his writing table.

(f) There was a lot of noise in the auditorium.

The musicians waited for the audience to become quiet so they could begin their concert.

(Combine the two sentences)

Ans. There was a lot of noise in the auditorium, so, the musicians had to wait for the audience to become quiet so they could begin their concert.

Q3. Correct the following sentences. There could be more than one mistake in each sentence:

(a) Cartoon teach us to laugh at ourselves.

Ans. Cartoon teaches us to laugh at ourselves.

(b) The new pilot were extremely nervous and his voice was trembled.

Ans. A new pilot was extremely nervous and his voice was trembled.

(c) The lady looked at me very strange and starts laughing loudly.

Ans. The lady looked at me very strangely and starts laughing loudly.

(d) Mahesh with his friends want to go for Shimla during their summer break.

Ans. Mahesh wants to go to Shimla with his friends during their summer break.

(e) Nobody could told how the ships disappeared during their voyage.

Ans. Nobody could tell how the ships disappeared during their voyage.

Q4. Write a paragraph of about 200 words on any one of the following topics:

(a) My visit to a place of historical importance

Ans. India is studded with many places of historical importance which tell us the past history of our country. Among them, Agra occupies an important position. The famous Taj Mahal has immortalised Agra. It was my long cherish dream to visit the Taj Mahal and it was fulfilled last year when the school organised an excursion to Agra.

The Taj Mahal is the queen of all buildings in the world and it is one of the wonders of the world. This great piece of art and architecture was built in the 17th century by the Mughal Emperor Shah Jahan in memory of his beloved wife Mumtaz Mahal. This historical monument is a symbol of love between Shah Jahan and Mumtaz Mahal. It is situated on the bank of the river Jamuna.

All of us were very anxious to have a look at the Taj Mahal and when we reached it we were spell- bounded by its beauty. It is a wonderful monument and it looks like a creation from the dream world. It is a dream in marble, a poem in marble and a symphony in stone. The Taj in its picturesque surroundings presented a wonderful sight. We went into beautiful and peaceful garden.

On the either side of the main pathway, there are cypress tree which are evergreen. There are beautiful garden and flower-bearing around this great building. In the middle of the pathway there are rows of fountains.

The Taj stands on raised platform. There are four lofty minars on all the four corners of this platform. In the centre stands the mausoleum. It is built of snow- white marble. We saw two graves there. One is in the centre and the other is just near it. The grave in the centre contains the mortal remains of Mumtaz Mahal and the other, those of Shah Jahan. Verses from the Holy Quran are written on them. Precious stones of different colours have been fixed on the walls. The beauty of this portion cannot be described by words. At the back of the Taj Mahal runs the river Jamuna. The reflection of the white Taj Mahal is still water of the Jamuna on a moon-lit proves a wonder sight. We visited each and every part of this superb piece of art and were deeply impressed by it as a work of profound skill and art. It is said that thousands of artists and workers worked for many years to build this monument at a cost of several crores of rupees.

The gleaming white marble, the black shadows, the dim light, the silence and the sweet-scented gardens on the moon-lit night made the Taj a sight never to be forgotten. The Taj Mahal has withstood of severities of time and weather through several centuries. It has still preserved its ancient and glory and splendor. Poets have praised it.

Common people adore it. Lovers of art from all over the world visit it. It is a sign of undying love. It is a symbol of culture and the pride of the architects. The visit of a foreign dignitary is not complete till he visits Agra to see the Taj Mahal. No tourists can afford to miss this beauty spot on earth. The Taj is a thing of beauty which words fail to describe. It was indeed my luck to visit this beautiful place. The memory of this visit will always remain fresh in my mind.

(b) Caring for the disabled

Ans. Just as no one person is like another, no person with a disability is the same as another, even if he or she has the same disability. A disability is a functional limitation that may interfere with a person's ability to walk, hear, talk, see, think, and learn but does not affect each person in the same way. In addition, some people may have multiple disabilities in varying degrees.

When speaking or associating with a person with a disability:

- Smile; be yourself.
- Focus on the person's capabilities. Don't be so focused on a person's disability that you don't see the person.
- Talk to the person with a disability—or with the person's caregivers, when appropriate—about how you can include the person in activities and what he or she is comfortable with.
- Be respectful. Offer assistance if asked or if the need is obvious. Do not move wheelchairs or other mobility aids without permission from the owner.
- Speak slowly and directly when talking to a person with a hearing impairment. Do not assume a person with a hearing or speech impairment has an intellectual disability.
- Be patient.
- Be considerate of that person's feelings when talking to others. Would you want what you are about to say being said about you?

Remember to speak softly unless the person has a hearing impairment. Speaking loudly does not improve understanding.

Terms considered appropriate often differ from group to group and from generation to generation. A good rule of thumb is to consider the person before the disability. For example, a person with a disability is not a "disabled woman" or "handicapped man." Nor is Sister Smith "disabled" or "handicapped." Rather, refer to the person first and, if needed, the disability second: "Sister Smith" or "Sister Smith has a disability"

Be patient as other members learn about disability issues and overcome misperceptions. Realize that most members of the Church are open to guidance on how to help and include those with disabilities. Recognize that others who care may also be prompted on how to help. The Holy Ghost can help family, teachers, and leaders reach out and be helpful.

(c) Role of youth in electing a government that is corruption free

Ans. "Youth is a more fluid category then a fixed age-group. "Youth is often indicated as a person between the age where he/she leaves compulsory education, and the age at which he/she finds his/here first employment by different countries/agencies and by some agency indifferent contexts."

Youth symbolises energy, and politics is about right, representation, justice, and change. Thus the synthesis of youth and politics is about hope, revolutionary ideas, transformations and a brighter future. The idea that a large proportion of youth in the population will lead to a greater role for youth in politics is based on the assumption that they constitute a distinct politicalconstituency- a section of population with distinct political preferences, attitudes and voting patterns.

Youth is hope of the future of the country. However only youths of character, intelligence, 'self sacrifices' and obedience can shape the destiny of the nation. Youth devoid of energy, suffering from inertia and dullness, without mental vigor and courage are bound to lead us nowhere. Youth meekly constituted in mind and body breeds only the generation of cripples. For this reason sometimes a great despair and despondency comes in the minds of those who rest the hope of future upon the shoulders of the young. Young and educated people from the backbone of a growing nation. Since they are young, their minds are fresh and innovative. They are more prone to take risk and accept challenges. They are less vulnerable to corruption. Therefore their work is inevitable for the growth of a nation. Their courage can contribute to the development of the society.

Youth politicians, young journalists, young students and leaders of the national polity must work as a role model for general public and revolutionise the whole system and fulfill Kalam's vision-2020. The role and relation of politics with youth is to be taken in constructive perspective, they are hope of corruption free society who will promote morality, effectively and honestly. Only positive approach will make sure that Indian youth will lighten the country which is under the dark clouds of bribery. It is the best medicine to cure the disease of future but also the key factor in the present scenario who will give us a systematic and full solution of the problem.

The role of youth is of most importance in today's time. It has underplayed itself in field of politics. Youth should become aspiring entrepreneurs rather than mere workers. Youth participation is important because youth are the country's power. Youth recognise problems and can solve them too. Youth are strong force in social movements.

Youth is one of the greatest assets that any nation can have. Not only are they legitimately regarded as the future leaders, they are potentially and actually the greatest investment for a country's development. They serve as a good measure of the extent to which a country can reproduce as well as sustain itself. The extent of their vitality, responsible conduct, and roles in society is positively correlated with the development of their country. Youth is a dynamic of any country that can do great good when used in a right way. They are the powerhouse and store house of infinite energy which brings laurels to the country.

India Youth as a category is extremely complex and difficult to ascertain as a time when there is no general consensus yet amongst on its minimal definition. The category or the social group referred to as 'India youth' many look simple as most of us identify this category by a certain age group, but it is not as simple as a one may think. The importance of youth as a demographic category due to its sheer size in the subcontinent is undeniable. The government of India had its own age bracket of 13-35 years as a definition of youth in different national youth policies. However in the most recent National youth Policy (2014) the age bracket was shrunk to 15 to 29 year, it was 16 to 30 according to National youth Policy (2012). Researchers who conducted studies on India youth have looked at a different age bracket- up around 25 years. The difference of opinion about youth is not only limited to different age groups, but also other demographic factors, such as location, gender, level of educational attainment, caste, region, religion, and economic class of the family to which the youth belong; all these throw up challenges in defining the category referred to as India youth.

(d) Advantages and disadvantages of living in a big city

Ans. Nowadays, large cities are becoming more and more inhabited. The majority of the population prefer living in a big town mainly because of the great advantages it has compared to living in the countryside. However, what are the benefits of this situation, and what are the drawbacks? In this essay, I will explore the pros and cons of living in alarge city and try to draw some conclusions.

Let's start looking at the advantages. One of the main positives of a big town is the large amount of shops available in every corner of the city. What I mean by this is that whenever you live, there are some useful stores like supermarkets, banks, tobacconists and clothing stores where you can easily buy everything you need without going to the city center. Secondly, living in a big town is a big challenge for evening parties. In London, for example, there are so many things to do in the evenings like going to the cinema, to the pub or to the park during the summer period.

Turning to the other side of the argument, traffic could be one of the major disadvantages of living in a big city. Many people take the car everyday and it has also been proved that the majority of the families have at least two cars. This means that you have to deal with rush-hour traffic on your way to work and on your way back. In addition, in a big town there is consequently a lot of smog and this can really affect people's health.

To sum up, living in a big city has great advantages but also some significant negatives.You have to weigh up to the pros of enjoying evenings' nights outside and the availability of many shops and the cons of cope with smog and traffic issues. Personally, I believe that the benefits of enjoying the city-life and the comfort of having shops at every corner, eventually overweigh the negatives.

Q5. Write a dialogue in about 200 words on any of the following topics:

As part of your college studies you took up a project on 'reading habits of youth'. You were asked to conduct a survey of some colonies in your neighbourhood to find out about reading habits of young people and how they spent their leisure hours. A newspaper reporter interviews you and asks you questions about your survey.

Ans. Newspaper reporter: Hello mam, today

I want to take some information about your survey.

I : Of course, I will share my experiences during survey.

Reporter: As I know that your survey is about "reading habits of youth". Is it interesting topic for you.

I : Yes, it is very interesting topic for me. As we know that reading is very important thing for our career growth and development.

Reading books will help you to learn new words and demonstrate different ways in which you can use them in your daily life.

Reporter: What were the answers of people about reading habits?

I : Some people said that reading is positive for us. We can learn many things from reading.

But Some people said that we get bored while reading.

Reporter: O.K

That's great you have done nice job.

Nice to meet you.

I : Same here

Or

You are Swati, working for a well-known organisation that has taken up welfare work for girls living in villages. It has started providing free education to the girls in a new residential school for them. Alia, a newspaper reporter wants to know about the project and asks you questions.

Ans. Alia: Hello Swati, I am very excited to know about your projects "free education to the girls."

I want to take some information about it.

Swati: Sure Alia, you know that I am working with an organisation which has taken up welfare work for girls living in villages.

Now we have started providing free education to the girls in a new residential school.

Girl education is very important for our society.

If every girl gets good education then society will develop.

Some girls can't afford expenses. Therefore, we provide free education to them.

Alia: Mam, you are doing awesome contribution for our society glad to meet you.

Swati: Same here

Foundation Course in English: BEGF-101
December-2019

Note: *Answer all questions.*

Q1. Read the passage given below and answer the questions that follow:

In Delhi, where Preeti Singh grew up, girls weren't allowed to take off their saris to learn how to swim. Preeti said, "My older brother learned to swim when he was 16. I was amazed when I saw him diving into the water. I was only 6 but I used to wish I could do it too."

In fact Preeti waited for 28 years until she was 34 and started living in England before she finally decided to take swimming lessons. At first, she was shy and scared about appearing in a one piece swimming costume. "And I didn't realise that I would have to put my whole face into the water. Although I knew I shouldn't breathe inside water; I used to forget and swallow a lot of water. After the third lesson I was fed up and I wanted to stop."

But now after 15 lessons from her 'very patient teacher', Preeti feels as if she has made progress. She added, "Now I feel a lot more confident inside the pool and I have mastered the free style. My next challenge is to be able to swim on my back. I don't want to win any medals, I just want to swim for pleasure and to keep fit."

(a) Read the following statements and say which statements are True and which are False:

(i) Preeti felt scared when she saw her older brother swimming.

(ii) She got an opportunity to swim after she left India.

(iii) Preeti gave up swimming after her initial classes.

(iv) Preeti has a good swimming instructor.

(v) Preeti swims well and is ready to take part in competitions.

Ans. (i)False, (ii) True, (iii) False, (iv)True, (v)False

(b) Answer the following questions:

(i) Why was Preeti unable to learn swimming when she was a child?

Ans. During her childhood, Preeti was unable to learn swimming because in her family, girls weren't allowed to wear swimming costume for swimming classes.

(ii) What was her main challenge when she started swimming?

Ans. Her main challenge when she started swimming is to be appeared in a one piece swimming costume.

(iii) What role did Preeti's teacher play in her journey?

Ans. After the third lesson of swimming, Preeti was fed up and decided to stop, but her teacher taught her swimming with patiently.

(iv) Discuss the role of our society in Preeti's experience with swimming.

Ans. During Preeti childhood, girls weren't allowed to wear swimming costume for swimming classes. In contrary, Indian's men are allowed to wear anything. Preeti waited for swimming classes until she went to England.

(v) Give an appropriate title to the passage.

Ans. Swimming journey of Preeti

Q2. Do as directed:

(a) Ishaan said, "It is going to rain tomorrow."

(Change into indirect speech)

Ans. Ishaan said that it was going to rain following day.

(b) Will he get through the examination? It is not certain.

(Combine the above sentences by using an appropriate writer)

Ans. It is not certain if he will get through the examination.

(c) For a healthy body we need to wake up.........time and take part.......some form of physical activity.

(Use appropriate preposition to fill in the blanks)

Ans. On, in

(d) I want to buy.......washing machine. I like......one I saw on TV yesterday.

(Fill in with appropriate articles)

Ans. a, the

(e) Yesterday when I.........(reach) home, the food....... (prepare).

(Use the correct form of the verbs given)

Ans. reached, was prepared

Q3. Correct the following sentences:

(a) I am having a nice laptop.

Ans. I have a nice laptop.

(b) My friend didn't came yesterday.

Ans. My friend didn't come yesterday.

(c) If you will be doing exercise, you are going to be fit.

Ans. If you will do exercise, you will be fit.

(d) My sister and I goes to school together.

Ans. My sister and I go to school together.

(e) Where you work?

Ans. Where do you work?

Q4. Write an essay in about 200 words on any one of the following topics:

(a) Smartphones are making people dumb.

Ans. The Smartphones have entirely changed the world of communication, and the impact of its introduction is visible on personal as well as professional lives. Smartphones come with multifunctional tools and several numbers of apps which bring uncountable benefits to businesses both large and small. It is the prime reason behind the name 'Smartphones'. However, there is a group which believes that Smartphones are making people dumb.

The greatest drawback of using smartphones is the adverse impact on people's memory. Nowadays, people tend to forget things due to excessive use of Smartphones. Previously, people didn't have any problem in remembering the telephone numbers and other tasks to do; however, it is not the same case now. The so-called useful tools including social networking apps, fully functional web surfing, games and many other mindlessly occupy the time of people. Instead of doing productive work, people keep on wasting their precious time. Financially, a smartphone can be bought under ₹20000 as well as above ₹40000. There is no doubt that the expensive ones have more features. But more than 80% of people don't even know what the features are. They just buy to show off, and hence are nothing but dumb. Smartphones make people dependent or rather say addicted to it. The users remain at the mercy of the notifications.

There is no dividing line between rational use and addiction, which results in stress and decreased productivity. Texting on Smartphones has deteriorated people's English grammar and spellings. Even on formal papers, they write either the SMS language or wrong spellings. This is another step towards being dumb.

Smartphones can be better defined as a tool that presents the latest conundrum of productivity. On one side, they force innovation to follow people wherever they go, and on the other side, they amplify the negative habits enter into the people's lives. Understanding how to reduce the bad while focusing on the good is the smart way of using a Smartphone. So, use it wisely, and don't allow anyone to comment 'Smartphone has made you dumb.'

(b) The importance of education in our society.

Ans. Education helps in spreading knowledge in society. This is perhaps the most noteworthy aspect of Education. There is a quick propagation of knowledge in an educated society. Furthermore, there is a transfer of knowledge from generation to another by Education. Education is also extremely important for employment. It certainly is a great opportunity to make a decent living.

Better Communication is yet another role in Education. Education improves and refines the speech of a person. Furthermore, individuals also improve other means of communication with Education. It helps in the development and innovation of technology. Most noteworthy, the more the education, the more technology will spread. Important developments in war equipment, medicine, computers, take place due to Education. People become more mature with the help of Education. Sophistication enters the life of educated people. Above all, Education teaches the value of discipline to individuals. Educated people also realize the value of time much more. To educated people, time is equal to money.

Education enables individuals to express their views efficiently. Educated individuals can explain their opinions in a clear manner. Hence, educated people are quite likely to convince people to their point of view. Education is a ray of light in the darkness. It certainly is a hope for a good life. Education is a basic right of every Human on this Planet. To deny this right is evil. Uneducated youth is the worst thing for Humanity. Above all, the governments of all countries must ensure to spread Education.

(c) My personal contribution to saving our planet-Earth.

Ans. Refer to December-2016, Q.No.-5 (a) [Pg. No.-227]

(d) Advantages and disadvantages of using public transport system.

Ans. Nowadays, many kinds of public transport can be seen on the road, even though people drive their own car. It is usually on time and economical. Firstly, one of the advantages is that using public transport is very economical. Taking buses and trains is cheaper than using private cars. If people have their own car, they have to pay a lot of money for service, repairs, and insurance. It maybe will cost all the money people earn. Moreover, there are many discounts for some individuals, like students, old people, and children. They can get cheaper prices by taking public transport. Students have to go to school almost every day, and they usually take public transport to school and home. It is more economical for students. In addition, a further advantage is that using public transport can preserve the environment. It can reduce pollution, because there are less cars driving on the road, and there are fewer fumes and also less traffic jams. Furthermore, it can increase the spaces in the city, because there are less cars parking. Taking buses and trains is able to keep the environment green, However, one of the disadvantages is that using public transport is inconvenient. It can be crowded. For instance, there are always too many individuals on the same bus in rush hour. Maybe thieves are on the bus they take. The public transport does not operate 24 hours a day. People have to follow the time table, so they must wait for it. Furthermore, sometimes, it does not travel to the suburbs, so individuals have to walk for a long time to reach the place they want to go. If people have an important work at the suburb, it is inconvenient. In conclusion, although there are some problems of using public transport, people should still take it to go to school or to travel to work, because the overall advantages of taking public transport are more than the disadvantages. Private cars should be used for urgent needs only. Otherwise, public transportations should be used. It will save our environment.

Q5. Two friends are having an argument on what they want to do. Write a dialogue giving about 5 turns to each speaker on one of the following situations:

(a) Neelu wants to go out to play but Shyam wants to play games on the cell phone.

Ans. Neelu: Hi Shyam! How are you?

Shyam: Hello: I'm fine. How do you do?

Neelu: Good. Let's go outside to play badminton.

Shyam: No, I will play PUBG on my cell phone.

Neelu: Don't play PUBG, because it's harmful.

Shyam: No, it's very interesting game. While playing badminton, you can only jump and hit the rocket. But in PUBG, I can fire, jump, rest and many more.

Neelu: Badminton is very good for health. You become active and lose weight. It also helps in improving metabolic rate. But while playing

PUBG, you can only lie down or sit down that will gain you weight. It also impact eyes.

Shyam: But we can also play PUBG during walking.

Neelu: It's more dangerous. Many people have lost their lives due of accident. Because while playing PUBG, they only concentrate on the game, not here and there.

Shyam: I think you are right. Let's play badminton.

Neelu: Yes. Let's go.

(b) Radhika wants to watch a play but her friend Anil wants to watch a movie.

Ans. Radhika: Hi Anil. How are you?

Anil: Good. What about you?

Radhika: Good too. Let's watch the play.

Anil: Play! I don't like. I will watch a movie.

Radhika: But I want to watch the play. Give me the remote.

Anil: No. First I will watch a movie then afterwards you will see your play.

Radhika: What? How it's possible? It broadcasts on a particular time only.

Anil: You can record the play and watch later.

Radhika: No. I will not be interesting. You can watch movie later.

Anil: Ok. Let's watch the play.

Radhika: Thanks.

Whatever you do, do with determination. You have one life to live; do your work with passion and give your best. Whether you want to be a chef, doctor, actor, or a mother, be passionate to get the best result.

Foundation Course in English: BEGF-101

June, 2020

Note: Answer all questions.

Q1. Read the passage given below and answer the questions that follow:

Charlie Chaplin was believed to have been born on April 16, 1889. There is some doubt whether April 16 is actually his birthday, and it is possible he was not born in 1889. There is also uncertainty about his birthplace : London or Fontaineblue, France. There is no doubt, however, to his parentage : he was born to Charlie Chaplin and Hannah Hill, both Music. Hall entertainers. His parents got separated soon after his birth, leaving him in the care of his increasingly \instable mother.

In 1896, Chaplin's mother was unable to find work; Charlie and his older brother Sydney Chaplin had to be left in the school for Orphans and Destitute Children. His father died an alcoholic when Charlie was 12, and his mother suffered a mental breakdown, and was eventually admitted temporarily to an asylum. She died in 1928 in the United States, two years after coming to the US to live with Chaplin, who was by then a commercial success.

Charlie first took to the stage when he was five years old when he performed with his mother. As a child, he was confined to bed for weeks due to a serious illness. In 1900, when he was 11 years old, his brother helped him to find the role of a comic cat in the Pantomime Cinderella at the London Hippodrome. In 1903 he appeared in 'Jim, A Romance of Cockayne' followed by his first regular job, as the newspaper boy Billy in Sherlock Holmes, a part the played in 1906. This was followed by Casey's 'Court Circus' variety show, and, the following year, he became a clown in Fred Karno's 'Fun Factory' Slapstick comedy company.

According to the immigration records, he arrived in the U. S. with the Karno troupe on October 2, 1912. There he met Stan Laurel with whom he shared a room in a boarding house. Laurel returned to England but Chaplin remained in the U. S. Chaplin's act was seen by film producer Mack Sennett, who hefted him for his studio, the Keystone Film Company.

(a) Read the following statements and say which statements are True and which are False:

(i) Charlie Chaplin might have been born some years earlier than is currently believed.
(ii) Chaplin's mother died before he became successful.
(iii) Chaplin first performed on stage when he was five years old.
(iv) His first serious job was delivering newspapers.
(v) His first partner on stage was the actor Stan Laurel.
(b) Answer the following questions:
(i) What were Charlie Chaplin's struggles as a child?
(ii) What role did his brother play in his career?
(iii) What kinds of roles did Charlie play before reaching the US?
(iv) Considering Charlie had a tough childhood, do you think it was easy for him to be a comedian? Discuss.
(v) Give a suitable title to the passage.

Q2. Do as directed:
(a) Asha said, "My mother is making something special today." (Change into indirect speech).
(b) It is quite late. I want to sleep. (Combine the sentences by using an appropriate linker).
(c) I love chocolates. I think I am addicted, them. What should I do to get rid this addiction. (Use appropriate prepositions to fill in the blanks).
(d) Diwali is important festival in India. (Use appropriate article).
(e) My classes start at 9 : 30 in the morning. (Form a 'Wh' question).

Q3. Correct the following sentences:
(a) I not good in mathematics. (b) Thanks to coming.
(c) He do many mistakes in English. (d) She can't able to do this.
(e) Over the years India change a lot.

Q4. Write an essay in about 200 words on any one of the following topics:
(a) Happiness is more important than money.
(b) Advantages and disadvantages of city life.
(c) The importance of a father's role in bunging up of a child.
(d) Social media has made us more isolated than even before.

Q5. Write a dialogue giving 5 turns to each speaker on any one of the following situations:
(a) Raji and Vijay want to do something interesting over the weekend. They make a plan to go to cinema but cannot decide which movie to see.
(b) Anjana wants to spend time at home while her husband Rajesh wants to spend time at a Mall.

Foundation Course in English-1: BEGF-101

February, 2021

Note: Answer all questions.

Q1. Read the following passage and answer the questions below it.

The art of tattooing goes back a long way. The Egyptians used to tattoo each other 3,000 years ago, and the oldest known example is on the body of a 4,000-year-old 'ice-man' who was found frozen in mountain snow on the Italian-Austrian border in 1993. The picture shows a tattoo on the upper arm of another ice-man, who died 2,500 years ago in Siberia, and who is now on display in a Moscow museum.

In more modern times, tattoos were reintroduced to Europe by Captain Cook and his crew on their return from Tahiti in 1771 — hence the traditional association of tattoos with sailors. The word 'tattoo' itself comes from the Tahitian word 'tatau' — onomatopoeic for the sound made by their tattooing instrument.

There are a number of major styles of tattoo, including Tribal (bold, simple patterns in black ink), Celtic (intricate knotwork, again usually black), Oriental (fish, clouds, dragons, etc.) and Portrait (images taken from photos, usually in black and grey ink). But nowadays almost any kind of image can be turned into a tattoo, in a full range of colours, and on almost any part of the body.

Technically, the only places you can't get tattooed are your hair, teeth and nails, but parts of the body which may change shape with ageing (such as the stomach, which tends to get bigger and sag) are best avoided. Arms and shoulders are the most popular, and one reason for this is that while these areas can be displayed in public, it is equally easy to conceal them under a shirt. For the same reason, many people choose the left wrist (which can be covered by a watch) or the feet and ankles. Some even use a shaved area of the head — and can then grow their hair to cover it up again if they want to.

The main disadvantage of tattoos is that they're permanent. It is true that they tend to blur (and possibly sag) with age — but they don't go away. So it is not a decision to be taken lightly. If you might want a job as a bank clerk in a few years' time, think twice before tattooing that fire-breathing dragon on your hand. And by all means tattoo a heart with your partner's name on your arm — provided you're sure you'll feel the same way for ever.

Tattoos can be removed, but it can be a painful process and it can leave scars. Only laser treatment can remove them completely, and this is very expensive. In other words, it is much easier to get a tattoo than to remove one. In a recent survey, one-third of men and women questioned regretted getting tattooed. So the undecided would be well advised to stick to those temporary tattoos that you put on for the evening and remove with baby oil the next day.

(a) (i) "The art of tattooing goes back a long way." Discuss.

(ii) Why are tattoos associated with sailors?

(iii) Discuss the difference between tattoos of the past and those of present times.

(iv) What parts of the body do people have tattoos on and why?

(v) Why does the author suggest the use of temporary tattoos?

(b) Make sentences of your own with each of the words/phrases given below. Do not copy the sentence from the passage.

(i) go(es) a long way back (ii) on display
(iii) traditional (iv) styles (v) disadvantage

Q2. (a) Fill in the blanks with the appropriate form of the verb given in brackets.

While Satish________(drive), his cell phone________(rang). He_______(talk) on the phone when he________(have) a car accident. He______(hit) a lamp post and fortunately he wasn't hurt.

(b) Do as directed :

(i) A : Is Susan married?
B : She__________ be married. She's wearing a wedding ring. (Use an appropriate modal)

(ii) __________ there are changes in immigration patterns, nearly one in five people will be an immigrant in 2050. (Choose the correct option: If, Unless, Because of)

(iii) When I was a child, I dreamt that________. (Complete the sentence)

(iv) When I got back to__________house, there was__________ letter on the doorstep. (Fill in blanks with a, the)

Q3. You are planning to go on a trek to the mountain areas. Discuss with your friend the preparations that are required and the gear you need to take along with you. Write the dialogue in about 10 – 15 turns.

Q4. You are the President of your college student union. The Principal of the college has asked you to give a speech about "Protecting Yourself From Pollution." Write the speech in about 200 – 250 words.

Foundation Course in English-1: BEGF-101

June, 2021

Note: Answer all questions.

Q1. Read the passage given below and answer the questions that follow:

(1) My father gets a faraway look in his eyes that's unmistakable. As he looks towards the horizons and his eyes seek out the bright flashes of snow-capped peaks, we all know that he's thinking Mountain tops have always had that magnetic effect on him.

(2) As I grew up I inherited some of my father's restlessness. I know many people think there must be some compulsion for the son of Edmund Hillary to climb mountains. They assume that I need to compete, or measure up as if there was some strong mark on stone that stays, "Thou shalt climb mountains"— and in particular Everest, whether you like it or not. But for me it is simpler than that. I think families are like factories: some manufacture lawyers while others produce landscape gardeners. The Hillary family is a limited production mountaineering establishment.

(3) Today at the age of 48, I am determined mountain man : love to climb them; love to dream about them. I have been on more than 30 mountaineering expeditions, from the Himalayas to the Antarctic. And yes I have climbed Everest—twice. I treasure the same things that drew my father to climbing–great feeling of friendship and trust among people who work together, sense of pleasure and excitement, especially in dangerous places where your life depends upon making the right call. I guess I am luckier than most because I can fall back on all that my father has taught me. One devastating day in 1995 this advice saved my life.

(4) Just below the summit of the mountain known as K2 or the "savage mountain" of the Himalayas—there is a steep ice channel called, "The Bottleneck". I was among a party of eight climbers heading for the summit, with just 400 metres left to climb. Perched there, 8200 metres above sea-level and looking east along the northern edge of the Karakoram Mountains to the Tibetan Plateau, I noticed curls of ominous cloud had began to move in suddenly and quickly with great force.

(5) As the weather worsened, I became very concerned. I stopped. Something didn't feel right. At that moment I clearly heard my father's voice–Down. Go down. Stick to your guns, Peter.

(6) Then, from above me, I heard another voice – a woman's "Come on up. Use the red rope". Alison Hargreaves, a fellow climber, was encouraging me to join her. "Not for you, Peter." Was that my father's voice again? The unsettled felling in me grew stronger. Finally I told Jeff Lakes, my climbing partner, that I was going down. He too was feeling unsure, but decided to go on ahead. As I headed down, I looked back at Jeff a couple of times, until a thick, threatening cloud blocked the view. Soon, the same fast-moving cloud would engulf the summit and plunge me into an isolated world of terror.

(7) Don't be afraid to make your own decisions. Don't be afraid to stand alone. That was my father's voice.

(8) Alone in body but not in spirit I descended. But with fear tapping upon my shoulders, I was caught in the frightening situation of the rising storm. The flanks of the mountain were out of control and so, perhaps, was I.

(9) Fear makes you careful. Fear makes you good. Fear, my father told me, is not something you manage. So I seized on what I could control; a well clipped descender and a taut rope. For hours I continued to go down rope after plunging rope–every rope one closer to the ice ledge at Camp-2.

(10) When I awoke in my tent the next morning, it was silent, sunny still. I along had successfully descended from the summit pyramid of K2 that night. The seven above were dead.

(a) (i) What does the son read in his father's eyes? Who is the father?

(ii) State two qualities of the father that have rubbed off on the son.

(iii) In what way does the author consider himself more fortunate than other mountaineers?

(iv) What was the father's opinion about 'fear'? How did it help the author?

(v) What was the fate of the seven companions who climbed the K2 summit? Why?

(b) Find words/phrases from the passage which mean the same as the following:

(i) captivating (Para 1)

(ii) to be as good as (Para 2)

(iii) can make use of (Para 3)

(iv) ruthless/terrible (Para 4)
(v) threatening/menacing (Para 4)
(vi) refuse to change (Para 5)
(vii) uncertain (Para 6)
(viii) extreme fright (Para 6)
(ix) came down (Para 8)
(x) very tight and completely stretched (Para 9)

Q2. Do as directed:

(i) Before .... the system, I'd like to review it completely. (Change) (Put the verb in brackets in the correct form)

(ii) Anita said, "I need to put the children to bed." (Change the sentence to indirect/reported speech)

(iii) People sometimes don't understand me because of .... (Complete the sentence)

(iv) You must do the homework .... you are absent.
Absence is no excuse for not doing the homework.
(Complete the sentence with the correct option : if, unless, even if)

(v) I came to this institution .... learn English (Fill in the blank with the correct option : becauses of, in order to, so that)

(vi) It is important for a new immigrant to the USA to know English therefore .... (Complete the sentence)

(vii) The home .... I grew up had a beautiful fireplace. (Fill in the blank with the correct option : where, that, which)

(viii) How do you get noticed when you are working as part of .... team, and are expected to blend seamlessly with .... rest? (Fill in blanks with appropriate articles : a/the)

(ix) The director will give us instructions. (Change into passive voice)

Q3. Write a paragraph of about 200 words on any one of the following topics:

(i) Caring for the aged.
(ii) Social media in actually disrupting our social life.
(iii) Creating a pollution-free world.
(iv) Problems faced by our population.

Q4. You are the secretary of a green club, "Nature Calls." Your club organised a massive tree planting drive. Write a report about this.

Foundation Course in English-1: BEGF-101

December, 2021

Note: Answer all questions.

Q1. Read the passage given and answer the questions that follow:

(1) Food is also one of the most complicated relationships that exist. Historically and culturally, food and social interaction are connected. We have always used food as a way to celebrate, remember, comfort, love and mourn together and we have been conditioned to do this over thousands of years. Our fondest memories would probably be associated with our grandma's dahi wadas or the first cake mummy baked for us. It's not an easy relationship to either understand or separate ourselves from.

(2) So I'm not asking you not to meet your friends and family over meals. But it could be very difficult to lose weight if you don't make changes to the way you interact socially. If you give food the same entertainment value as a movie or a show, or if food is how you pass your time, your body will hit back with heart disease, gastro-intestinal infections, acidity, bloating, pre-diabetes and obesity. If not worse.

(3) It is a proven fact that we eat more in the presence of others. Social pressures make us drink recklessly and consume more than we should. Why do women gain weight after they get married? Studies suggest that newly married women eat with husbands who have larger appetites and they are subconsciously trying to match up to them.

(4) Reduce the importance of food in your social life. Take it down a notch. Skip lunch at a fancy, high-priced restaurant. Catch up with your friends over coffee instead. You'll eat less. Call those distant relatives home for chai instead of dinner. If you have kids, meet other friends with their kids and go to the park together. Want to double date with another couple? Forget meeting over drinks or dinner. Instead, go bowling or catch a movie.

(5) You see what you're doing here? You're meeting the same people, spending the same amount of time with them, and losing weight in the process. A dinner takes, what, 90 minutes? So will tea or coffee. Calorie intake over dinner? At least 1200. Calorie intake over coffee

or tea? If you don't order a high-cal beverage with whipped cream, you won't be consuming more than 100 to 150 calories. See the difference? And I'm not even going into how much money you will save.

Answer the following questions:

(a) (i) How have humans interacted with food in the past? Discuss.

(ii) Why is the writer asking us to make changes in our relationship with food now?

(iii) Why do women gain weight after marriage, according to the writer?

(iv) Mention two changes in our lifestyle that the writer suggests we should make.

(v) Give an appropriate title to the passage.

(b) Pick out words from the passage which mean the same as the following:

(i) complex (para 1)

(ii) mix with others (para 2)

(iii) abnormal fat that presents a risk to health (para 2)

(iv) foolhardy fashion without thinking of the consequences (para 3)

(v) elegant and high-priced (para 4)

(c) Make sentences with the following words/phrases:

(i) mourn

(ii) entertainment value

(iii) consume

(iv) take down a notch

(v) catch up

Q2. (a) Fill in the blanks with the correct propositions:

(i) At last she succeeded __________ climbing Mount Everest.

(ii) I absolutely insist __________ paying for the meal.

(iii) Would you be interested __________ the folk festival?

(iv) He's not used __________ going anywhere on his own.

(v) I don't mind you phoning me _______ work.

(b) Rewrite the following sentences making corrections wherever necessary:

(i) Where you spent your holidays last year?

(ii) I asked her when was she going abroad.

(iii) When I had reached the station, the train had left.

(iv) I could not solve the paper because I was not understanding the questions.

(v) This year's paper was more easier than last year's.

Q3. Write a paragraph on any one of the following topics (about 150 words):

(a) Social media has destroyed real heart-to-heart communication

(b) Ways to improve our mental health during COVID times

(c) My way of protecting the environment

(d) Gandhi's relevance to the present times

(e) My favorite cultural event

Q4. Write a dialogue on any one of the following. Take about ten turns.

(a) Your younger brother is very careless about switching off lights and fans, saving water, etc. Explain to him the importance of preserving the environment.

(b) Your younger brother is not taking adequate precautions now that the COVID-19 cases are down. Explain to him why such precautions are necessary.

Foundation Course in English-1: BEGF-101

June, 2022

Note: Answer all questions.

Q1. Read the following passage and answer the questions below:

The art of tattooing goes back a long way. The Egyptians used to tattoo each other 3,000 years ago, and the oldest known example is on the body of a 4,000 year old 'ice-man' who was found frozen in mountain snow on the Italian-Austrian border in 1993. The picture shows a tattoo on the upper arm of another ice-man, who died 2,500 years ago in Siberia, and who is now on display in a Moscow museum.

In more modern times, tattoos were reintroduced to Europe by Captain Cook and his crew on their return from Tahiti in 1771 – hence the traditional association of tattoos with sailors. The word 'tattoo' itself comes from the Tahitian word 'tatau' – onomatopoeic for the sound made by their tattooing instrument.

Technically, the only places you can't get tattooed are your hair, teeth and nails, but parts of the body which may change shape with ageing (such as the stomach, which tends to get bigger and sag) are best avoided. Arms and shoulders are the most popular, and one reason for this is that while these areas can be displayed in public, it is equally easy to conceal them under a shirt. For the same reason, many people choose the left writs (which can be covered by a watch) or the feet and ankles. Some even use a shaved area of the head – and can then grow their hair to cover it up again if they want to.

Though not pleasant, the process is not dangerous, provided the tattoo is applied by a qualified artist in a clean and properly supervised environment. Infections can, however, result from using a 'scratcher' – someone who's bought a tattoo gun by mail order and has no idea how to use it safely. For this reason, many US states have strict safety regulations concerning tattooing, and four have banned it altogether.

Tattoos can be removed, but it can be a painful process and it can leave scars. Only laser treatment can remove them completely and this is very expensive. In other words, it is much easier to get a tattoo than to remove one. In a recent survey, one third of men and women questioned regretted getting tattooed. So the undecided would be well advised to stick to those temporary tattoos that you put on for the evening and remove with baby oil the next day.

(a) Answer the following questions:

(i) Is tattooing an old art? Discuss.

(ii) Where has the word 'tattoo' come from?

(iii) Why should certain parts of the body not be tattooed? Discuss.

(iv) Research has shown that later people regret getting tattooed. Why?

(v) Give a title to the passage.

(vi) Would you like to have a tattoo? Why/Why not?

(b) Pick out words from the text which mean the same as the following:

(i) frigid due to immense cold (Para 1)

(ii) a group of people who work together, especially on ship (Para 2)

(iii) to hang down (Para 3)

(iv) rules which must be followed (Para 4)

(v) felt sorry that they did something (Para 5)

(c) Make sentences of your own with each of the following words/phases:

(i) on display

(ii) to conceal

(iii) banned

(iv) scars

(v) undecided

Q2. (a) Rewrite the following sentences making necessary corrections:

(i) Sunil had gone to Mumbai yesterday.

(ii) Whose mobile phone this is?

(iii) She is so weak to do difficult chores.

(iv) You will be late until you hurry.

(v) She being engaged on other work, is no excuse.

(b) Do as directed:

(i) Complete the sentence with the most appropriate verb:

Would you mind .... the door, please?

(ii) Fill in the gap with the correct modal verb:

We all hoped that he .... take the advise he had been given.

(iii) Fill in the gap with an appropriate preposition:

Most people disagreed .... what had been suggested.

(iv) Fill in the gap with an appropriate phrasal verb:

All communication with the outside world has been .... (discontinued).

(v) Fill in the blank with the correct question-tag:

You won't tell them what happened, ...?

Q3. Write a paragraph in about 150 words on any one of the following:

(i) The hazards of noise pollution

(ii) An autobiography of my childhood

(iii) Eating too much junk food

(iv) The importance of our cultural heritage

(v) My grandma's house

Q4. You participated in a cultural programme in your college. Write a letter to your friend in another city:

– describing the event

– the long hours of practice for the event

– the friendships that happened as a result

– importance of cultural events

Foundation Course in English-1: BEGF-101

December, 2022

Note: Answer all questions.

Q1. Read the passage given and answer the questions that follow :

(1) We've all been there. We have searched endlessly for solutions to life's problems at the bottom of a bag of potato chips. We've looked for God at the end of a stack of pakodas. We've tried to find the true meaning of life in decadent, rich chocolate. But when it's done frequently and excessively, without us realizing it, emotional eating can affect weight, health and overall well-being. Using food as a way to always escape our feelings is a tried-and-tested way of making sure we'll never get back into shape. It's also one of the hardest habits to break.

(2) A common myth about emotional eating is that it's initiated by negative feelings. While people do turn to food when they're stressed out, lonely, sad, anxious or bored, they also do so in love, excitement and happiness. Remember how your grandfather used to give you chocolate as a reward for being a good child? Or when your mum made your favourites when you did well in your exams? Studies have shown that emotional eating is behaviour that we have learned, through which we develop the habit of reaching out for the same foods in happy or sad moments.

(3) It also doesn't help that certain foods are designed to be harder to resist. For example, chocolate has a common mood elevator which produces a high similar to the one you feel when you're in love or on top of the world. Certain foods are embedded with natural or man-made chemicals that make you happy. Your brain starts to associate that food with 'happiness' or 'celebration' and you reach for it the next time you want that feeling.

(4) Emotional eating is pointless because the same high you get with chocolate or another favourite food will be reversed an hour or two later when your sugar levels crash. Which is why, in so many cases, binges make you feel worse than when you started. You also start to feel guilty about binge eating, and sometimes use food again as

a way to deal with that guilt. It's a vicious cycle. And it doesn't address what's really bothering you.

(5) It has been said that nothing in life is permanent except change. Well, in today's times, you could say that nothing in life is permanent except stress. It's always going to be there. And eating our stress away with chocolates and samosas isn't going to help.

(a) Answer the following questions :

(i) Which is one of the hardest habits to break and why ?

(ii) When do humans usually turn to food ? Discuss.

(iii) Name the foods that are difficult to resist. Why ?

(iv) Why is "emotional eating pointless" ? Discuss.

(v) Give an appropriate title to the passage. Give reasons for it.

(b) Pick out words from the passage which mean the same as the following :

(i) self-indulgent (para 1)

(ii) started/commenced (para 2)

(iii) refrain from/avoid (para 3)

(iv) to uplift (para 3)

(v) become low suddenly (para 4)

(c) Make sentences of your own with the following words/phrases :

(i) tried-and-tested way

(ii) get back into shape

(iii) reward

(iv) reaching out

(v) binges

Q2. (a) Select the correct alternative and complete the passage given below :

Hindustan Times ________ (is/are) the paper that brought out the news of the birth of the quadruplets. According to the news each of the babies ________ (weigh/weighs) about 500 grams and ________ (is/are) doing well. Three of them ________ (is/are) girls. Everyone is surprised since neither of the parents ________ (has/have) any history of twins in the family.

(b) Choose a comparative or superlative form of adjective :

(i) The Marriage of Figaro is ________ (beautiful) of all Mozart's operas.

(ii) The new car is ________ (fast) than my old one.

(iii) My mother and her sisters are all ________ (short) than their children.

(iv) I think Sarita is ________ (intelligent) person in our class.

(v) Let's meet in the library – it's ________ (quiet) than all the other rooms.

Q3. Write a paragraph on any one of the following topics in about 150 words :

(a) How to lead a healthy and fit life ?

(b) Being an environmentally responsible tourist

(c) Planning for a Beach holiday

(d) An invention that has changed the world for the better

(e) An autobiography of an important year of your life

Q4. Write a dialogue on any one of the following.

(a) While Covid had lots of negatives, it also taught humans a lot of life lessons. Discuss with your friend.

Or

(b) You are going on a trek with a friend. Discuss the weather, items of clothing, food, and other essentials.

(In both dialogues, you need to take about 10 to 12 turns)

www.ingramcontent.com/pod-product-compliance
Ingram Content Group UK Ltd.
Pitfield, Milton Keynes, MK11 3LW, UK
UKHW021706190726
13853UKWH00001B/439